D. Michael McIntrye

The Rosegarden Companion

© 2005 bomots verlag

cover design: bomots verlag

cover photograph: Nathalie Dautel

ISBN: 2-915925-18-6

Table of Content

I dedicate this work to Graham Percival, my Linux mentor and friend, for sending me my first taste of the amazing thing the Linux and Open Source phenomena have become.

Thanks to Chris Cannam and Rich Bown of Fervent Software, and to Guillaume Laurent, principal developers of Rosegarden, for their years of tireless, frequently thankless efforts bringing this magnificent software to light. Thanks particularly to Chris for making the initial suggestion that proved to be the seed which grew into this book. Finally, thanks to everyone in the Open Source and Linux Audio communities, for giving us all the tools we need to build this software, to use it, and even to write about it.

1 What is Rosegarden?

Rosegarden, is a versatile, Open Source music creation tool. It combines the aspects of a MIDI (Musical Instrument Digital Interface) sequencer, an audio sequencer, and a notation editor into one convenient, powerful, easy-to-use package that provides users with a consistent and intuitive interface.

Rosegarden makes use of two powerful and flexible subsystems available to Linux. For MIDI operations, Rosegarden employs the ALSA (Advanced Linux Sound Architecture) MIDI sequencer infrastructure for routing in-coming and out-going MIDI events. It can record from any number of inputs simultaneously, and out-going events can be routed to any of a myriad MIDI clients.

For audio recording and playback, Rosegarden is one of numerous applications that make use of the Jack Audio Connection Kit, or JACK, a low-latency sound server designed from the ground up to meet the demands of professional musicians. Hand in hand with JACK, Rosegarden can apply LADSPA (Linux Audio Developer's Simple Plugin API) plugins to audio streams on the fly, providing effects ranging from EQ to reverb and virtually everything in between. These plugins can be layered on top of each other for yet more possibilities.

Bridging the gap between these two technologies, Rosegarden is the first MIDI sequencer to employ the new DSSI (Disposable Soft Synth Interface) plugin architecture. MIDI events are routed through ALSA into DSSI synth plugins, and audio produced by these plugins can in turn be routed through LADSPA plugins and thence to JACK.

Rosegarden provides three distinct ways of viewing, editing, and entering MIDI events, including a powerful notation editor that provides many advanced features not typically found in the notation facility of MIDI sequencers. Underneath these three editors, Rosegarden provides a segment-based mechanism for arranging blocks of MIDI and audio data on a canvas that brings something akin to the flexibility of a layer-based image editing program to the realm of music.

All of this flexibility means you can use Rosegarden as the center of a very powerful home studio and music composition solution for Linux.

1.1   About This Book

This book will take you, the reader, on a tour of Rosegarden. It will introduce you to its features, and then show you a variety of ways to use these features in real-world situations.

The Linux novice will have questions that this book does not answer. I leave you to turn to the support community for your particular flavor of Linux for help with matters of installation, hardware configuration, and so forth. I assume that you have general knowledge of how to maintain your Linux box on a day to day basis, and that you have already installed Rosegarden-4 1.0 or later. (If you installed a "rosegarden" package, and the application you see does not resemble the one covered in this book in the slightest, then you have found Rosegarden's ancient ancestor.)

Each chapter is loosely divided into two parts. The first half details the mechanical side of making use of various controls in order to manipulate data in some way. The latter half focuses on demonstrating how to use these controls to achieve common musical goals. There are special NOTE: and TIP: sections set off throughout the text to draw special attention to tips, tricks, caveats, and, in some cases, workarounds.

Menu options and references to dialog pages or tabs are formatted in bold, with arrows indicating the progression through the layers of menus. For example, if I say to use *File -> Import -> Import MIDI File* this means to begin at the "File" menu, find "Import" on this menu and hover on it until the submenu opens out, then click on "Import MIDI File."

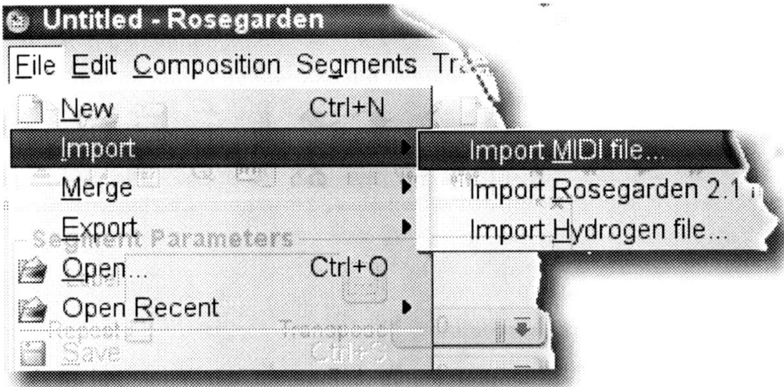

1.2   Equipment and Software Required

Many people are running Rosegarden successfully on older, slower hardware. However, your CPU can't be too fast, and you can't have too much RAM or hard disk space. I suggest a 1.0 GHz machine with at least 256 MB of RAM as a minimum starting place. You can get by with less if you do not do much audio work, and if you have a CPU-friendly way of playing MIDI. The more resources your computer can bring to the table, however, the more you will be able to do successfully and enjoyably with Rosegarden. The following is a quick list of basic requirements you will need to satisfy in order to be able to do different kinds of work with Rosegarden.

For MIDI recording:

- a MIDI capable keyboard, guitar, or other device, along with:

- an ALSA-supported, properly-configured hardware MIDI interface for connecting MIDI devices to your computer, such as:

- a soundcard joystick port MIDI box or Y cable, and/or

- a dedicated MIDI port card, and/or

- a USB MIDI interface

- or a virtual keyboard such as Virtual Keyboard

For MIDI playback:

- a properly configured, ALSA-compatible soundcard or MIDI interface, and

- an external MIDI device such as a keyboard or sound module, and/or

- an ALSA-supported hardware synth, such as the Sound Blaster Live! (emu10k1) and its descendants, with an appropriate soundfont loaded into it, and/or

- an ALSA software synth, such a QSynth with an appropriate soundfont loaded into it (audio output via ALSA or, preferably, JACK), and/or

- a DSSI synth plugin such as the FluidSynth DSSI plugin, with an appropriate soundfont loaded into it, and/or any of several available synth and sampler plugins, both of which require a working JACK server for audio output

For audio recording:

- a properly configured, running JACK audio server, and

- a JACK-compatible soundcard, and

- a microphone, or one or more devices capable of producing sound and piping it into an appropriate jack on the soundcard, and

- plenty of available hard disk space

For audio playback:

- a properly configured, running JACK server, and

- a JACK-compatible soundcard

2 Producing Sound

Many users have written to ask why they are unable to get Rosegarden to make any noise. It is the most common question asked on the rosegarden-user mailing list by far, and is especially troublesome for those newly migrating to Linux from Windows. Before we start Rosegarden for the first time, I want to explain what is necessary to pave the way, and have a good first experience. Some of you already know all this, and those of you who do are invited to jump ahead to the next chapter, where the interesting part begins.

The topic of sound covers two distinct areas that may or may not be co-dependent, depending on the hardware and software you have available. One the one hand, there are several requirements that must be met in order to play MIDI with Rosegarden, and on the other, it's necessary to get the JACK server up and running reliably in order to make use of Rosegarden's audio features. A working JACK server is also required to play MIDI with synth plugins, or to play more than one ALSA software synth at a time. Getting Rosegarden to make noise can be a complicated business, but hopefully I can help you deal with whatever set of circumstances you have before you. I cannot, however, cover every detail of getting every card working with every distribution. I'm afraid I have to leave some questions unanswered, lest this chapter become a book unto itself.

Here is a roadmap showing all the possible ways to produce sound with Rosegarden at a glance. It's quite daunting, I know, but I hope I can help you make sense of it:

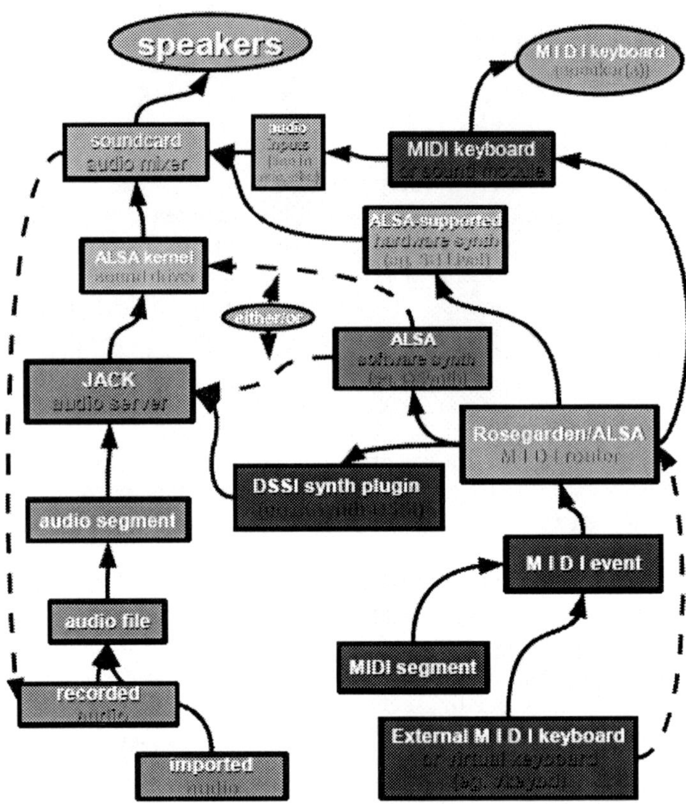

2.1   Playing MIDI

MIDI under Linux is quite a complicated subject. The available hardware falls into three broad categories, each with its own special considerations. External MIDI hardware, internal hardware with ALSA support, and internal hardware without ALSA support. The latter category splits into ALSA soft synths and synth plugins, which are similar, but slightly different.

2.1.1 What's in My Computer?

If you have no idea what you have inside your box, and you have no idea how to configure any of this stuff, one good place to start is to have a look and see how far your distro has gotten you for free. Most modern distros should load ALSA in preference to OSS (an older sound system which predates ALSA), and they should detect and configure a wide variety of soundcards for you automatically.

KDE has a useful information center that can display information about your sound configuration. It will typically be found on the KDE menu under *System -> Info Center*, or you can run it manually by typing kinfocenter into an *Alt+F2* run command box. Here is a sample of its output, with explanations superimposed on the screenshot:

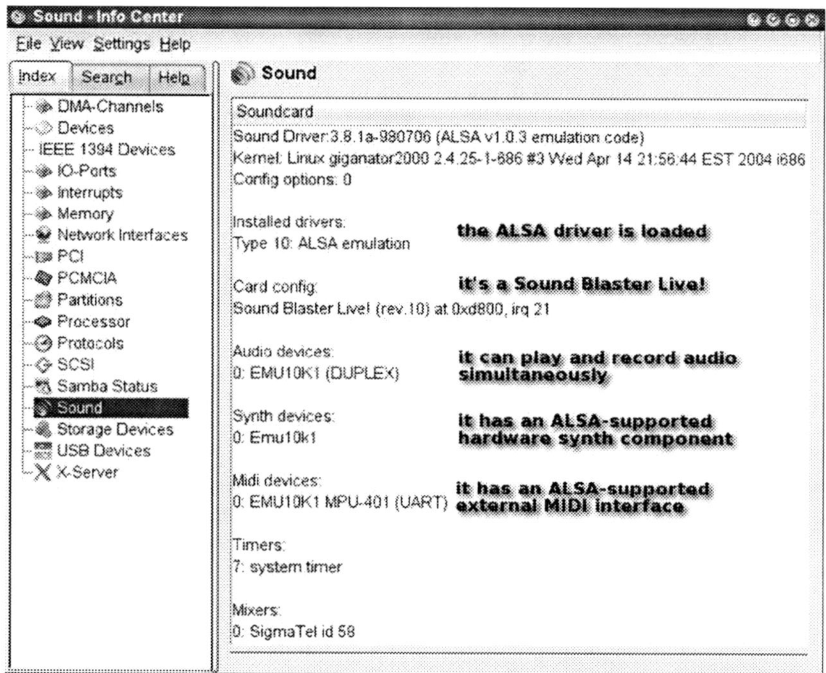

Different soundcards will have different features. Most of them, for example, will list nothing for "Synth devices."

2.1.2 External MIDI Interfaces

By far the least complicated, and most expensive way to play MIDI under Linux is to use real MIDI equipment. This can include keyboards, sound modules, and perhaps even MIDI guitars. A wide range of equipment is available for this purpose, ranging from comparatively inexpensive consumer keyboards to professional quality gear. The cost ranges from hundreds to thousands of dollars however, and this is not the way to go unless you are serious about MIDI.

If you're fortunate enough to have such equipment, then you probably already have some idea how to hook it up to your computer. If the equipment has the ability to produce sound on its own, as some MIDI keyboards do, then you may wish to use those speakers for MIDI playback. If your MIDI equipment has no speakers, or if you intend to record the audio output from this equipment, you may wish to connect the audio output from your keyboard or sound module to an audio input jack on your soundcard. This will allow you to route everything through the soundcard's mixer. There are several choices for external MIDI interfaces.

Joystick Port MIDI Adapters

The simplest, least expensive route is the joystick port MIDI adapter. These plug into the joystick port found on many common AC97 soundcards, and on some on-board audio solutions. The most typical adapter you will find in music stores is a simple Y cable, but nicer products are available which have LEDs to show MIDI activity. With the right adapter in hand, all that remains is to plug the adapter into your joystick/MIDI port, connect your equipment to the box or cable using standard 5-pin DIN MIDI cables. With most AC97 soundcards, including the Sound Blaster Live!, it's only a matter of making sure the snd-seq-midi and snd-rawmidi modules are loaded (using whatever mechanism your particular distribution provides for that function.)

USB MIDI

USB is supplanting traditional MIDI cabling, and several manufacturers are producing keyboards that plug directly into your computer using standard USB cables. There are also devices available which provide multi-port MIDI interfaces. These interfaces attach to your computer using a USB cable, and they provide several traditional 5-pin MIDI sockets.

USB Keyboards

Evolution (http://www.evolution.co.uk) manufactures several models that are known to conform to the standard USB MIDI specification, which are therefore compatible with Linux. Chris Cannam, one of the core Rosegarden developers, uses an Evolution-2 keyboard, and reports that it works using the snd-usb-audio module, which should probably be loaded automatically by hotplug. He imagines that most other manufacturers' wares are similar.

USB MIDI Interfaces

The Edriol UM-2 and mAudio MidiSport 2x2 are known to work under Linux. I have no experience with such things myself, I'm afraid, so I can only provide second-hand information. Pedro Lopez-Cabanillas, a contributing Rosegarden developer, reports that getting the Edriol UM-2 working is as simple as plugging in the USB cable and loading the snd-usb-audio module, which should probably be loaded automatically by hotplug.

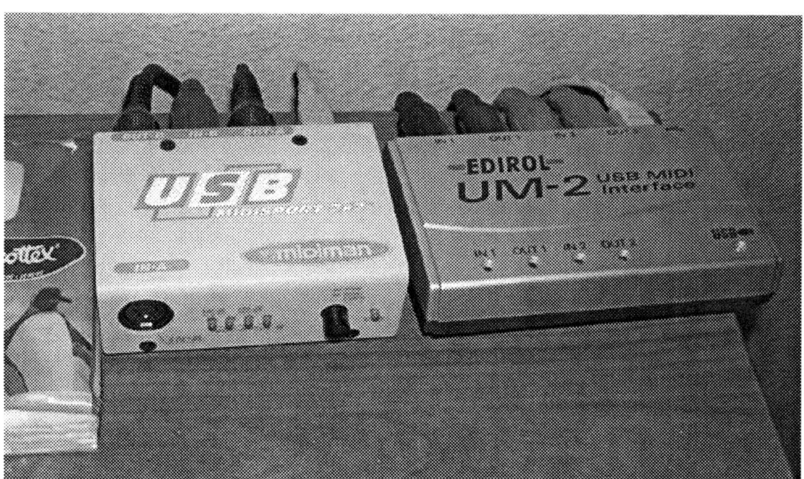

Pedro Lopez-Cabanillas's MIDI Interfaces.

Pedro and Chris both report that the mAudio MidiSport interfaces are more difficult to get working. Pedro reports that "some of them require a firmware program to be loaded into the device's RAM before you can use it. There are GPL firmwares (package ezusbmidi) for the 1-port and 2-port devices (up to Midisport2x2), they are provided as RPM packages for Red Hat by CCRMA, and for Mandrake by Thac. There are also ready to use packages from AGNULA/Debian and Gentoo. Or you can tweak and compile the firmware from its sources." Chris reports that users with 2.6-series kernels may have difficulty using these devices. Pedro suggests that you have a look at the "zero config environment" information available from CCRMA if you are running Red Hat or Fedora.

2.1.3 MIDI without External Hardware

For those without external hardware to use, there are two remaining categories. A few soundcards have a built-in MIDI playback capability that ALSA can use. Everyone else will have to use some kind of software synth. Unfortunately, if you are coming from a Windows background, there is a very good probability that your soundcard used to play MIDI perfectly well under Windows, but it has no ability to do so under Linux out of the box.

The difference is that most such soundcards (in fact, the vast majority of common soundcards on the market) have a software synthesizer built into their Windows driver, so that the user is never really aware that the MIDI playback capability is coming from software. In Linux, you have the choice to run any of several software synthesizers to provide this same capability, but you will have to take steps on your own to bring this about, because it is not automatic or transparent.

Cards That Do Have Synth Support under ALSA

This is the next easiest way to get MIDI working. So far as I know, this category only applies to those with soundcards based on an Emu chipset, such as the Sound Blaster Live!/Audigy series (snd-emu10k1), and the AWE 32/64 (snd-emu8000). I have a Sound Blaster Live! Value Edition myself, and can report that it's easy to get working, and it sounds reasonably good. If you have a slower computer, and you lack stand-alone MIDI equipment, purchasing one of these may be your best, most inexpensive option.

SB Live! Modules

First, you'll need to ensure you have the proper kernel modules loaded, and that you are using the ALSA modules, which have "snd" in the name. If your distro has a nice utility for this purpose, use it. I have been unable to locate a graphical module-reporting utility that's universally-available. The only alternative I can give you that's assured of working across all distros is to head for the dreaded command line to issue a command like:

```
lsmod | grep snd
```

I have the following modules loaded for my own SB Live!:

```
snd-seq-oss    snd-seq-midi    snd-emu10k1-synth    snd-emux-synth

snd-seq-midi-emul    snd-seq-virmidi    snd-seq-midi-event snd-seq

snd-emu10k1 snd-pcm-oss  snd-mixer-oss  snd-pcm  snd-timer

snd-hwdep  snd-util-mem  snd-page-alloc  snd-ac97-codec

snd-rawmidi snd-seq-device snd soundcore
```

If you don't see "snd" you almost certainly have the wrong (OSS, an older sound system) modules loaded, or no sound modules at all. Addressing that is beyond the scope of this book, due to there being so many differences between distros. I fear I have to refer you to whatever help resources your distro provides in that event.

Set the Mixer Volume

Next, you'll need to check to make sure you've turned up your mixer volumes. I will cover this card's rather complicated mixer in detail when I talk about managing various inputs and outputs for the purpose of audio recording. For the moment, it should be sufficient to ensure the "Music" channel volume is turned up. My mixer of preference is QAMix. Unfortunately, it is not widely available outside of SuSE and Studio..to go!, and you may well have to compile it for yourself. I would love to be able to recommend something more commonly available, but try as I might, I can find nothing else that works reliably in every situation I've thrown at it. Every time I try to standardize on something else, I run into a problem I have to use QAMix to fix.

(QAMix can be downloaded from *http://alsamodular.sourceforge.net/*, but compiling and installing it are, unfortunately, well beyond the scope of this book.)

Load a SoundFont

Finally, you'll need to load a soundfont into the card. These cards use *.sf2* soundfonts that are readily available. I'm not aware of a soundfont free enough to be included with any distribution of Linux, so you will most likely have to obtain one from the web, or perhaps from the CDs that came with your soundcard, or you could, of course, simply purchase one.

Once you have obtained a soundfont, you need to load it into the card. There really isn't any user-friendly way of managing this. Your two choices are to run the command line utility *asfxload*, or to configure Rosegarden to load a soundfont for you at startup, via *Settings -> Configure Rosegarden -> Sequencer -> General.* You must still have asfxload installed for this to work, and you will need to tell Rosegarden where to find it if it is not in the place it expects (asfxload is usually part of the package called awesfx).

Cards That Do Not Have Synth Support under ALSA

This is really the "everything else" category. It includes too many soundcards to list; each with its own set of modules. Almost all of these will show up as some flavor of "ac97" in addition to whatever chipset-specific name they have. The Sound Blaster PCI and Ensoniq AudioPCI cards (ens-1370, ens-1371, ens-1373), and integrated snd-intel8x0 and snd-via82xx are probably the most common, but soundcards that fall into this category are legion. The process for getting them to play MIDI is similar in all cases.

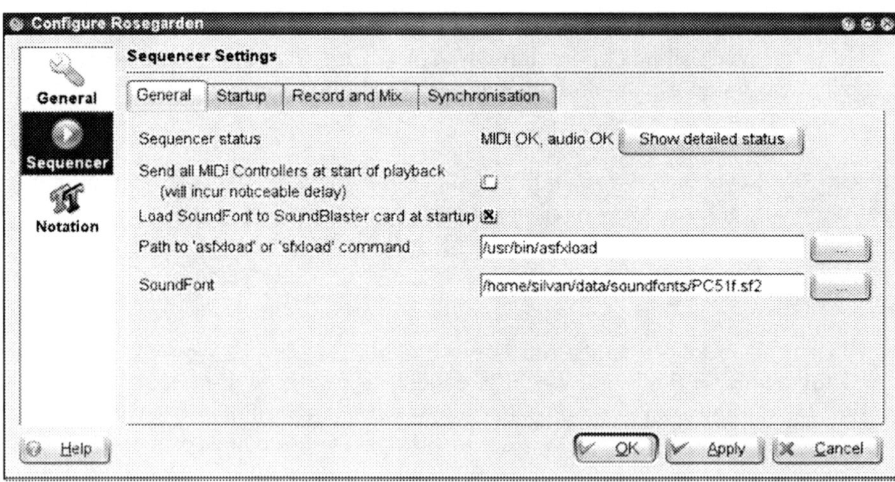

Check your Modules

First, you need to ensure you have the necessary ALSA MIDI infrastructure by loading the following kernel modules in addition to whatever other modules you require for your particular hardware:

```
snd-seq midi snd-seq-virmidi snd-seq-midi-event snd-seq
snd-timer snd-rawmidi snd-soundcore
```

If these "-midi" modules are not loaded, then you can often get the MIDI subsystem up by simply issuing a modprobe snd-seq-midi command, which pulls in all or most of the other modules it needs. Check back with KInfoCenter, or a similar utility, to see if you have something listed for "Midi devices" now, or issue a pmidi -l command, and look for something with "64:0" in the name. If this modprobe command has the desired effect, check into your distro's particular mechanisms for configuring your system to load these extra modules at boot time, which often involves editing files in the /etc directory.

QSynth

The least complicated way to get one of these cards to play MIDI is to use QSynth. It is a simple-to-use ALSA soft synth that takes MIDI data as input and uses *.sf2* format soundfonts to produce audio output. In its simplest configuration, it can use ALSA for audio output, avoiding the need to run JACK. If you already need or want to run JACK, it can connect its output to JACK instead. In this configuration, you can also use a variety of other ALSA soft synths such as Hydrogen and Aeolus, all sharing the same audio output. QSynth is the most useful for general music production, and so it is my focus here, but the others are well worth your time to check out (In particular, I wish I had had time to cover Aeolus. It is a pipe organ simulator that does a simply spectacular job).

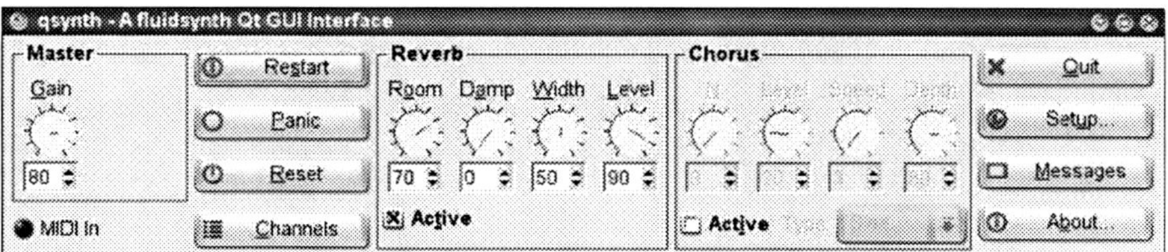

Configure the Audio Driver

The first decision you need to make is whether to use ALSA or JACK for output. I will cover starting and configuring of the JACK audio server in detail in a moment. If you have a slow computer, you may not be able to run QSynth through JACK, and you will have to run without JACK, and run Rosegarden without its audio or synth plugin capabilities enabled. No matter which option you choose, both are configured via the *Setup* button. In this example, I'm using JACK. Take special note that I have adjusted the sample rate to match the sample rate I'm using with JACK, which is 48,000 Hz (for reasons I will explain directly.) Also note that I have checked *[x] Auto Connect JACK Outputs*. This allows QSynth to make its own default connection with JACK, which is very convenient.

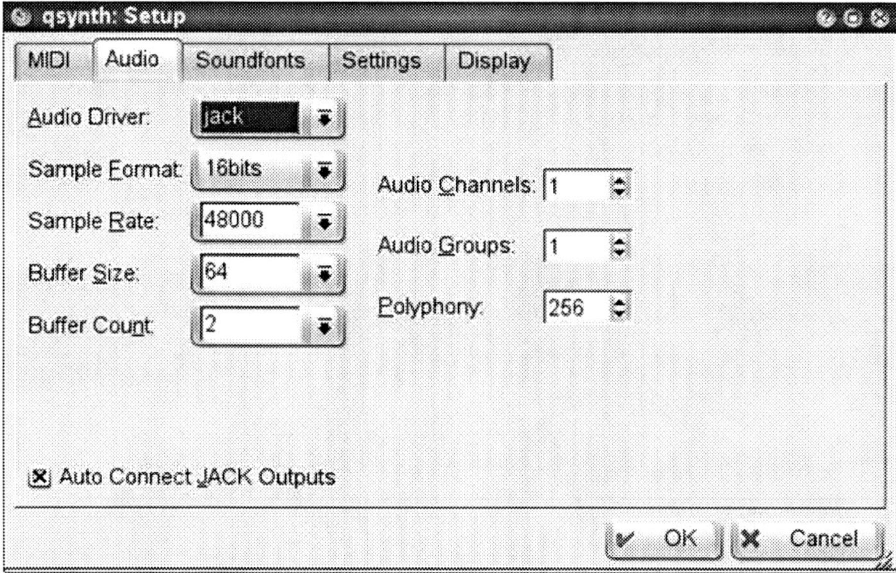

Loading a Soundfont

Finally, it's necessary to load at least one soundfont. These are the same *.sf2* soundfonts used by the SB Live! series of cards, and they are loaded via a different tab on the same setup page.

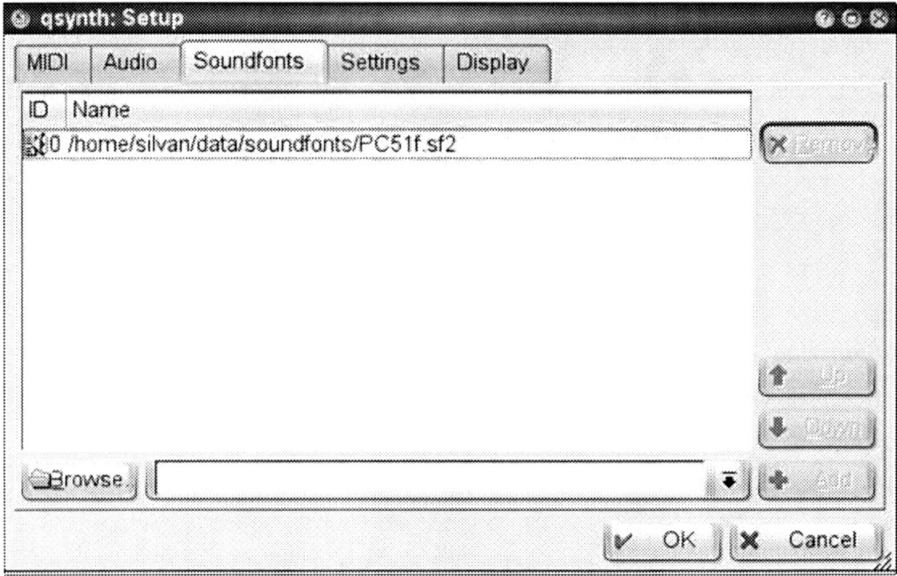

Synth Plugins

It is also possible to play using synth plugins. There is a FluidSynth-DSSI plugin that provides essentially the same functionality as QSynth, except that it's integrated directly into Rosegarden. I will describe it in detail when I talk about assigning instruments to tracks, because its configuration and use is entirely internal to Rosegarden. For the moment it is sufficient to know that it exists, and that it requires a working JACK audio server in order to function.

2.2   Playing Audio

In order to play audio you will need to run JACK.

2.2.1 What is JACK?

JACK is short for the "Jack Audio Connection Kit". JACK is a flexible audio server that allows its client applications to share the audio hardware seamlessly, and to share a common transport. It provides flexible mechanisms for routing inputs and outputs to and from client applications using a jack-and-cable metaphor. It is geared toward the audio professional who wants to get the lowest possible latency and the best possible performance out of his or her hardware. Whether your own goals are professional or not, you still need JACK to get audio out of Rosegarden (although you can still do MIDI work without it under most circumstances.)

2.2.2 Look After Your Kernel

It is theoretically possible to run JACK and Rosegarden with an ordinary stock kernel as installed by any distro, but I have never obtained acceptable results, even on machines with quite high specs. It is simply impossible to throw enough CPU after the problem, and you will not obtain acceptable results until you look after your kernel. I strongly recommend that you leave aside the kernel question entirely, and run something like Fervent's Studio..to go! (*http://www.ferventsoftware.com*), AGNULA's DeMuDi (*http://www.agnula.org*), or Planet CCRMA (*http://ccrma.stanford.edu/planet ccrma/ software/*). You can also obtain suitable kernels from either AGNULA or the Planet to retrofit existing installations.

I think that perhaps in another year or so, this question will be easy for anyone to solve using any off the shelf distro, merely by changing a few configuration options along the way. In the meantime, running, or borrowing packages from a specialized music distro is a great way to save yourself having to deal with the headaches that still exist as of this writing. For my own part, I use the 2.4.25-multimedia kernel from AGNULA, because it was installable as a retrofit package for my existing Debian system. However, Studio..to go! ships with a suitably tweaked up 2.6 kernel that works quite well. The difference between these two is a toss-up as of today, but I expect that the newer 2.6 kernels will quickly become the better choice.

2.2.3 Starting and Tweaking JACK

The simplest way to control your JACK server is to use QJackCtl. It is a very useful utility that provides a convenient way to start and stop your JACK server, to play with various configuration parameters to find the best combination for your hardware, and to manage JACK connections between applications.

2.2.4 Configuring the JACK Server

To change how your JACK server is configured, use the *Setup* button. The process that follows will probably be tedious and time-consuming, but once you have discovered the "magic numbers" for your hardware, everything should continue to work thereafter. The tweaked kernel you installed allows JACK to have higher than normal priority, and this requires root privileges. You should configure JACK to start using "jackstart" so that you can run Rosegarden and JACK as an ordinary user.

If "jackstart" does not work, then your kernel needs attention. You do not have "capabilities" enabled. "Capabilities" allow you to run certain applications as your user, while giving them the root-level privileges they require for proper performance. This allows you to run as your user, creating files as your user, and discourages you from doing more with root than is absolutely necessary.

If you are running Studio..to go! then you can probably skip this section entirely, because it should find the best settings for you automagically, and should boot with JACK already up and running.

The settings displayed are those that work best for me on my Sound Blaster Live!, and you may well have some fiddling to do from here. If you have more than one soundcard, you may need to twiddle the "Interface" setting. I don't actually have any experience in such a situation, so you are on your own to experiment in that case.

Discovering the best combination is a process of playing with the "Frames/Period", "Sample Rate" and "Periods/Buffer" settings. Your objective here is to find the lowest possible latency, as reported in the lower right-hand corner of the dialog. As you change settings, this number will show the results yielded by that combination. You want the sample rate high, and the frames/periods and periods/buffer low.

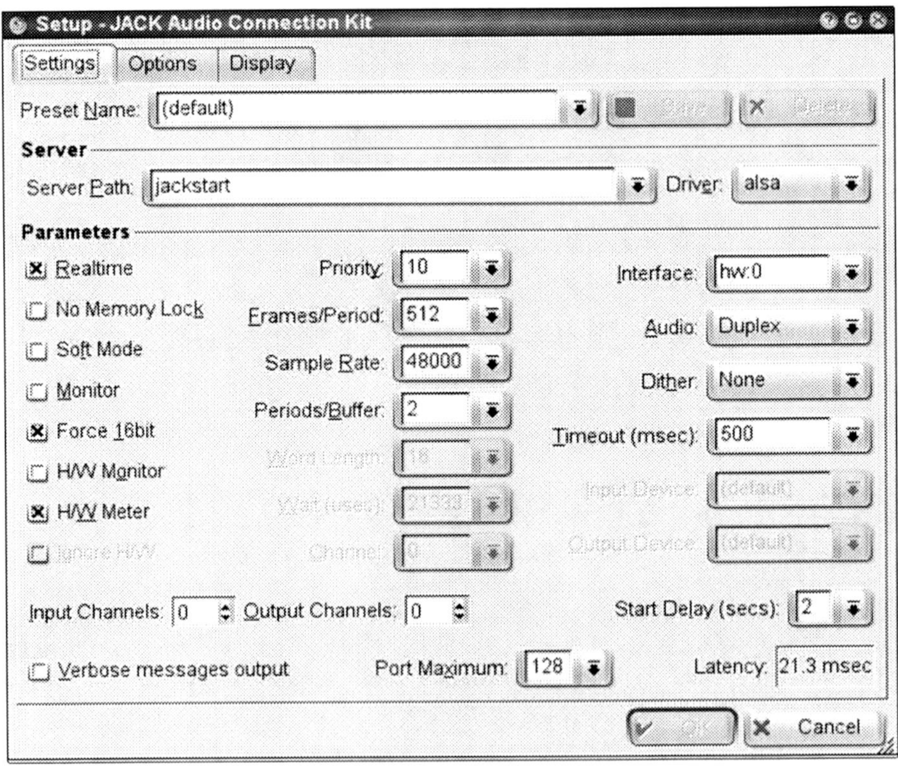

I suggest you dial up the lowest possible latency, click on *OK*, then try to start the JACK server with the *Start* button on the main dialog. If the server fails to start, come back to this dialog and keep working up, one setting at a time, until you find a combination that works. Many combinations of settings will probably cause JACK to fail immediately. You should quickly begin to get an idea of the range of possible values you can use that will actually work, and then you can home in on the ideal settings from there. (For example, it is impossible to start JACK on my hardware with a periods/buffer other than two, so there is nothing for it but to use that setting and move on to a different parameter.)

The Evil XRUN

It is very important to avoid xruns. If you find a combination of low-latency settings that allow the JACK server to start, but which produce a flood of xruns, you're aiming too high. Xruns are reported in the main QJackCtl dialog. Ideally, you should see 0(0) in green, like this:

If, on the other hand, you see something like this, in red, you have trouble ahead:

You never want to see this much red. Seeing any red at all is really unacceptable to the purist, but I have tested this with some reasonably fast (2.0 GHz or better) computers, and have done everything possible, short of buying high end professional quality hardware, to reduce my xruns. It is not possible, in my experience, to banish the xrun completely, but it is possible to manage the problem more or less effectively by ensuring that you do not perform CPU- or disk-intensive tasks while playing or recording audio.

2.2.5 Managing JACK Connections

Rosegarden will establish sane default connections automatically. So will QSynth and Hydrogen, if you've configured them to do so. ZynAddSubFX, Time Machine, and perhaps the majority of other JACK-aware applications do not do this. To see and change the connections, click on the *Connections* button. Making or breaking connections is a process of highlighting one or more items in the left pane and one or more items in the right pane, then using the *Connect* or *Disconnect* buttons as required.

Items in the left pane are output ports, and items in the right pane are input ports. Some applications, such as Rosegarden, make both input and output ports available, so they appear in both lists. Others, such as Hydrogen, only provide output, while still others, such as Time Machine, only provide input.

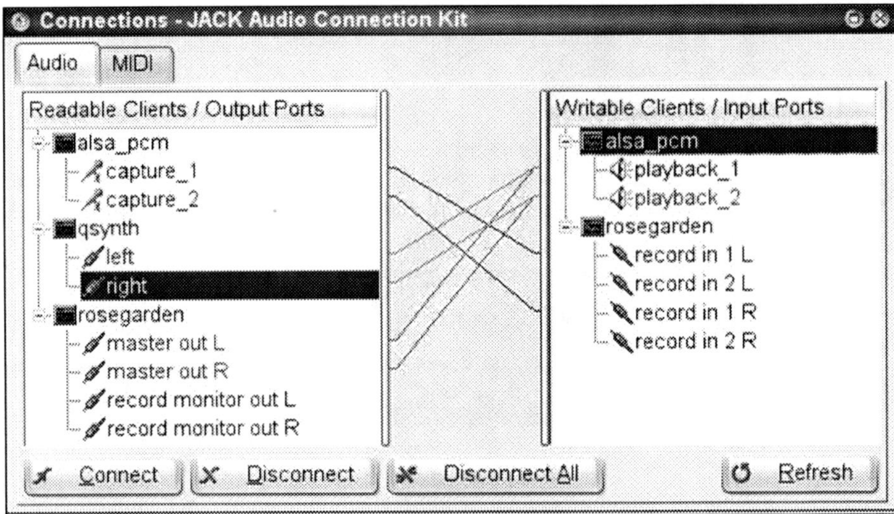

NOTE: You can also use QJackCtl to manage ALSA MIDI connections. Unfortunately, this MIDI manager is not compatible with Rosegarden 1.0, and you must use Rosegarden's own internal connection manager exclusively. A fix for this inconsistency is is under way on the unstable, development branch as of this writing.

3 The First Look Around

Let's begin by starting Rosegarden, and having a look at the main window. This is where you get an overall view of your work, and control a number of settings and parameters.

3.1 The Main Window

A Rosegarden document is called a composition. The main window is primarily dedicated to editing at the composition level, so most of these tools affect your document in a broad way. This is where you name tracks and assign instruments to them, create and manipulate segments, and watch a broad overview of playback. I will explain these concepts in more detail later on. This is also where you configure segment parameters such as label and color. Tempo and time signature settings exist at the composition level, and they may be edited here in the main window using the tempo ruler.

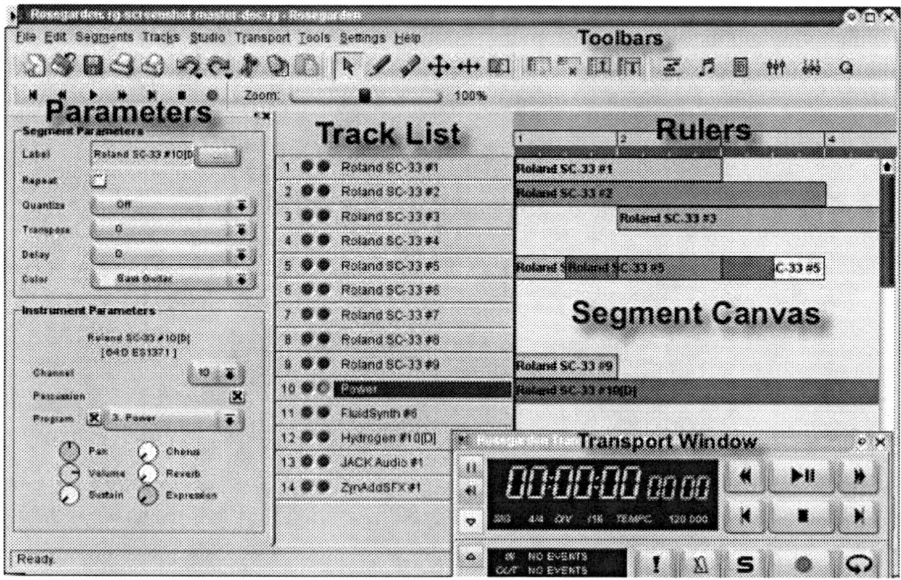

3.2 Special Toolbars

One of the first things you might notice about Rosegarden is that there are several toolbars at the top of the main window. In addition to the usual standard controls shared by most KDE applications,

there are several toolbars specific to Rosegarden. You'll choose various tools for selecting and manipulating segments from the Tools Toolbar (Select, Move, Resize, New, Erase, Split),

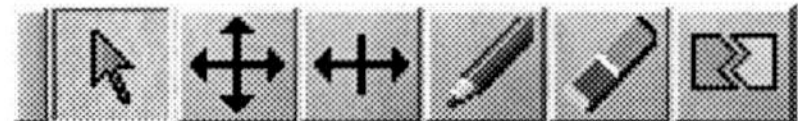

a subset of transport tools available in the Transport Toolbar (toggled off by default),

tracks can be added, deleted or moved with the Tracks Toolbar,

and once a segment has been created, you can use the Editors Toolbar to open it in one of the three available editors. You'll also find icons to start the Quantizer, the Studio configuration dialog, the Synth Plugin manager, the audio file manager, and the MIDI and audio mixers.

At the end of it all is the Zoom Slider, which is used to change the magnification of the Segment Canvas:

3.3   The Tracklist

Rosegarden is a track-based sequencer. Each entry in the tracklist is a separate track that can have individualized settings for several different parameters. Each track has a label and an output assignment, and can be used to record, play, and manipulate either MIDI or audio data, but never both.

3.3.1 Instrument vs. Name

The tracklist can be configured to display either the name you've assigned to the track, or the name of the instrument to which it is connected. Toggle this behavior with *Settings -> Show Track Labels*. I will explain more about this later on, in *Managing Instrument Parameters*.

Here we see how instrument assignments are displayed on the tracklist. In this example, the tracks are configured to play using instruments #1 and #2, respectively, on the "Roland SC-33" device.

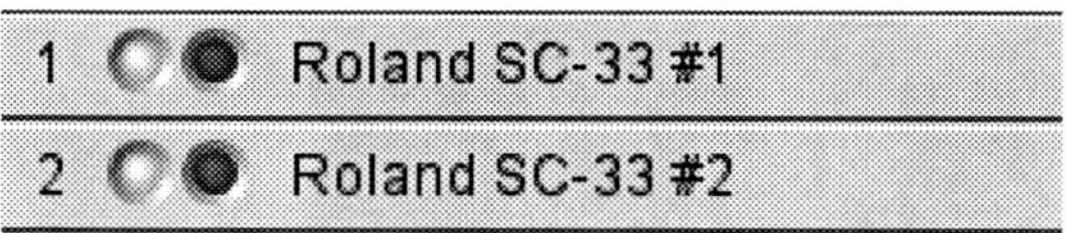

3.3.2 Track LEDs

Here we see the labels. One track has not yet had a name assigned, so it remains "<untitled>". Each track has two LEDs. The blue one is the track mute. If the blue LED is glowing, the track will be heard during playback. All of the blue LEDs can be turned on or off all at once with *Tracks -> Mute All and -> Un-Mute All*. The red LED lights up to indicate that the affected track is armed as the destination for recording operations.

TIP: The mute LEDs can also be used to control which tracks are included when exporting the composition into another format. Muted tracks will typically be ignored during export, though this varies slightly by the export method chosen.

3.3.3 Changing the Track Name

To change the track name, double click on the label. A dialog should appear, allowing you to enter a new name.

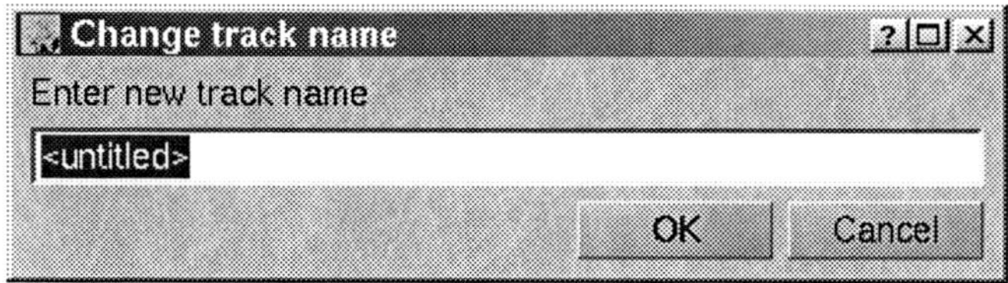

3.3.4 Adding, Removing, Moving Tracks

The tools on the Tracks Toolbar can be used to move tracks up and down, to delete them, or to create new tracks. It is not possible to copy an entire track.

3.4   Segments and Segment Parameters

Rosegarden compositions are made up of *segments*, and editing at the composition level involves dragging them around and rearranging them within tracks. Segments are a universal container that may hold either MIDI events or audio data. Segments are rather similar to layers in an image editing program such as the GIMP. MIDI segments can be cut, pasted, split, recombined, overlapped, flattened, and pretty much rearranged at will, and are very flexible. Audio segments behave in many of the same ways, but they are more limited in the ways they can be modified.

3.4.1 Creating a New Segment

You can begin recording (audio or MIDI) to create a segment, but I'll get into that a bit later. For now, why not draw one from scratch?

Use the [pencil] tool to create a new segment. Click and drag it out to the desired length:

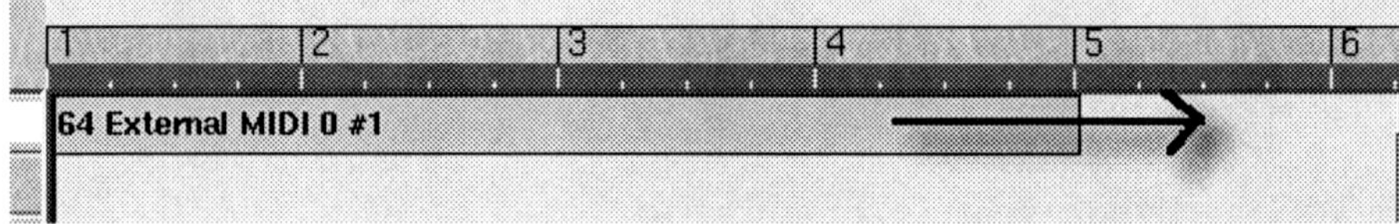

Now that a segment exists, you can open it with one of the three editors. I will return to that idea later on.

3.4.2 Moving and Copying

Use the [cursor] cursor to select a segment:

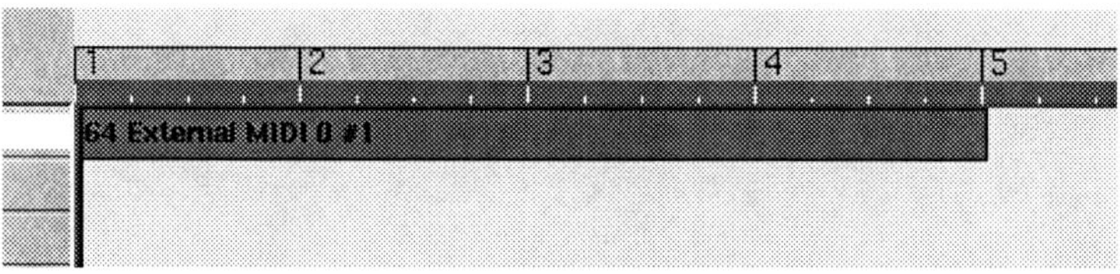

Drag it to a new track:

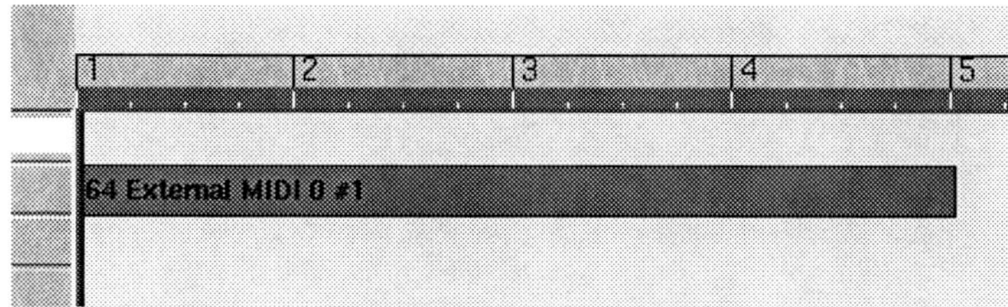

Hold down *Ctrl* while dragging it back,and make a copy:

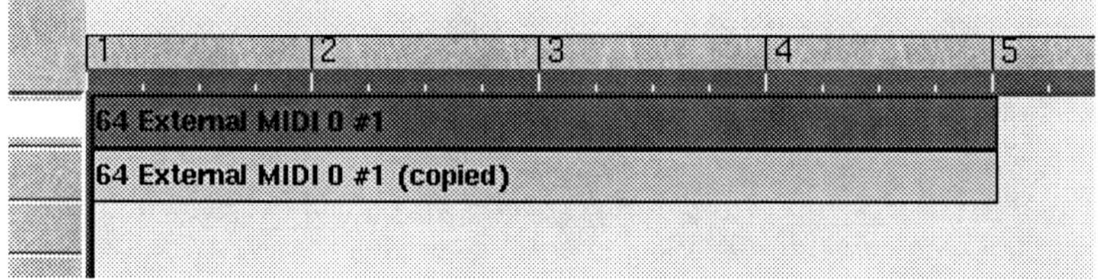

3.4.3 Splitting and Joining

Use the [cursor icon] cursor to split one of the segments, then switch to the [pointer icon] and drag one of the pieces so that it overlaps the segment on the other track. By default, this will snap to whole beat positions within the bar, but you can override that behavior by holding down the *Shift* key while dragging.

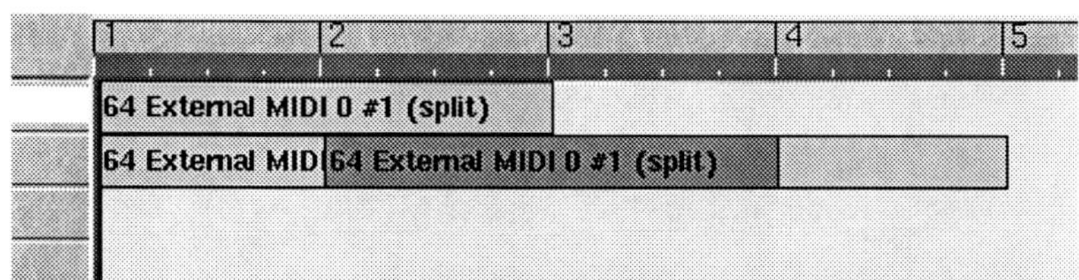

Highlighting the smaller of two overlapping segments can sometimes be a bit tricky, but once accomplished, you can use *Segments -> Join* to combine several segments into one, rather like flattening the layers in an image editing program. This can also merge MIDI events from several different tracks into a single segment. The events will combine, and merge onto a segment on whichever track is currently active.

Audio segments can be split, but they cannot be resized, joined or merged. If you split an audio segment, you can undo that operation to revert it to its original state, but you cannot, for example, cut out the middle and splice the ends back together. Neither can you merge two overlapping audio segments into one, nor merge audio and MIDI segments together. Audio segments are always associated with a file on disk, usually in the audio path for this particular composition, and changing the length of the segment does not affect the underlying file in any way.

Split by Pitch

If you have a segment where the treble and bass parts are jumbled together, you might wish to split this at middle C or thereabouts. You can use *Segments -> Split and Join -> Split by Pitch* and then make your selections for split point, clef handling, etc. from the resulting dialog. By default, this feature attempts to split the segment intelligently, so that you can hopefully avoid winding up with treble notes in the bass part, and bass notes in the treble part.

Once split, the two segments will overlap exactly on the same track. It is impossible to select a segment that lies completely underneath another segment, so it is probably a good idea to move one of the two halves into a different track.

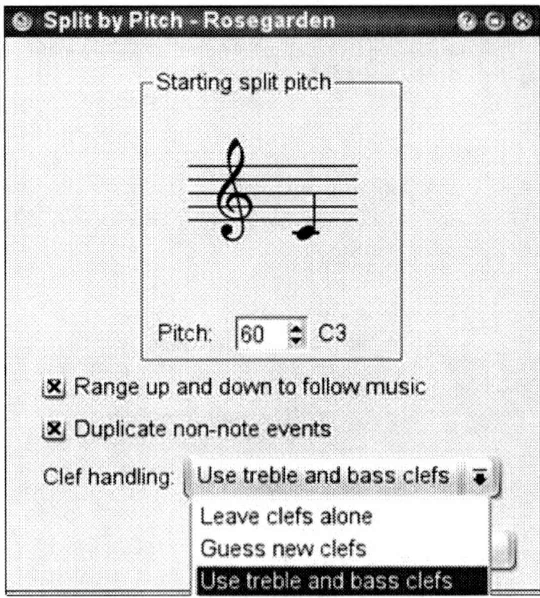

3.4.4 Segment Previews

You can get some sense of what that bit of music is like just by looking at the segment display, which is a useful visual aid when dragging things around. If this feature is not turned on, turn it on with *Settings -> Segment Previews*. This displays a miniature "piano roll" for MIDI segments, and a drawing of the wave form for audio segments.

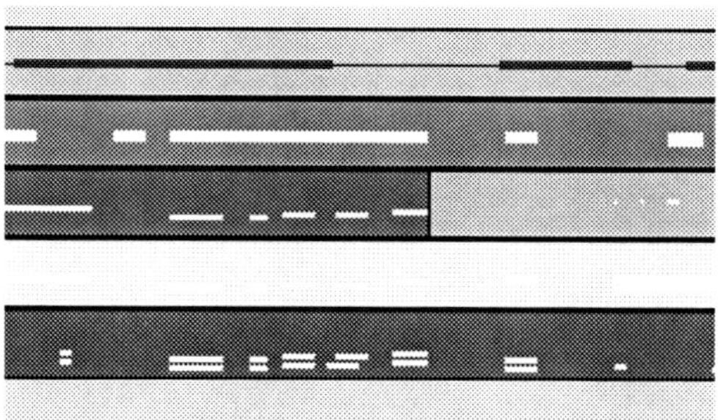

3.4.5 Segment Parameters

After you have created a segment, you can edit various parameters from the *Segment Parameters* box to the left:

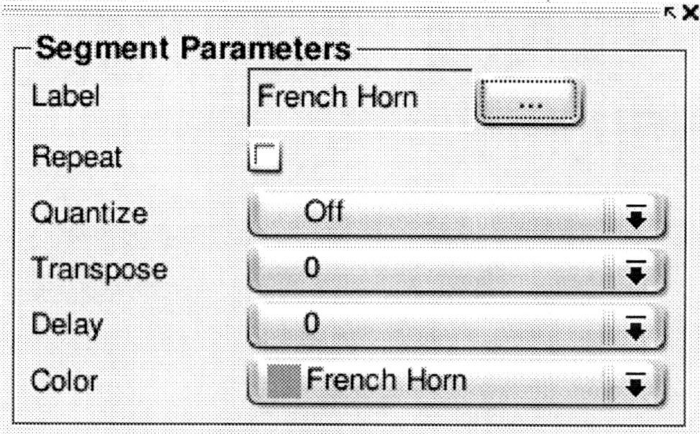

Every segment can have a unique label and color. In this example, I've chosen the most obvious color to use for this French horn part, but colors are entirely user-configurable, and these defaults are only suggestions. I'll explain how to configure custom colors later on, in the Studio chapter.

3.4.6 Repeats

Every segment can be made to repeat. It will keep repeating until the end of the document, or until another segment is encountered in the track; whichever comes first. These are displayed between repeat signs (|: :|) in the notation editor.

You can turn all repeats into copies at once with *Segments -> Turn Repeats into Copies*, or you can turn individual repeats into copies by double clicking on the light colored repeat rectangles.

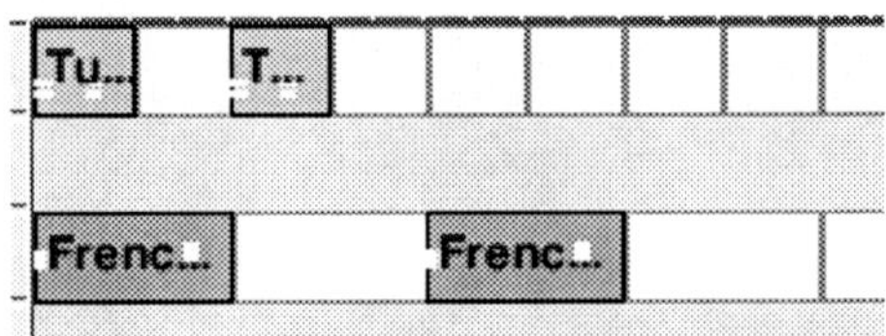

3.4.7 Segment Quantizer

Changing the setting in this box will immediately quantize all notes in this segment to the selected grid position. It will move the start times forward or back to align them with the next closest beat at the desired resolution. It will not change note durations in any way.

3.4.8 Transposing Instruments

If you wish to write notation for transposing instruments, you can dial a transposition setting into the *Transpose* box. This will cause the part to sound in a different range from written. A typical Bb trumpet part, for example, should have -2 here.

3.4.9 Delay

The *Delay* setting allows you to knock the timing of a segment out of sync on purpose. There is no negative delay, so if a situation arises where you wish to create a negative delay, you can accomplish this by putting a positive delay on all the other segments.

3.5   Getting Around in the Composition

If you've been following along thus far, you don't actually have anything useful to play. This might be a good time to load one of the sample files from the Rosegarden Library. The first time you use the *File -> Open* menu, you should be looking at the Library. If not, there should be an icon in the SpeedBar that will direct you to these files.

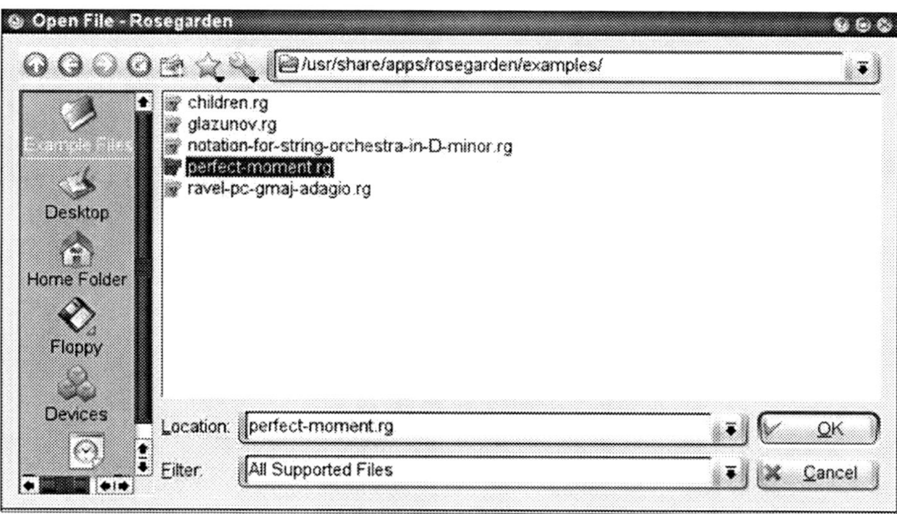

The highlighted file in the above screen capture is my own creation. "Perfect Moment" is the name of a yellow rose, and it also describes my mood at the time I composed that. It was the first composition I ever completed using Rosegarden.

3.5.1 The Playback Pointer

Notice that there is a vertical blue bar running vertically across the segment canvas. That bar is the *playback pointer*, and as it sweeps across the canvas, you'll hear the events as it passes over them.

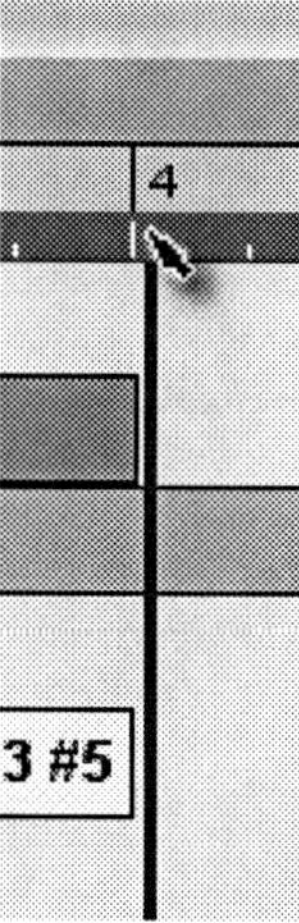

While you can't grab it and move it around directly, you can position it at any arbitrary point in the composition by clicking along the dark gray portion of the ruler at the top, or you can use the transport to move it around. If you don't see it, play with the transport or the ruler until you coax it out of hiding.

3.5.2 Loops

You can loop a portion of the composition. Set the loop region by holding *Shift* and clicking on the gray portion of the ruler, then dragging the white bar.

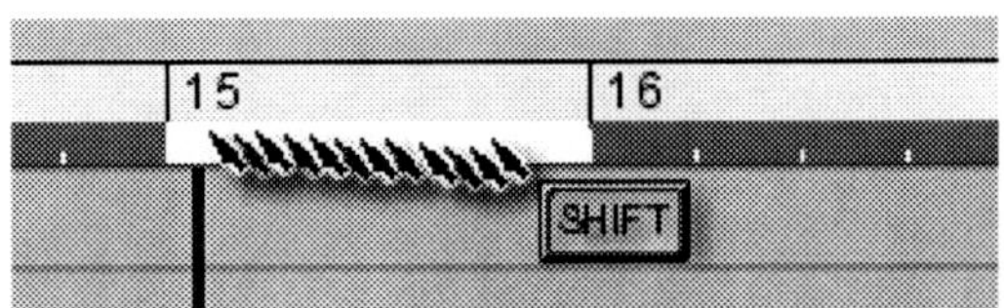

3.5.3 The Transport

You should have a separate, floating *Transport* window like this one. If it's not visible, then toggle it on with *Settings -> Show Transport*.

Most of these should be self-explanatory. If you can't figure out what any of the buttons do, hover over them a bit, and context-sensitive help will pop up.

The ❚❚ button switches between various display modes, including a visual metronome that flashes beats at you in color. Of special note are the panic, metronome, and solo buttons. If they're missing, toggle the extra controls via the △.

The panic button will stop any instruments that have gotten stuck droning for some reason (as sometimes happens when a synth loses track of the state of it's sustain controller, for example).

The metronome does what you'd probably expect. The button controls two separate metronomes. One sounds during playback, the other during recording. Pressing the button while recording toggles the recording metronome. At all other times, the button affects the playback metronome. They share common settings for what device to use for playback, what pitches to use, and several other parameters, which are configured at *Composition -> Studio -> Manage Metronome*.

The solo button forces the Transport to play only whatever track is currently selected at the moment, independently of its mute state. (To "solo" more than one part, you'll need to set the mute for tracks individually, or by using *Tracks -> Mute All Tracks* and then un-muting the parts you desire). The loop button causes the Transport to loop within the white region defined on the ruler.

3.6   Time and Tempo

As I mentioned, the time signature and tempo are global to the entire composition. I'll discuss another way to manipulate these in another chapter, but here and now you can manipulate both time signature and tempo to your heart's content from the main window.

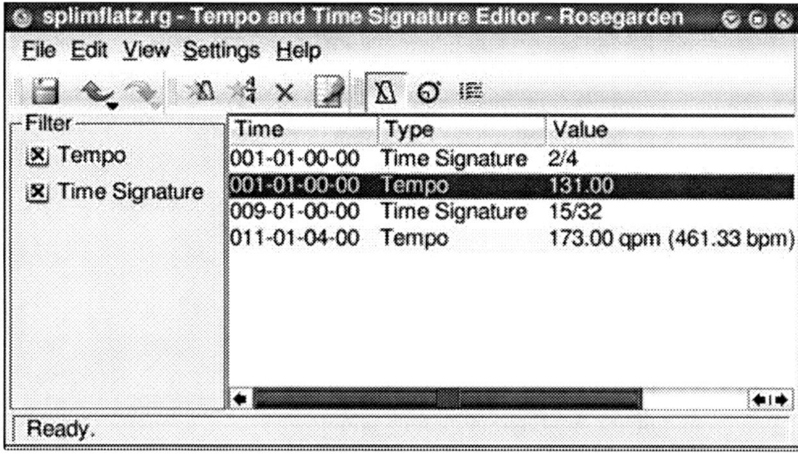

The tempo ruler changes color to indicate changes in tempo. When a change occurs, the tempo is displayed along the top half of the ruler, and the time signature is displayed across the bottom. If you double click this ruler, the Tempo and Time Signature editor will appear.

3.6.1 New Tempo

To add a new tempo, click the icon, and you'll be presented with a dialog like this:

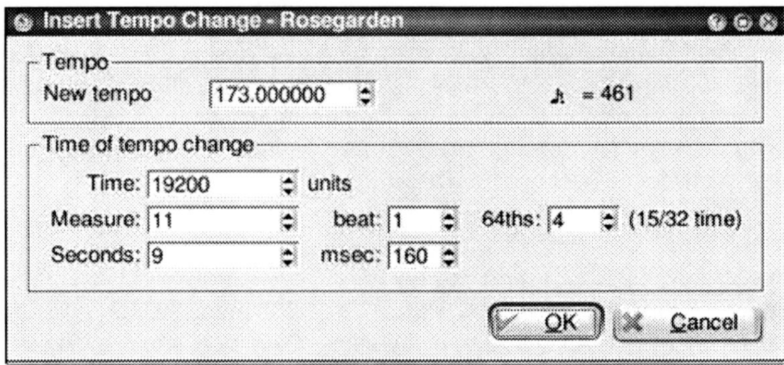

By default, new events you add here will be inserted at the point in time where you clicked to open the Tempo and Time Signature editor. You can change this by adjusting the "Time of tempo change" parameters, if you wish.

3.6.2 New Time Signature

Use the icon, and you'll be presented with a dialog like:

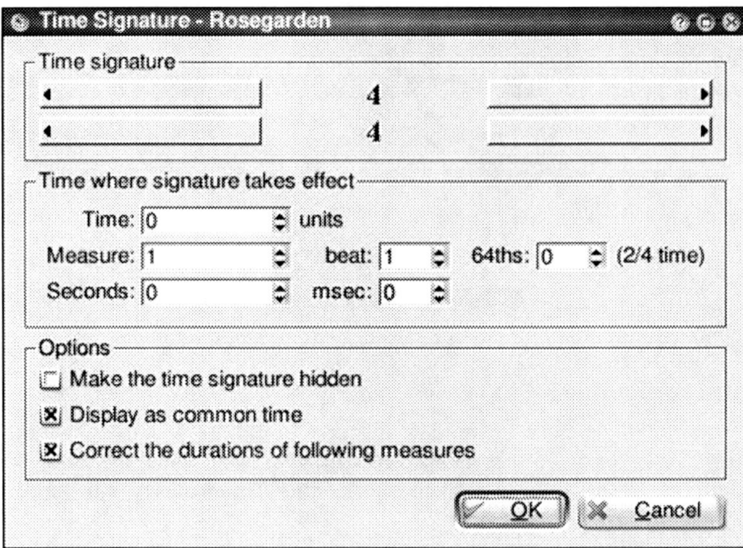

You can display the time signature as cut or common time, and make the time signature hidden. You should probably always leave "Correct the durations of the following measures" checked unless you have a good reason to do otherwise.

3.7   Document Markers

Markers are special events that can be used to mark particular passages in the music at a composition level. They appear on the ruler, and can be edited from *Composition -> Edit Markers...* Issuing this command summons the marker editor dialog. In this example, I've already created a sample pair. The "Marker Name" portion is what appears on the ruler, and the "Marker description" is for the informational purposes of the composer only.

3.7.1 The Manage Markers Dialog

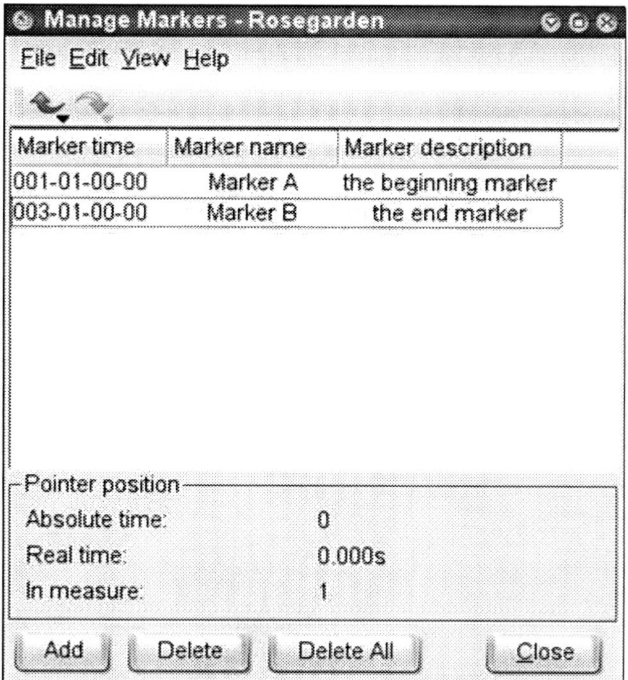

3.7.2 Creating a New Marker

Click on the *Add* button to create a new marker. A raw default marker will appear on the list spontaneously.

Marker time	Marker name	Marker description
001-01-00-00	Marker A	the beginning marker
001-01-00-00	new marker	no description
003-01-00-00	Marker B	the end marker

To edit it, or to edit an existing marker, double click on it. An editor like this will appear, allowing you to set the name and description, and adjust the time at which this marker will display.

> **NOTE**: Markers cannot be dragged around or otherwise edited from the ruler. They must be positioned and edited from this pair of dialogs, using the above controls. The same applies to tempo and time signature changes as well. Repositioning any of these elements is a royal pain.

3.7.3 Markers In Position

After closing out the manager dialog, the markers you created will appear on the ruler.

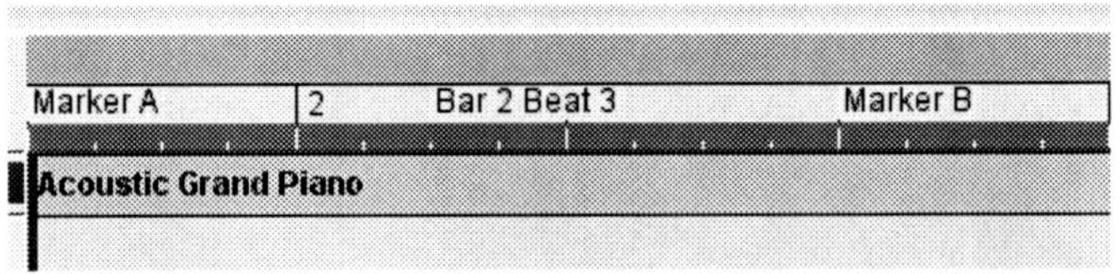

3.8   Miscellany

There are a few main window features that don't quite fit in anywhere else, yet which bear special mention.

3.8.1 Importing and Merging Other Compositions

Several options are available for importing and merging material from other sources. On the *File -> Import* menu, you can import standard MIDI files (**.mid*) and Hydrogen (**.h2song*) files. On the *File -> Merge* menu, you can merge these and other data sources (including native Rosegarden composition (**.rg*) files) into the existing composition.

3.8.2 Autosave

If you have a power outage or the like, the next time you start Rosegarden and attempt to load the file you were working on, you'll be presented with the option of loading the autosave file instead. If you hadn't yet saved the file, you'll find it in your ~/autosave directory with a basic name of "untitled."

The autosave interval defaults to 60 seconds. Configure it via the Settings menu. If you notice Rosegarden grabbing a lot of your CPU time for no apparent reason, it is probably autosave, and you might want to increase the interval, or turn this feature completely off. It can become quite cumbersome when working on very large compositions.

4   The Studio

Now that you have a general idea how Rosegarden works, it now is a good time to think about telling Rosegarden something about the MIDI equipment you wish to use. People who intend to use Rosegarden purely for audio work are free to skip this chapter entirely.

Before we get started, some of you might need some basic background information so that you can dive into this with some understanding of the concepts I am about to explain. If you are new to MIDI, or if anything in this chapter leaves you scratching your head, you might want to read through my MIDI Primer in Appendix B.

4.1   What is a Studio?

Every native Rosegarden composition (*.rg*) file contains a studio definition in addition to all the nuts and bolts stuff of music. The studio is a definition of every MIDI device Rosegarden can detect during the course of editing the composition. (Everything that was there at the start, plus any new devices that become available during the course of editing; as when starting something like ZynAddSubFX or Aeolus in the middle of working on a composition, for example.) It comprises information about the device itself, and about how data is routed into or out of it.

4.1.1 What is a Connection?

Rosegarden has an integrated MIDI router to manage the flow of raw MIDI events into and out of ports provided by the underlying ALSA infrastructure. You can think of this as something like the sort of router often used to share a broadband internet connection. Unlike ethernet, however, MIDI is not bidirectional over the same cable.

As a consequence of this, all connections in Rosegarden are unidrectional; even if both connections belong to the same physical piece of hardware. Connections will be displayed as one of "read," "write," or "duplex." In this diagram, connections are represented by black arrows that point in the direction data will flow through them. Rosegarden's MIDI router allows you to rearrange these connections as you require, to change what is connected where.

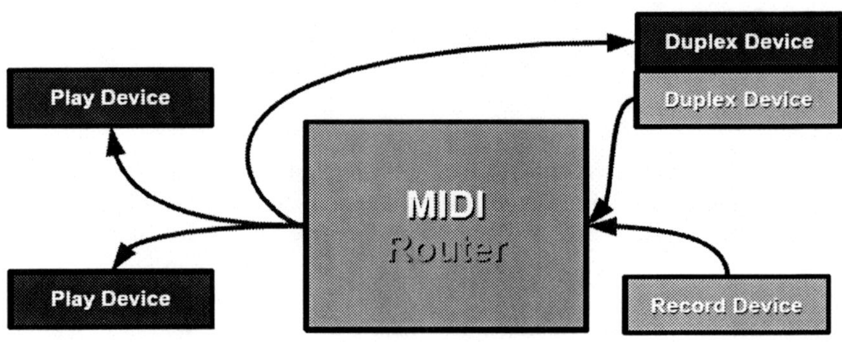

4.1.2 What is a Device?

A device is a sort of virtual model of an individual piece of MIDI equipment. Equipment, in this sense, can be full-fledged external MIDI hardware, internal hardware like the Sound Blaster Live!, or virtual hardware like QSynth or Virtual Keyboard. Each device encapsulates information about the capabilities of a piece of equipment, and allows you to make use of those capabilities from within Rosegarden. In effect, the better the job you do of describing a particular device in Rosegarden, the better control you will have over that device.

For example, if you have a nice keyboard attached to your computer, but you accept Rosegarden's default General MIDI device definition for it, you will be unable to make use of any of the keyboard's advanced features from within Rosegarden until you make your device definition more accurate. Conversely, telling Rosegarden you have a Roland JV-88 does not make it so, and if you assign any *instruments* to programs that are not actually available on the connected equipment, you will hear no sound (more about instruments in the next chapter).

A device like the following is typical of either QSynth or a Sound Blaster Live! after loading an uncomplicated soundfont. It includes a basic set of controllers (which are dependent on the capabilities of either QSynth or the Sound Blaster, both of which do support a limited number of controllers, and actually have nothing to do with the soundfont per se), a set of standard General MIDI programs loaded into bank 0 0, and a set of Roland GS-style extra drum kits loaded into bank 1 0.

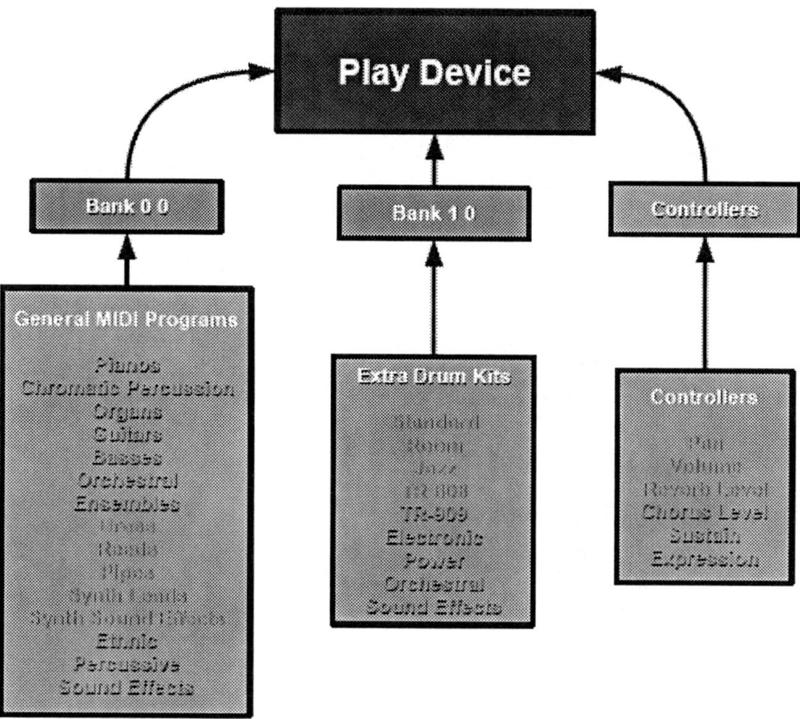

4.1.3 Putting Connections and Devices Together

A studio can consist of just one device, and perhaps for many of you that is all the complexity you will ever need. The real power, however, lies with Rosegarden's ability to manage numerous devices simultaneously. A studio is, in effect, a collection of device descriptions and a routing table ensuring that the right devices are connected to the right MIDI equipment on the other end.

A Simple Sound Blaster Live! Studio

Even on the comparatively simple and very inexpensive end of the hardware spectrum, it is quite possible to have more than one device to manage. The Sound Blaster Live! falls into this category, with four separate write connections available, and four separate play devices. (Actually, there are five write connections once you include the duplex external MIDI port, but that is not depicted here.) They all share the same soundfont on the hardware side, but Rosegarden doesn't know that until you configure the studio that way, by loading programs out of the soundfont into each of the four play devices. (More on that last point in a moment.)

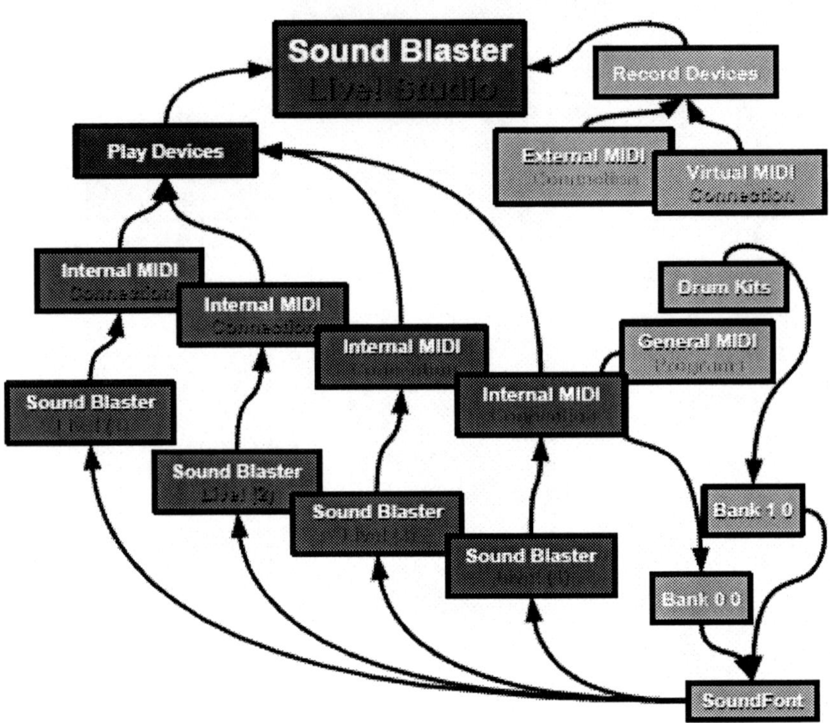

A Typical QSynth Studio

Another typical, simple setup involves using QSynth for MIDI playback and VKeybd for
input. You can start either of these after starting Rosegarden, and Rosegarden will detect
them and make a play connection and a record connection available, along with an
empty play device.

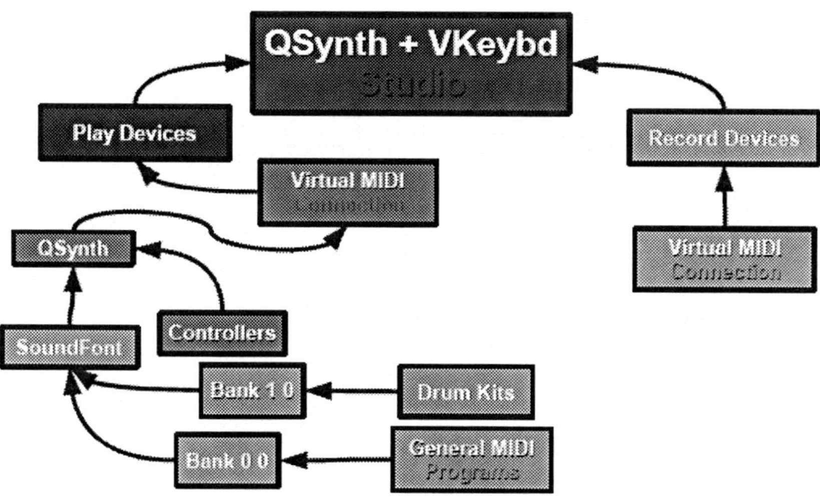

A More Complex Studio

This is what my own studio looks like when I have QSynth, Hydrogen, and ZynAddSubFX running, along with my Roland Sound Canvas and my Sound Blaster Live!. It looks horribly complex on paper, and it would look even worse if I drew out every single bank of GS variations, and did a better job of representing the fact that, while the same soundfont happens to be loaded into both the Sound Blaster and QSynth, that doesn't have to be the case. No matter how it looks, this is actually quite simple to use day to day, believe it or not. Rosegarden makes this easy.

Notice that I have controllers for the Sound Blaster, for QSynth, and for the Roland (the "External MIDI GS Synth"), but I do not have any controllers defined for Hydrogen or ZynAddSubFX. That's because, to the best of my knowledge, neither of those soft synths knows how to do anything with controllers. They both have their own control panels that must be twiddled manually, and that sort of thing can't be automated from within Rosegarden.

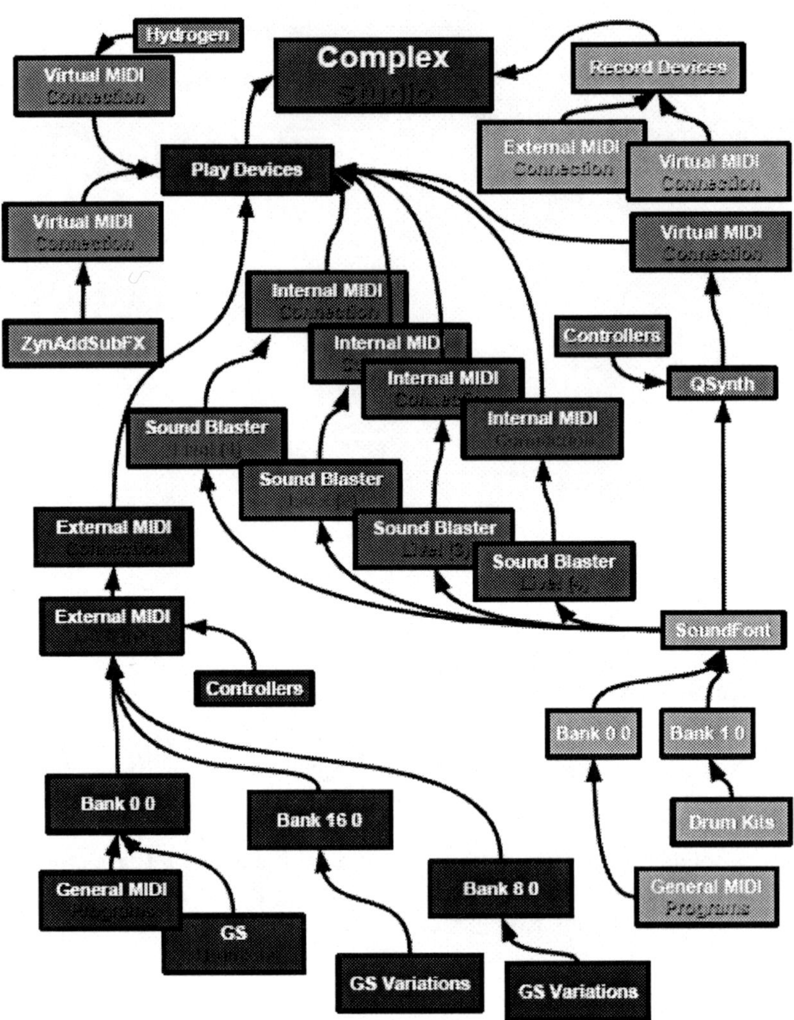

4.2   Configuring Your Own Studio

The first step in this process is to open the main Studio dialog *Composition -> Studio -> Manage MIDI Devices...* or by clicking on the [icon] icon.

You'll be presented with a dialog that resembles this one, except, of course, that this one has already largely been configured to suit my own default studio. It is divided into two sections; one for play devices, and one for record devices, and their associated connections. It also shows you how each of these devices is connected to internal, external, and software synths.

In this example, I have a device named "Roland SC-33" connected to "64:0 EMU101K MPU-401 (UART) (duplex)" and four "SB Live (n)" devices connected to each of 65:0 through 65:3, which are the four output ports on my SB Live!, with their associated write connections. I also have three generic spots reserved for soft synths, named "Soft Synth 1" through "Soft Synth 3", one of which is currently connected to KAMix, an ALSA mixer client that can be controlled via MIDI. These are empty devices that I created with the *New* button.

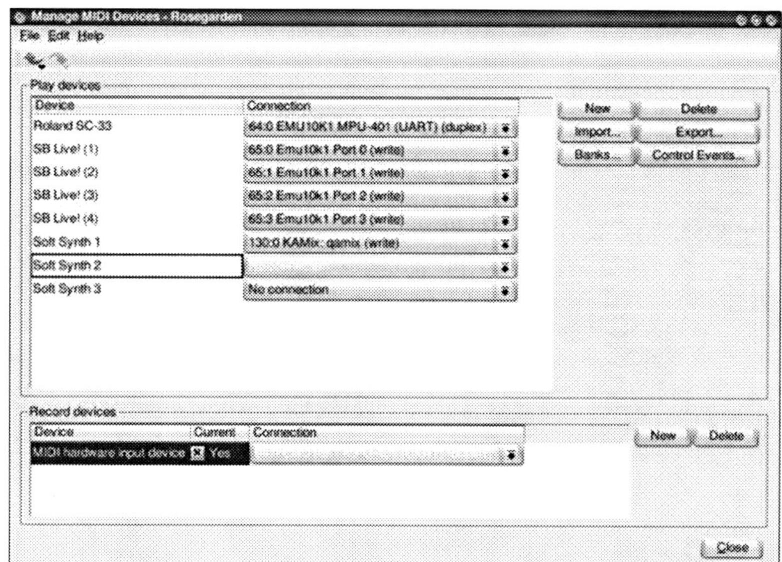

4.2.1 Connections

The reality of Rosegarden's MIDI router is a bit less intuitive than the diagram I presented earlier. Here is that same diagram with the ALSA port numbers included.

NOTE: The diagram does not exactly represent the same set of devices and connections depicted in the dialog box snapshot above.

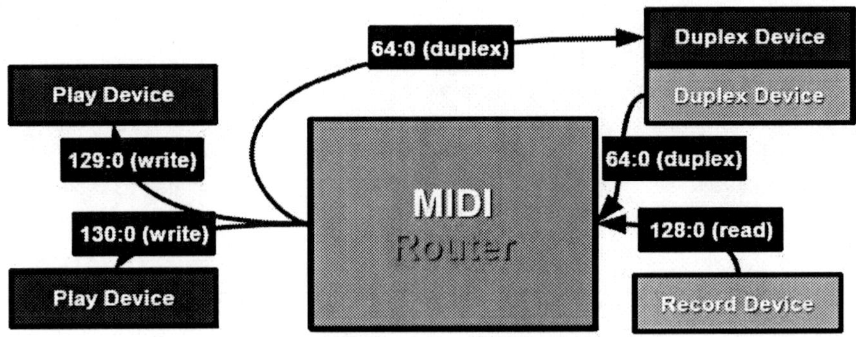

You might wonder about the strange names and numbers. ALSA assigns numbers to ports in three ranges. 64: means it is an external MIDI port on the first soundcard, which might be connected to a MIDI keyboard, sound module, or other noise producing gadget through some sort of cable. 65: means it is a virtual port with a supported internal synth such as the Sound Blaster Live! on the other side. Software synths like Hydrogen, ZynAddSubFX and the like will take numbers at the time they're started, on a first-come, first served basis starting at 128. In addition to the number, most of these will have some kind of vaguely descriptive text component, such as "Emu10k1 Port 0 (write)." These names are provided by the underlying kernel driver, and don't always make a lot of sense. That's why Rosegarden allows you give your devices a proper name.

4.2.2 Record Devices

Record devices are MIDI keyboards, virtual keyboards, MIDI guitars and the like. As record devices are rather less complicated, I will cover them first. With a record device, you have no capabilities to describe. The only thing Rosegarden can do is read data from it, or not. You may name these if you wish, but the *Record devices* section of this dialog is the only place where you will see the names, and I never bother to name mine.

Rosegarden can record from any number of inputs simultaneously. It will create a record device for every read connection it detects. Each of these can be set to be an active record device by toggling the associated checkbox.

In this example, I have both a hardware record device and a software record device. These devices were created spontaneously when Rosegarden detected the associated duplex read and virtual read connections. I have marked both of them "Current" and I can record events from either one of them, or both of them at the same time.

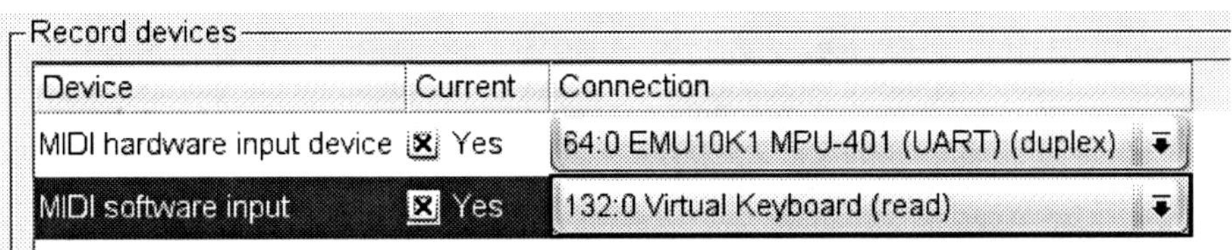

> **NOTE**: Rosegarden does not always automatically mark a record device as "Current." If you have a keyboard or similar device, and Rosegarden isn't recording anything, this dialog is the first place to look for troubleshooting the problem.
>
> Rosegarden 1.0 is not capable of treating data received from these various multiple inputs separately. However, an internal record of where which events came from is a part of the data, and it will eventually be possible to make use of this information in interesting ways.

4.2.3 Play Devices

Play devices are where all the fun, and all the complexity is. As I have mentioned elsewhere, they can be MIDI keyboards, sound modules, software synths, samplers, and pretty well anything else that can take MIDI input, such as KAMix. (Synth plugins are somewhat different. There is a single synth plugin device into which any and all plugins are plugged, and it is not a MIDI play device. I will cover synth plugins in the next chapter.)

The Easy Road (General MIDI Only)

If you have only one play device, and it only uses straight General MIDI programs, then you are probably ready to go out of the box. If you start Rosegarden with no file to open, it opens a default blank document, called *autoload.rg*. Initially, this will be the system default that was installed with Rosegarden. It will load a set of basic General MIDI programs and controllers, and will route output from this device to the first available play connection. The device at the top of the list is always the default device.

Typically this play connection will be routed to the correct destination for your MIDI data. If not, all you should have to do is adjust the routing table by dialing appropriate connections into the associated combo boxes. For example, if Rosegarden defaults to routing your output to "64:0 (duplex)" and you do not have any external equipment attached to your computer, you probably want to change this to point to either 65:0 or something like 128:0 as appropriate.

The Harder Road (Loading Device Definitions from the Library)

If you have some need beyond the simplest one-device, only-General MIDI scenario, you will have to use the bank editor; even if you do not intend to edit any banks directly. To load or create a device click on the *Banks...* button to pop up the bank editor dialog.

In this example, you can see that I have already imported some programs from the soundfont I use on my SB Live!, and I have named the four devices "SB Live! (1)" through "SB Live! (4)" for my own convenience. This soundfont has programs available in four banks, which are displayed as the branches of the tree. The LSB column is not visible in this snapshot, but the bank names tell most of the tale. I named the last one "Percussion" to set it apart, because that is where this soundfont stores the drum kits.

You can also see that I have a device called "Soft Synth 2" highlighted, and I'm looking at the empty list of programs that make up Rosegarden's virtual model for this device. Unlike internal and external MIDI equipment, Rosegarden assigns connections to soft synths on a first come, first serve basis, based on the order in which the applications are started. It is very easy to wind up with something named "Hydrogen" that is actually connected to QSynth. I find I prefer to give these things generic names and assign the connections manually as required, because I start and stop soft synths as I need them.

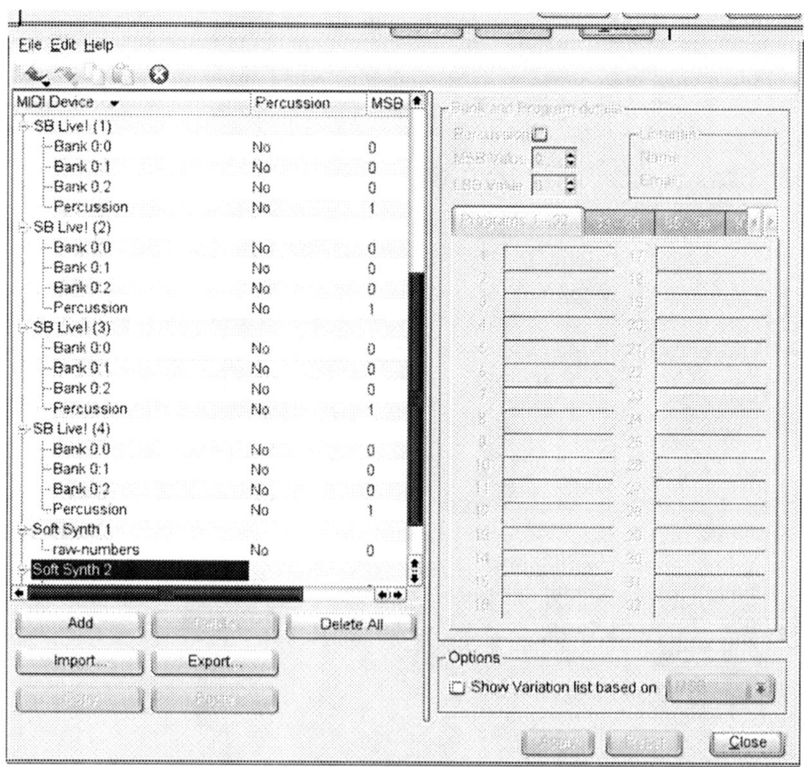

Loading a Device from the Library

If you're lucky, the growing Rosegarden Library already contains a set of bank and program definitions to suit your hardware. To try your luck, click the *Import...* button. You will initially be presented with a list of *.rgd* files from the Library, which was installed along with Rosegarden itself, but you can, of course, browse to other locations. You can import banks from both regular Rosegarden Composition (*.rg*) files, and from Rosegarden Device (*.rgd*) files. If you don't find anything suitable, you will probably have to start from scratch, as I will explain later on.

Turning a Soundfont into a Device

"Soft Synth 2" in the above example is a soundfont based card or soft synth. The simplest, most accurate way to define a device model for a synth of this type is to load the banks of program names directly out of the soundfont's *.sf2* file itself. Simply set the *Filter*: to "Soundfont" and browse to the location of the soundfont you've loaded into your synth.

NOTE: Defining a device by loading programs out of a soundfont is in no way related to actually loading that soundfont into either a Sound Blaster Live! or into QSynth. You are merely reading the directory inside the *.sf2* file that describes how the various samples are arranged into banks, and importing that textual information into Rosegarden as a time saving measure. It is perfectly possible to load, say. *foo.sf2* into the Sound Blaster Live!, and then load the programs out of *bar.sf2* into Rosegarden. The two actions are unrelated, and keeping things in sync is your job. Some users have found this confusing.

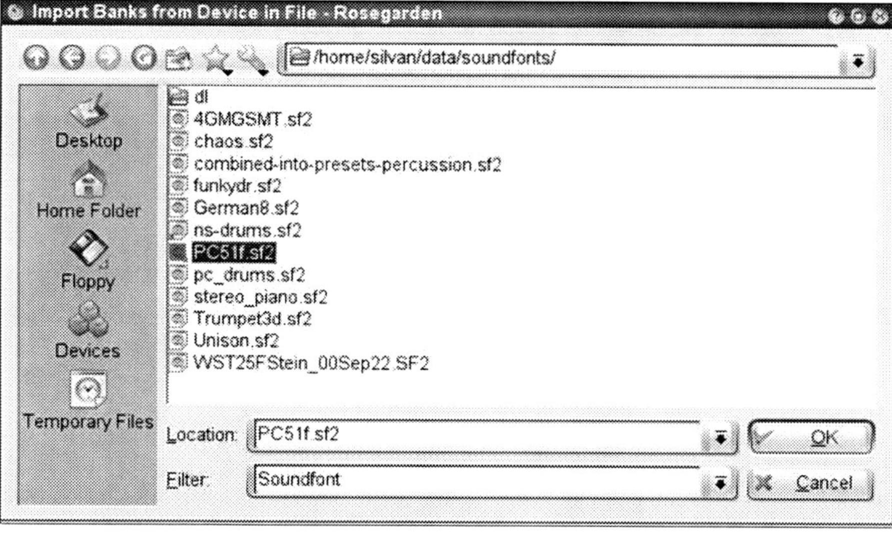

Once You've Made Your Choice

Regardless of whether you elected to load a stock device from the Library, or loaded the programs out of a *.sf2* file, you will need to make a few decisions how to proceed.

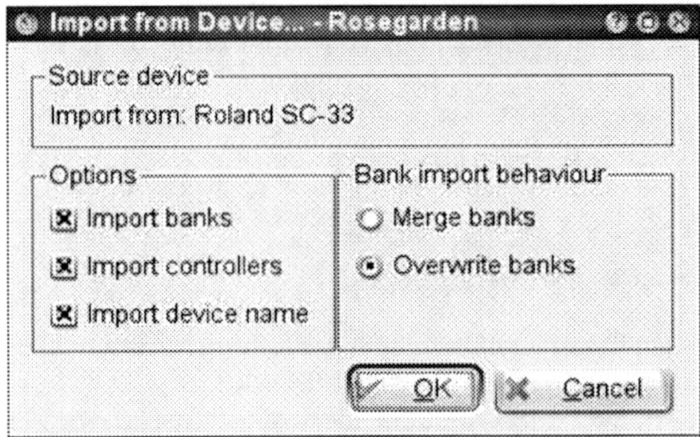

If the file contains models of more than one device, you can choose which one to import. You also have various choices about which bits to import, and whether to merge new banks into existing ones or replace them completely. Everything should be self-evident after a little experimentation.

The Hardest Road: Creating a List of Programs from Scratch

If none of the device models in the library are suitable, and you can't turn the program names from a soundfont into a device, then you will need to get to work creating your own. You can use an existing file from the library as a starting point, or you can create a new device definition completely from scratch.

Even if you have no real need to start from scratch, you may wish to read through this material anyway, in order to better understand how some of the devices in the Library are put together.

Naming the Device

So that you can avoid confusion, you probably want to replace Rosegarden's default "Anonymous MIDI Device 3" type name with something more meaningful. Simply double click on the existing name and give your virtual model a more descriptive one.

Now that your "Anonymous External Device" has become a "Roland SC-33" or what have you, you probably want add a description of its available programs and controllers to Rosegarden's model.

Why Name Programs and Controllers?

Depending on the capabilities of this device, it might not matter whether you define named program changes or not. However, if you do intend to transmit programs, bank changes or controllers to the equipment -even if you only want to use numbers--you need to define something here. Rosegarden's model of your equipment will only include what you define here, and anything you leave empty will not be available for your use. If you don't let Rosegarden know that program number 97 can play something, it will never allow you set a track to use that program number.

Gathering Information

The key to success here is having as much information about the equipment as possible. You need to know what programs it can use, and how the banks are numbered. If you have no idea, you may have to try loading "raw-numbers.rgd" from the Library, which I created as a way of providing a generic everything to everyone placeholder just to fill up the slots and allow program changes to be transmitted. Beyond the essential fact that you must understand your equipment to describe it, there are really only two special cases worth mentioning here.

Variations

Some equipment uses a method of sorting programs into banks in such a way that the programs in bank 0 0 are the standard General MIDI instruments, and the programs in the remaining banks are variations on those instruments. Roland's GS standard is a prime example of this. Bank 0 0, program 1 is "Piano 1" and bank 0 8, program 1 is "Piano 1w." In order to make it easy to take advantage of this relationship, Rosegarden offers the ability to display programs in secondary banks as variations. You may choose to enable this, and to show the variation list based on either the LSB or MSB value.

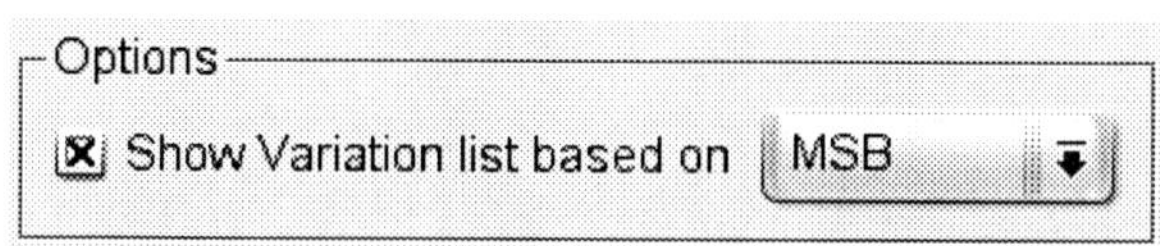

The Percussion Checkbox

The *[x] Percussion* checkbox is used to tell Rosegarden that a particular bank contains named drum kits, rather than more conventional programs. In many cases, this will be true for the 1:0 bank. Checking this box will tell the *Instrument Parameters* box (which you will see a bit later on) which banks have drum kits in them.

Finally, you may have noticed that Rosegarden only allows you one set of program changes per bank address. The exception to this rule is that you may define a parallel set of program changes if the *[x] Percussion* box is checked. For example, if you have a synth that interprets standard program changes in bank 0 0 on channel 10 as drum kit changes (like GS) then you can tell Rosegarden how to use them.

The process is a bit fiddly. First you have to use the *Add* button to create a new, empty bank. It will take a number other than 0 0 because 0 0 is already in use. Check the *[x] Percussion* box for this new bank, and then dial its LSB and MSB values back down to 0 0 (or wherever they need to be for your implementation) and enter the names of drum kits as programs.

DI Device ▼	Percus	MSB	LSB
Roland SC-33			
⋯Percussion	Yes	0	0
⋯Capital Tones	No	0	0

Send in Your Device Descriptions

Once you've defined the names for your program changes, you can save the device definition to disk with the *Export...* button. If you think anyone else might benefit from having the instrument definition, you can mail it to me at *dmmcintyr@users.sourceforge.net* and I will add it to our growing collection of user contributions.

> **NOTE**: Doing this job within Rosegarden can be tedious if you have a very complicated device to describe. If you prefer a faster, although less user friendly approach, you can bypass the GUI entirely, and build an .rgd file from a simple text file using the procedure outlined in the "mini-HOWTO" at http://www.rosegardenmusic.com/resources/documents/rgd-HOWTO.shtml.

4.3   *Custom Controllers*

Rosegarden should create a few basic default controllers for you. If you have special requirements, or if some of these controllers don't function on the piece of equipment for which you're defining the device, you may wish to edit these defaults by clicking the *Control Events* button.

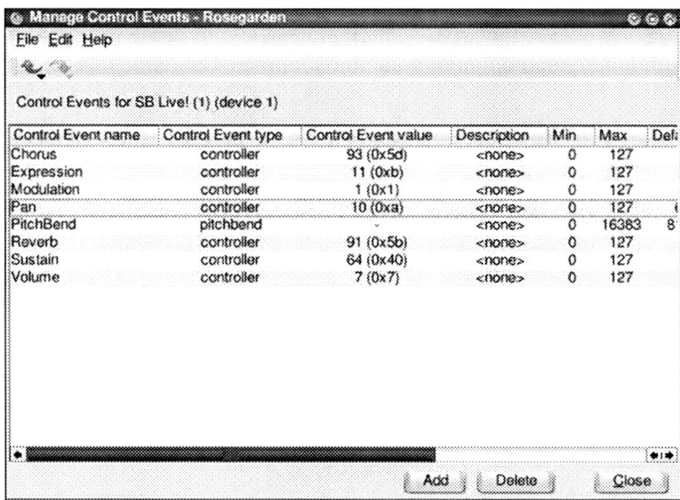

If your equipment can't use any of these controllers, you probably want to delete them. If there are controllers missing, you can add them one by one. Use the *Add* button. This will create a new entry using default values. Double click it, and you should be presented with a dialog similar to this one.

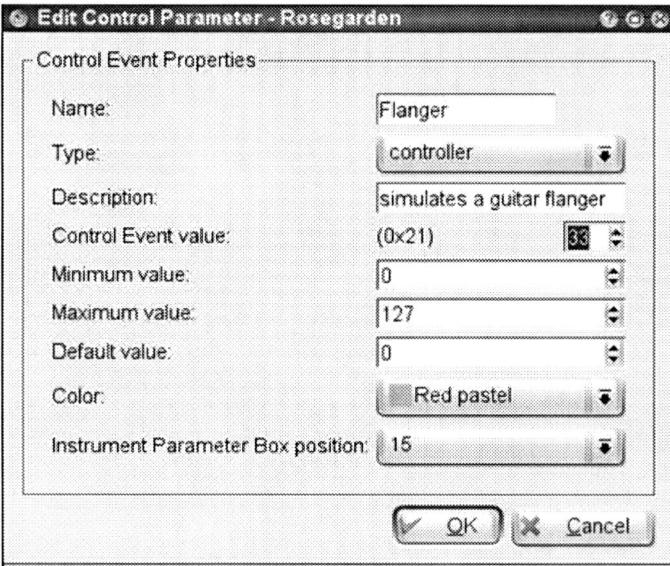

Most of these parameters should be obvious to you based on the particular needs of the equipment you're describing, but the last two bear special mention. The *Color:* parameter is the color this controller's knob will have on the *Instrument Parameters* box in the main window, and the position: determines whether this controller will show up, and how it will be arranged relative to the other controllers.

4.4   Default Document Properties

Before you make this document your default, you might want to have a look at some other document-specific settings. These aren't a part of the Studio, but they're saved in *autoload.rg*, and any new documents you create will start life with these defaults. To edit them, use *Composition -> Edit -> Document Properties*.

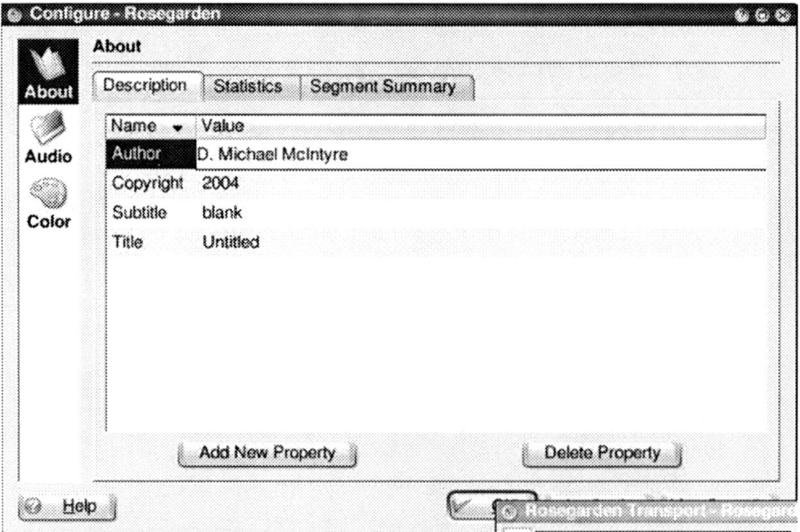

4.4.1 Lilypond Headers

The *About* tab starts off with some default properties. You can modify or delete these, and you can add new properties. The four defaults will be translated into Lilypond during an export. If you wish to use any other strings in your Lilypond headers, you can add them here by creating properties of that name, then binding your custom strings with them.. For example, "instrument," "dedication," or "poet." (Get the source code and have a look at gui/lilypondio.cpp for a complete list of the currently- supported headers, if you require more information).

4.4.2 Audio Directory

From the Audio tab, you can configure a new directory for audio files. Rosegarden will use this path for recording new files, and it's the first place it will look when you import audio segments. By default, this is ~/rosegarden. If this path doesn't exist, you won't be able to record audio, so either create that directory or configure Rosegarden to look somewhere else here.

You should get in the habit of creating a new audio directory for each document you create in which you intend to use audio segments, as I will detail in another chapter.

4.4.3 Custom Colors

Rosegarden can colorize segments and controllers. Custom colors are defined here.

4.5 Saving Your Studio as the Default

Now that you've gotten your studio configured, you'll want to make it your default, so that you can avoid having to go through this entire ordeal every time you start a new composition.

Composition -> Studio -> Save Current Document as Default Studio will save the current document as your local *autoload.rg* file. This becomes the default for all new documents you create, but it will have no effect on documents that you've already created, or documents you load from other sources. The studio belongs to each individual composition.

This default studio is just like any ordinary *.rg* file, and that means any segments, track labels, instrument assignments, etc. that you have in the current document will be saved, and will subsequently be loaded each time you create a new document.

> **TIP**: If your own studio does not change much, or often, and if you regularly load files created by people who have considerably different studios, you may wish to consider configuring Rosegarden to always load your own default studio, rather than the studio contained within the individual file you are loading. This handy option is hiding at *Settings -> Configure Rosegarden -> General*, on the *Behavior* tab, as *[x] Always use default studio when loading files*.

5   Managing Instruments

You want to play a particular track using a hammered dulcimer, or else you've got an audio track that needs some EQ. In either case, you need an introduction to the *instrument*. Instruments are configured with the *Instrument Parameters* box, and any number of tracks can be assigned to play via the same instrument.

5.1   Instruments

The previous chapter introduced you to the *device*, which is a construct Rosegarden uses to encapsulate information about what lies on the other side of a play or record connection, and make the capabilities of that equipment available to you. Hand in hand with the device is the instrument.

Every device has 16 instruments numbered #1 through #16. When working with MIDI playback devices, each of these instruments encapsulates a MIDI output channel (the same channel as the number of the instrument by default, although this relationship is not fixed), a bank/program/variation assignment, and any initial controllers you wish to affect the associated channel. These instruments allow you to assemble up to 16 collections of programs/controllers per device and assign these combinations to any number of tracks. If your JACK server is running (and if your distro compiled and packaged Rosegarden properly), you should have both an "Audio" device and a "Synth plugin" device in addition to however few or many MIDI devices you have available. Each and every one of these has 16 instruments.

When working with audio and synth plugins, these instruments serve the same purpose as MIDI channels, allowing you to configure up to 16 different combinations of LADSPA plugins, volume and pan settings, programs (for synth plugins) and so forth, and then apply these combinations to any number of different tracks.

I'll try to illustrate the point with some diagrams depicting the three general types of instruments. Here we have a sample MIDI instrument that will play using a hammered dulcimer program. All tracks assigned to play via this instrument will play using the first output port on the Sound Blaster Live!, using program 16 from bank 0 0, with an initial volume of 100, and an initial reverb level of 97. This instrument will show up as "Sound Blaster Live! (1) #12 (Hammered Dulcimer)" on the menu.

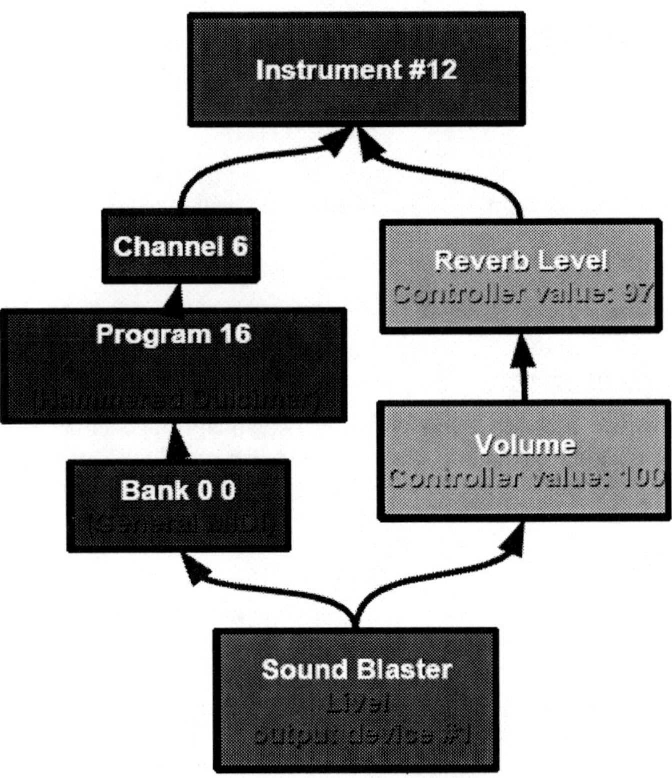

NOTE: While the instrument number and channel do coincide by default, it's possible to change this relationship. I have done so in this example. Instrument #12 plays using channel 6.

This is a typical synth plugin instrument. The sound it makes will depend on the synth plugin used, but all tracks assigned to play via this instrument will make the same sound. Its output will be piped through the EQ and Reverb plugins, and this instrument will show up as "Synth plugin #12" on the menu.

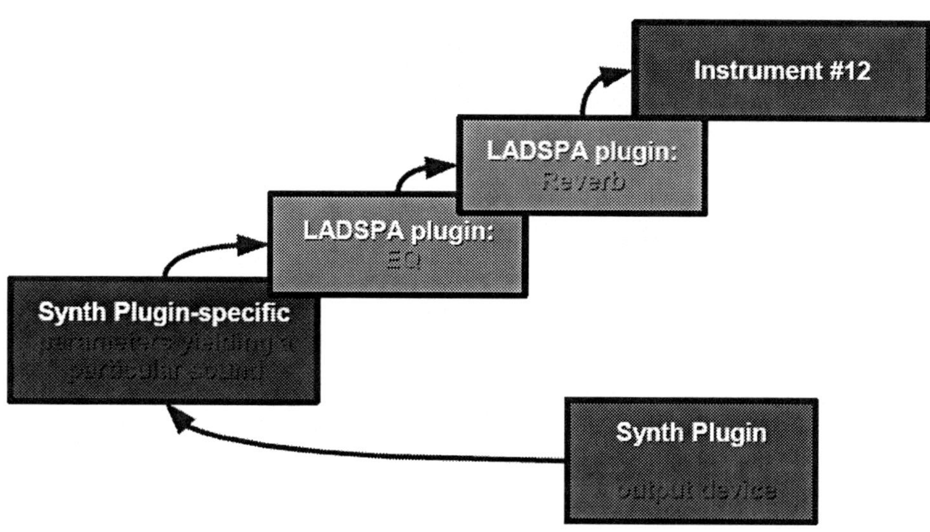

This is a typical audio instrument. Any audio tracks assigned to play via this instrument will have their output piped through the EQ and Reverb plugins, and this instrument will show up as "Audio #12" on the menu.

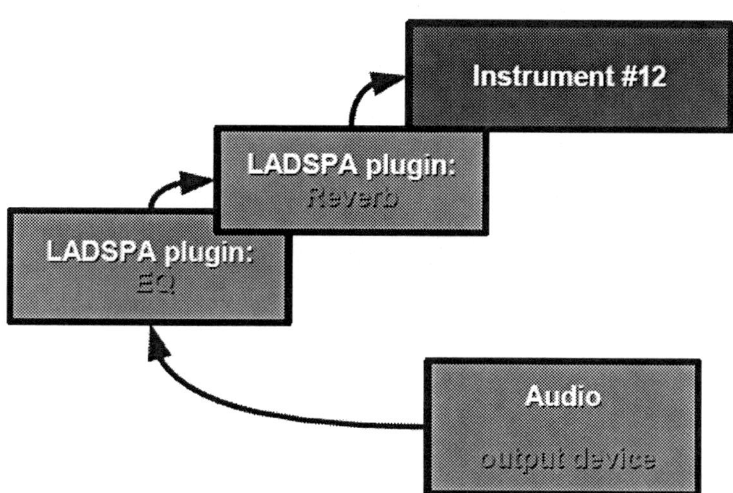

Notice that all of the above examples were "instrument #12," and yet all three of them will produce quite different results, because each of them is the "instrument #12" of a completely different device.

5.2   Routing a Track to a Device and Instrument

The first step in the assignment process is to route a track to a particular device. The device you use will determine whether you can play audio or MIDI data on this track. In order to make this device assignment, begin by clicking the mouse cursor in this area, and holding a moment until a context menu appears.

You should be presented with a series of two menus that allow you to choose first the device and then the instrument for this track. In this case, I chose to route it to my "Roland SC-33" device, which is ultimately connected through my Rosegarden studio to play through ALSA port 64:0, and thus the Roland Sound Canvas I have plugged into the box physically attached to my computer.

Then I assigned it to that device's instrument #6. Prior to taking this snapshot, I had already configured this instrument to play using the "Piano 1" program with the Instrument Parameters box (more on that in a bit), and so that name appeared in parenthesis in the second menu. If an instrument hasn't already been directed to make use of a particular program, only the instrument number will appear on this menu, as is the case for most of the other instruments depicted.

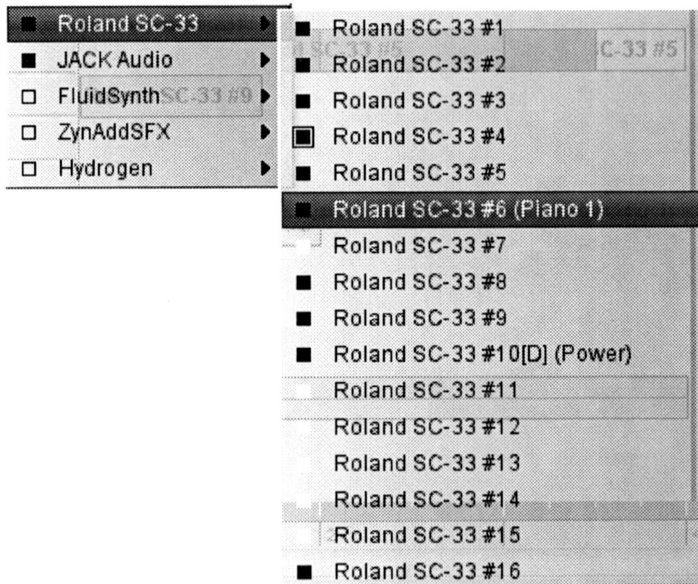

Notice also that instrument #10 has (D) in parenthesis, indicating that this instrument is normally used for playing drums. (Whether it actually plays drums depends on the capabilities of the MIDI equipment or software synth represented by this device, and probably depends on this instrument continuing to remain at the default channel assignment of 10.) In this example, I arranged beforehand for this instrument to play using the "Power" drum kit.

The remaining instruments are not assigned to anything in particular yet, and on most General MIDI-compliant equipment (or software synths) these instruments will probably play using a factory default piano program, with volume and other controllers set to neutral default values. Some equipment may not actually produce any noise until you explicitly assign a program to any instruments you use.

5.3   MIDI Instrument Parameters

Now that the track has had its output routed to a MIDI output device and instrument, and is therefore a MIDI track, the *Instrument Parameters* box will display controls similar to these. They allow you to reassign the channel for this instrument, and to dial in a program. Depending on how your synth/soundfont is set up, you may have to deal with a few different scenarios here.

5.3.1 Simple General MIDI Instruments

At the simple end, assigning a "Harpsichord" program to a basic General MIDI device only requires that you use the *Program* combo box to pick out the appropriate name.

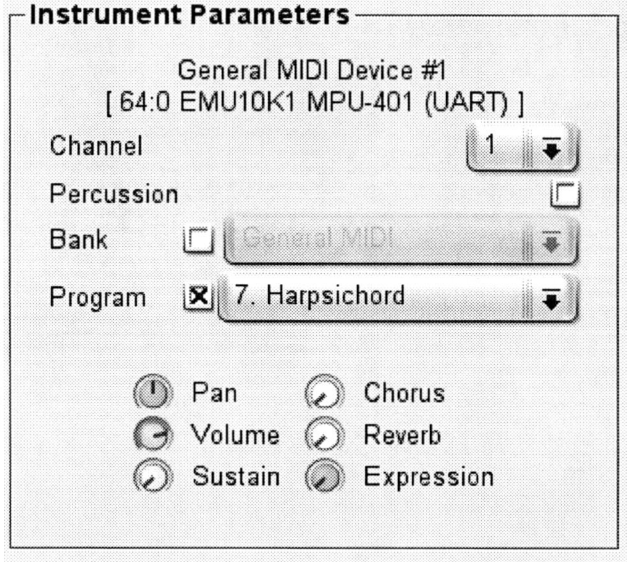

5.3.2 GS Program and Variation Instruments

With any of the GS devices from the Library, you can dial in both the program and variation. For example, "Church Org 3" is a variation of "Church Org 1." In order to get here, dial "Church Org 1" into the *Program* combo box, and then dial through the possible variations with the *Variation* combo box.

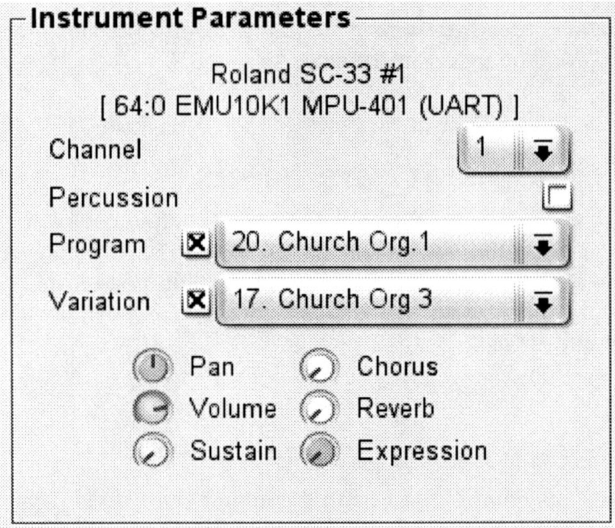

5.3.3 Drum Instruments

Most MIDI equipment has some way of playing drums using a bank of percussion sounds that are mapped to various pitches on the keyboard. Basic General MIDI equipment has only one standard drum kit, and you most likely need not do more than assign an instrument to output on channel 10 in order to make use of it. Most higher-end equipment and many soundfonts offer alternatives to this standard kit.

If your studio is correctly configured, you should be able to dial up a drum kit simply by toggling the [x] Percussion checkbox, and then dialing in an appropriate program. In order for this to work, at least one bank has to have its own bank editor level [x] Percussion box checked. The two checkboxes are interrelated.

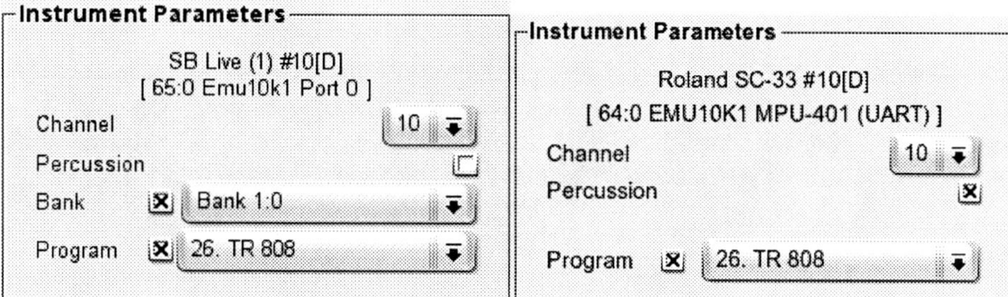

5.3.4 Controller Knobs

You may change the default controller values by adjusting the knobs. The tool tip explains how to use them just as well as I could.

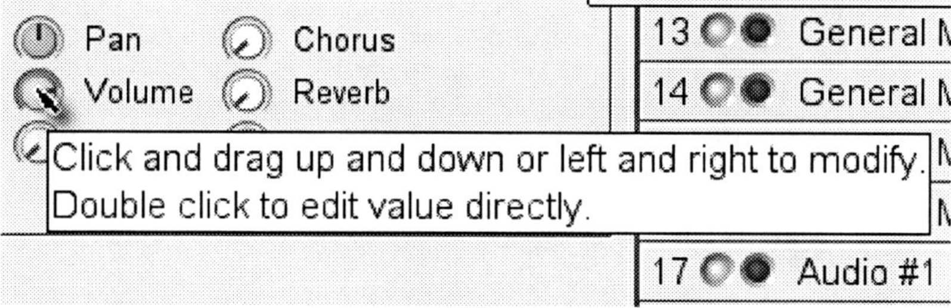

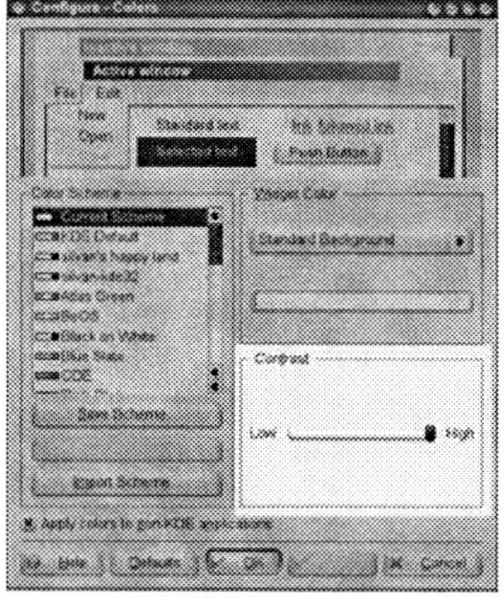

TIP: If your knobs do not have a crisp, clear appearance like the ones above, you might need to increase your KDE color contrast to a higher setting. Low contrast produces rather fuzzy, indistinct knobs. Adjust this with KDE's Control Panel (kcontrol), under *Appearance & Themes -> Colors*. Sadly, I have no idea how this might or might not affect people who are running Rosegarden from GNOME, or some other desktop environment.

5.3.5 Setting Initial Track Volume and Other Parameters

These initial controllers here inside the instrument provide the mechanism whereby you configure initial volume, pan, and similar settings for the track (if supported by the equipment, and properly configured into the device.) Any tracks that are routed to play through this instrument will share this instrument's parameters.

If you change these knobs in the middle of playing a composition, the new settings should take effect immediately. However, they are still only initial settings for the instrument, and the new setting will be in effect after you've rewound the composition to the beginning. If, for example, you want to change the pan setting in the middle of a composition, you must do it by inserting controller events from the event list editor, or from a controller ruler in either the matrix or notation editors, as I will explain in due course.

NOTE: If you notice that your initial controllers are not taking effect, as can sometimes be the case when you have changed a controller value in the middle of a composition, and have rewound it to the beginning, you may need to check *Settings -> Configure Rosegarden -> Sequencer -> Send all MIDI Controllers at start of playback [x]*. As the warning implies, it will, indeed, cause a noticeable delay.

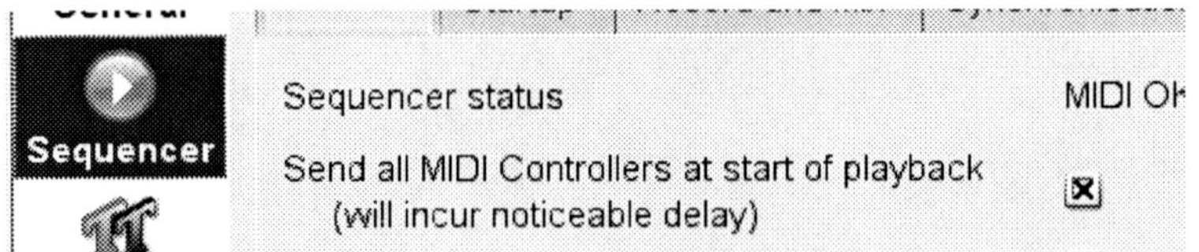

NOTE: The sustain controller for a particular MIDI channel remains wherever you last put it, and this is not affected by, for example, loading a different composition into Rosegarden. If you stop playback with the pedal on a particular channel down, it will stay down. If the *Instrument Parameters* sustain knob is set to 0, it does not seem to cancel out a stuck sustain from two compositions ago, even while the above configuration option is checked. The panic button should cure this annoying, and all too common condition. (The persistent state of sustain on a MIDI channel is not a bug, but a fact of life that causes problems for all MIDI sequencers.)

5.4   Audio Instrument Parameters

If you want to use a track for audio, you'll need to make it an audio track by routing it to the "Audio" device. (If you do not have an "Audio" device available, please ensure that your JACK server is running.)

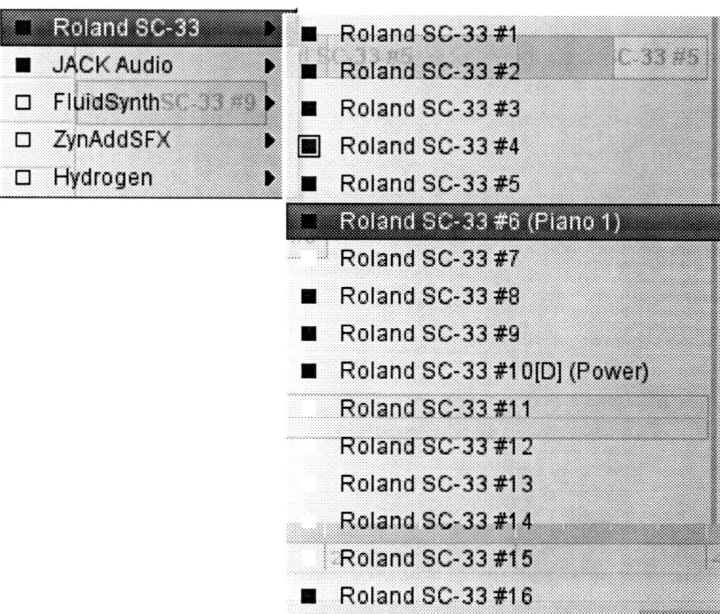

Audio instruments have different controls available in the *Instrument Parameters* box.

They have a mono/stereo toggle, (,) and various controls for adding plugins and adjusting levels.

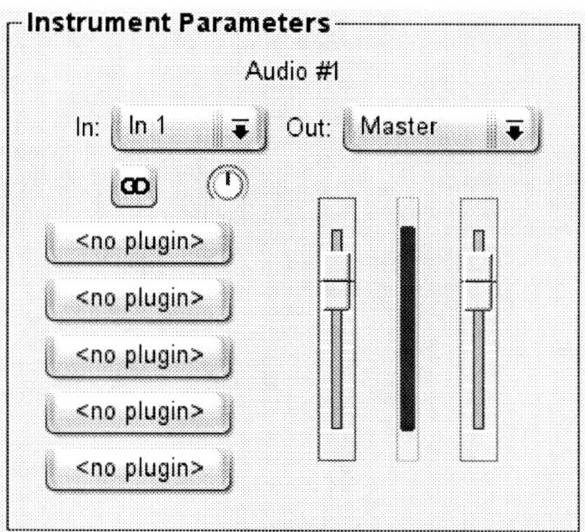

If you wish to assign LADSPA plugins to the instrument, you may use one of the "<no plugin>" buttons to summon a dialog similar to this one. You can narrow in on what you want using the Category: selector, and then dial in a particular plugin with the *Plugin:* selector. As you dial through these, the knobs in the bottom half of this dialog box will change to reflect the controls that are available for this particular plugin; ranging from one knob to a screen full of them. You can layer up to five plugins for each instrument in the "Audio" device, hardware allowing. Some plugins are particularly expensive in their use of your system's resources, so using too many may cause performance problems.

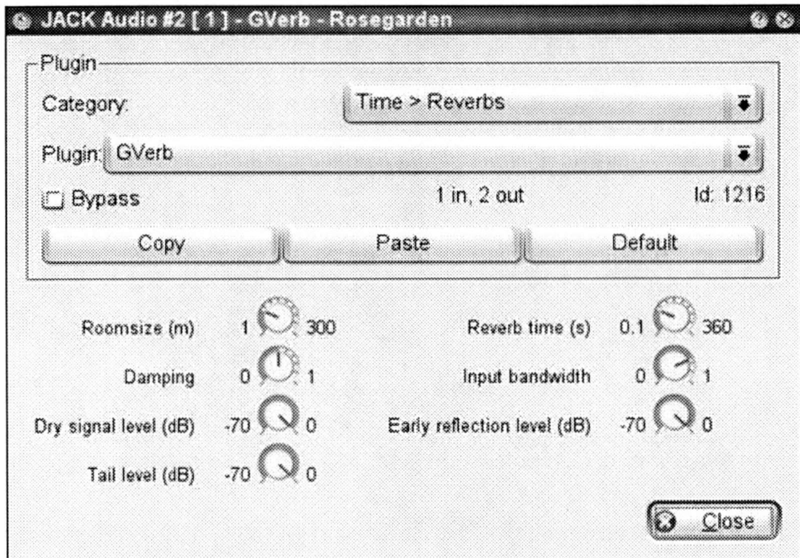

5.5   *Synth Plugin Instrument Parameters*

As mentioned in the introduction, Rosegarden was the first sequencer for Linux to employ the new DSSI plugin architecture. If you have your JACK server running, and your Rosegarden package was built with DSSI support enabled, you should have a "Synth plugin" device available. Each of the 16 synth plugin instruments can take a different synth plugin, and can have up to five LADSPA plugins layered on top of the basic sound the synth plugin produces. Begin by routing a track first to this device, and then to one of the 16 available instruments.

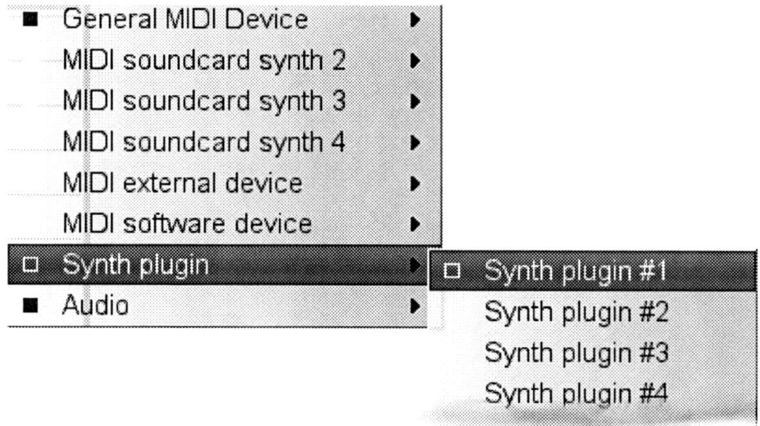

5.5.1 Select a Synth Plugin

After routing a track to a synth plugin instrument, the *Instrument Parameters* box will show a new set of controls. These are similar to the controls for audio instruments. To configure this synth plugin instrument, begin by clicking on the "<no synth>" button.

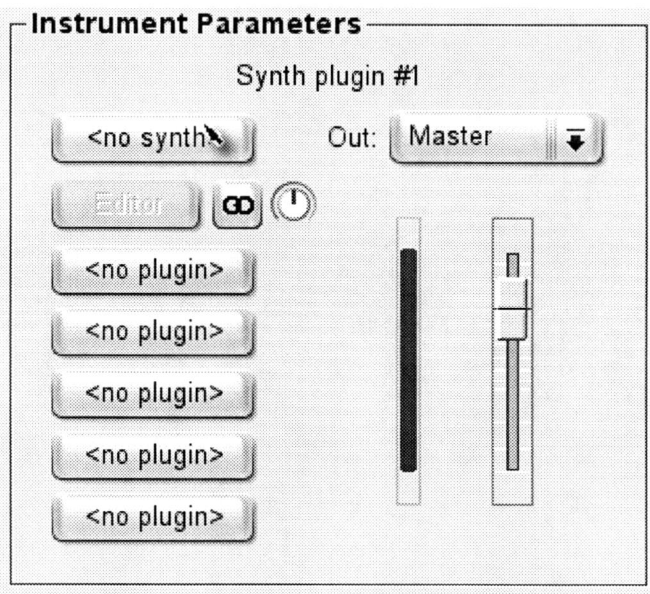

After first clicking the button, you will need to dial in one of the plugins you have installed. I cannot possibly cover all the plugins available, but the concepts I am demonstrating with these select plugins apply broadly to any of them.

Xsynth

After dialing the *Plugin* combo box to "Xsynth DSSI Plugin" the dialog box will transform itself into something like this:

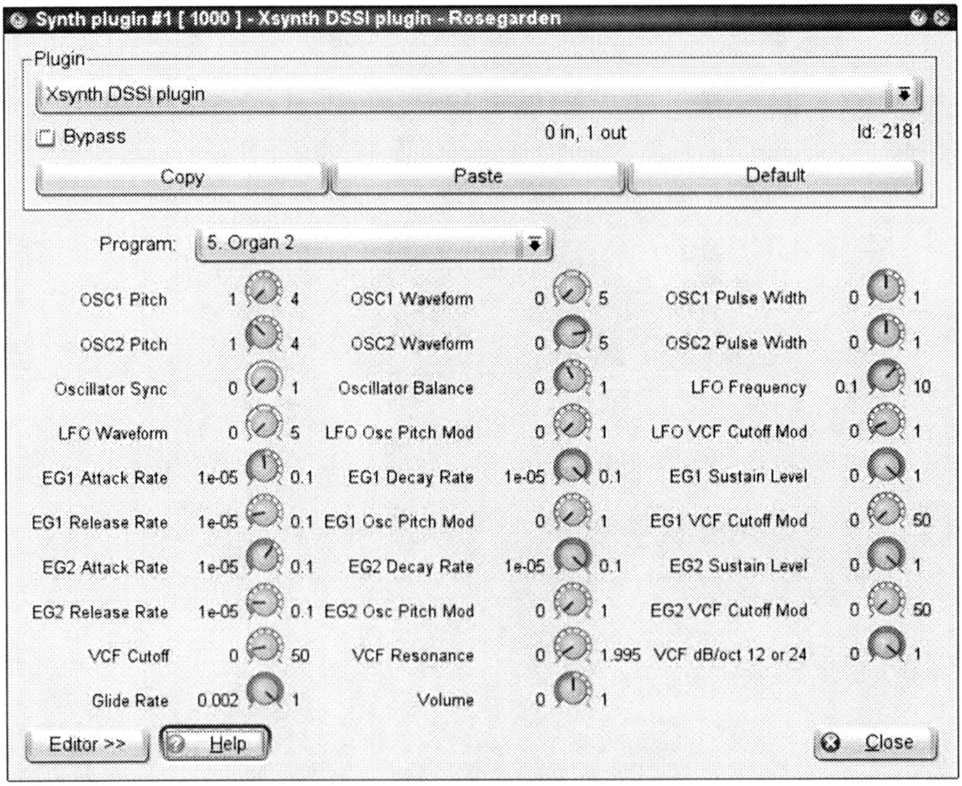

I have to leave it up to you to play with the knobs and discover how to twiddle this into making interesting noises. This synth plugin is not nearly as complex as something like ZynAddSubFX, for example, but having it effectively built right into Rosegarden has some advantages.

- no need to tinker with JACK routing, since it plays through Rosegarden's JACK connection

- settings for the knobs are saved with the composition, which allows you to dial up custom patches and save them with your file without having to fool with the external editor

- with 16 plugin instruments, you can have 16 Xsynths if you want, each with its own patch, and its own set of LADSPA plugins

Xsynth's External Editor

If you click on the **Editor >>** button you can use Xsynth's external editor to manage its controls in a different way, change several parameters, and to manage your collection of custom patches. While it isn't necessary to do this, you may find it useful to save named presets to disk, and you might find the plugin's own native GUI is slightly more informative with respect to what the various knobs are for. (In particular, the native GUI tells you what kind of wave form the various numbers represent, while Rosegarden's plugin interface does not.) The GUI is an independent module unrelated to Rosegarden, which is why the look and feel are so different.

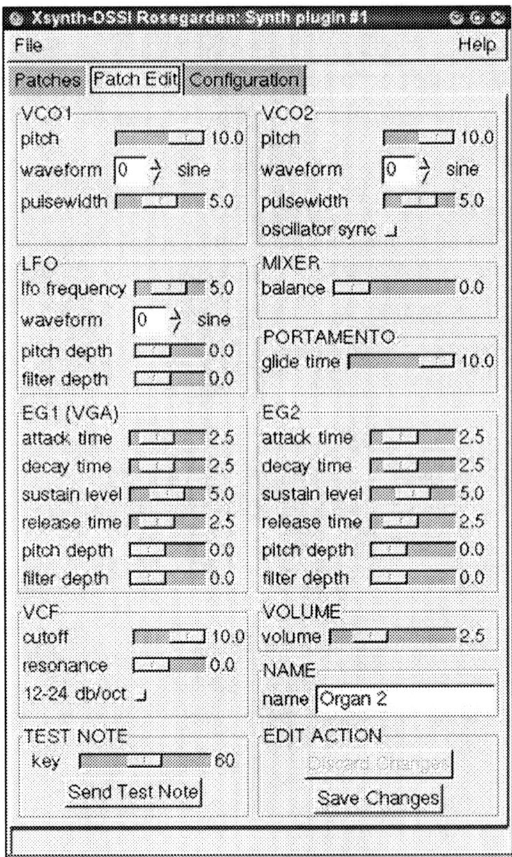

> **TIP**: This thing is uncomfortably large for my screen. If you have the same problem, remember that you can drag it around even when its title bar is hidden off the top of the screen. Hold down the Alt key while clicking on the window with your mouse, and reposition it as necessary to get to all of the controls.

FluidSynth

FluidSynth-DSSI is a plugin built around the same underlying engine that powers QSynth. The plugin implementation isn't quite as friendly to use as QSynth, but it affords most of the same functionality in a package that's integrated directly into Rosegarden's user interface. After dialing the *Plugin* combo box to "FluidSynth-DSSI Plugin" the dialog box will transform itself into something like this:

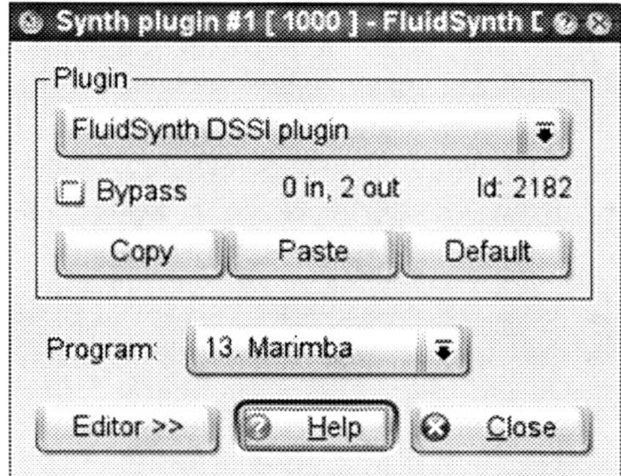

FluidSynth's External Editor

There are no knobs for this one, and everything must be done using the external GUI.

Click on the Editor >> button. You'll need to load a soundfont into it with the Select Soundfont button.

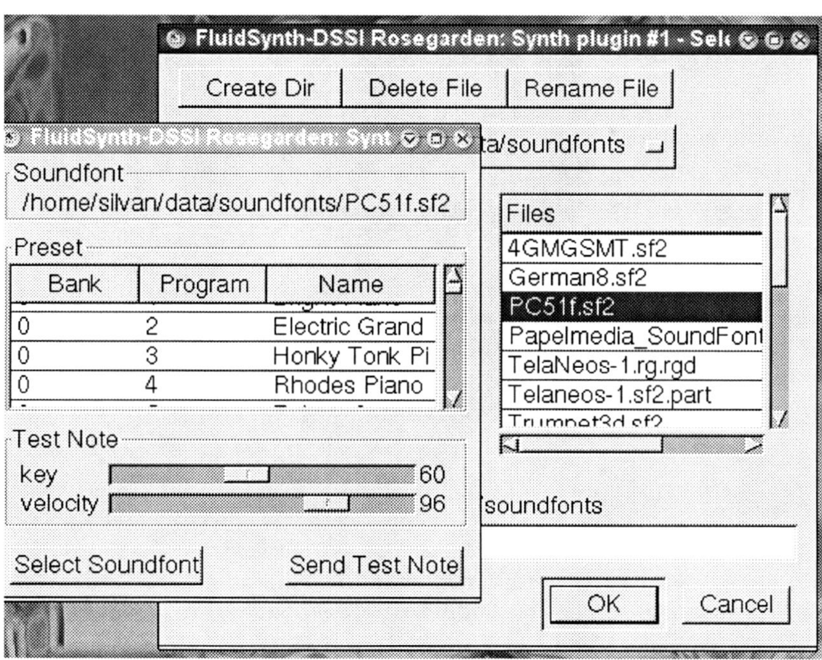

Selecting a Program

After you have loaded a soundfont, you can use the *Program* combo box to dial in any of the programs available in the soundfont. This interface does not separate them into individual banks in the same fashion you saw elsewhere. Instead, all available programs in the entire soundfont are presented within one top to bottom list.

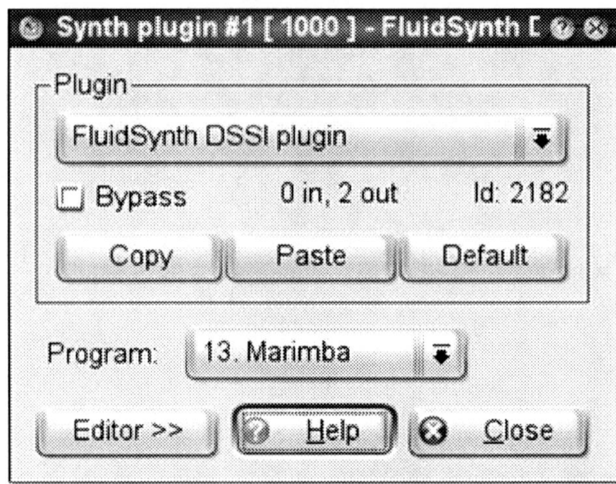

> **NOTE**: In the case of the particular soundfont I have loaded in the example above, the extra drum kits that are normally found in bank 1 0 (using QSynth or the Sound Blaster Live!) are instead located starting at program number 128. There is, in effect, only one gigantic bank.

Obviously, you can only have one program per plugin, so if you want to play both a flute and a guitar, you will need to assign two different tracks to the *Synth plugin* instrument, and configure both of these to use Fluidsynth-DSSI. The plugin itself is smart enough to run only one instance of itself in this situation, so you will not be running two copies of the plugin, both competing for system resources.

Other Plugins

You may also want to check out "Hexter," a cool Yamaha DX-7 emulator, and the "Trivial Sampler" which really isn't very trivial at all. Many other freestanding soft synths are considering joining the DSSI bandwagon, and making plugin versions of themselves, but as of this writing, none are yet available.

6   Recording

There are three different ways to record with Rosegarden. If you come from a MIDI background, the most obvious thing to do is plug in your MIDI keyboard and hit the record button to record a MIDI segment in the currently selected track. If audio is your aim, you'll want to set your mixer recording source and get to work. On the other hand, if you are not very good at playing keyboard instruments, you might be more interested in step recording.

I will cover step recording later on. For now my focus is on recording operations that can be performed from the main window.

6.1   Recording MIDI

You can record MIDI from any source that Rosegarden recognizes as a record device, as I mentioned in some detail in a previous chapter.

To recap briefly, click the 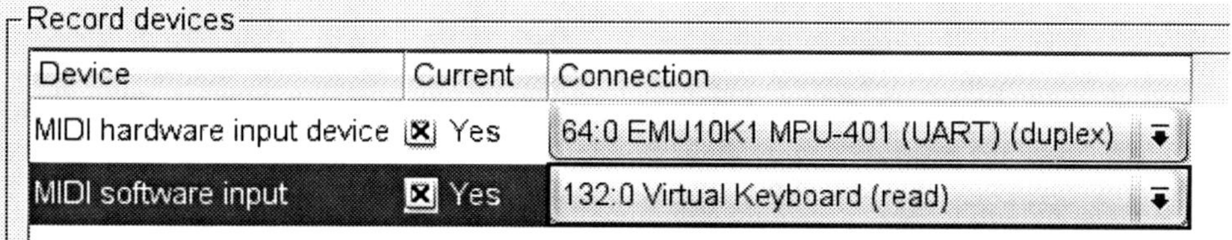 icon to have a look at your current studio, then look at the "Record devices" section of the dialog. Any inputs you have available will appear in this list, and you may set any number of them as active recording sources by toggling the *Current* checkboxes for each of them. In this example, I have both the external MIDI port on my soundcard and Virtual Keyboard available, and marked as active.

Record devices		
Device	Current	Connection
MIDI hardware input device	☒ Yes	64:0 EMU10K1 MPU-401 (UART) (duplex) ⬇
MIDI software input	☒ Yes	132:0 Virtual Keyboard (read) ⬇

6.1.1 Create a MIDI Track

You most likely already have plenty of MIDI tracks, but it bears mentioning for the sake of completeness that you must route a track's output to a MIDI or synth plugin device in order for that track to become a MIDI track, and therefore capable of serving as a destination for MIDI recording operations. Please review previous chapters if you have any questions about instrument assignment.

6.2   Recording Audio

Audio recording is considerably more involved than MIDI, but it can become second nature after a bit of practice getting everything in order beforehand.

6.2.1 Set a New Audio Path!

If you wish to record audio, the first thing you should do is create a new directory for the files, and set the audio record path for this composition to that directory via *Composition -> Edit Document Properties -> Audio*. This dialog also shows you how much space you have remaining on the target storage device (typically a hard disk, though it might be a USB memory stick if you are using Studio..to go!), and estimates how much room you have to store audio files.

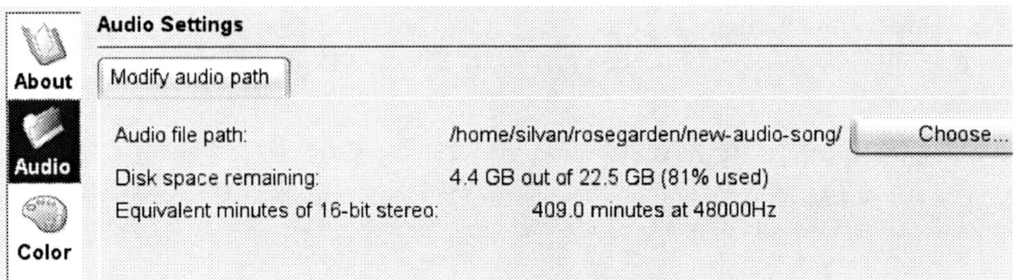

Rosegarden writes files with names like "RG-AUDIO-00001.wav" to this directory. Every botched take, every empty recording where you got the mixer set wrong, every goof in the world will get a new filename with a new number. If you don't sort your audio files into directories grouped by project, you'll eventually wind up with a horrible mess to sort out, with little choice but to audition each and every one of them to find out what is what. Discipline in remembering to choose a new audio path for each new project really pays off in the long run, by allowing you to avoid this problem. (After years of ignoring this advice in my own work, I now have a 2 GB ~/rosegarden directory full of who knows what, with completely meaningless filenames. Learn from my mistake!) Additionally, if you keep all files associated with a particular project in one place, it greatly facilitates going back at the end of the day to clean up any bad takes, so they don't waste disk space. I will deal with a bit of that later on.

6.2.2 Create an Audio Track

You may already have audio tracks, but in the event that you don't, merely route a track to an instrument belonging to the Audio device, as previously described.

6.2.3 Configure the Mixer

If you want to record audio, you need to have an audio source available, and you need to configure your mixer to record from this source. Getting everything tweaked up in order to achieve the desired results (for example, recording a guitar plugged into the line-in jack without also recording the metronome) can actually be quite involved. I fear that this is not an area where Linux wins any awards for user friendliness. Mixers are full of incomprehensible controls with names like "IEC958 Capture" or "Sigmatel Surround Phase Inversion Playback" and discovering how to use them to accomplish useful objectives can be maddening.

The KMix Handbook refers you to the ALSA documentation for information about what these names mean, saying "If you are uncertain about the meaning of a control, please ask your soundcard driver supplier (for most current Linux distributions this is ALSA from *http://www.alsa-project.org*)." Unfortunately, if there actually is anything there to help address the mixer question, it is certainly not obvious or easy to digest.

I had intended to survey a variety of different soundcards, sort out these mysterious names, and publish a precise road map that everyone who uses one of the four most common soundcards could use to reveal the mysteries of his or her particular mixer. Unfortunately, I have not been able to obtain the necessary hardware to make this possible. The only card for which I can publish a detailed recipe for managing the mixer is the Sound Blaster Live! Value Edition. Much of this will scale to other emu10k1-based cards, and some of it will scale to the extremely common, dismally bad AC97 soundcards as well. If you have an mAudio or Hammerfal soundcard, the good news is that you have an above average mixer application available (envy24control and hdspmixer, respectively,) but the bad news is I am unable to tell you anything about how to use it.

The Sound Blaster Live!/Audigy Mixer

I have tried every mixer application I could lay my hands on. Out of the entire spectrum of software, the only mixer that has all of the necessary controls to manage this card consistently every time is a little known application that can build into either QAMix or KAMix (*http://alsamodular.sourceforge.net/*, look for "QAMix"). This mixer is available for SuSE, and for Studio..to go!, but it is not readily available for other distros. If you wish to follow along with the next few sections, you will have to obtain this mixer application for yourself. Otherwise, you will have to muddle through with whatever else is in front of you, and hope you have better luck with it than I did.

Capture vs. Playback

The recording side of the mixer is configured via the *Capture* tab.

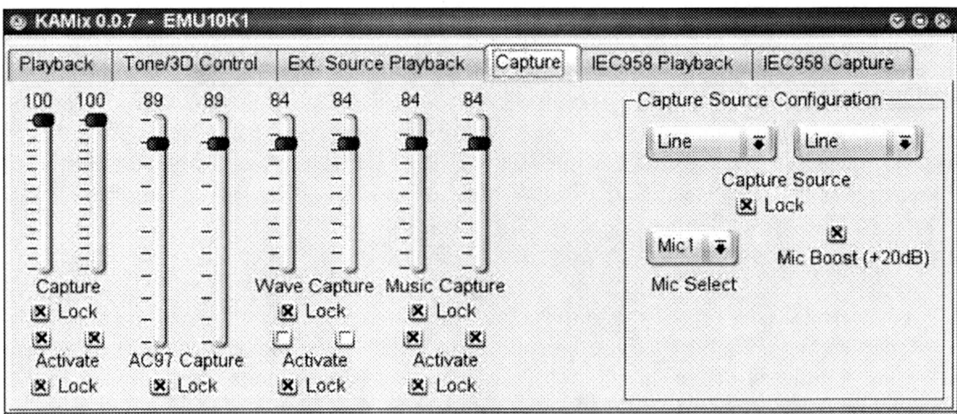

On the Sound Blaster Live!, there are a variety of capture options. The *Capture* slider controls the overall capture level. To record the on-board Emu synth, activate the *Music Capture*. To record other audio streams that JACK might be playing, activate the *Wave Capture*. The remaining capture options are all associated with the *AC97 Capture* slider. This can be used to record from a microphone (*Mic*) or from a line level audio source such as an external mixer, a guitar effects box, an external synth, or the like (*Line.*) It can also be used to capture the entire mix (*Mix*) and several other sources. Only one of these can be selected at a time, so if you wish to record from your microphone and the line-in simultaneously, you have no choice but to capture the entire mix.

Playback is configured via the *Playback* and *Ext. Source Playback* tabs. On my Sound Blaster Live!, the *Master* and *PCM* sliders are completely useless. I think perhaps it might be due to my using the coaxial digital out to connect to a cheap home theater. Everything on the *Ext. Source Playback* tab is useless except *AC97*, which plays whatever that source is capturing. The playback side of this is useful during recording because, for example, you can capture the microphone without playing back its output. This allows you to avoid feedback problems, and other unintended consequences.

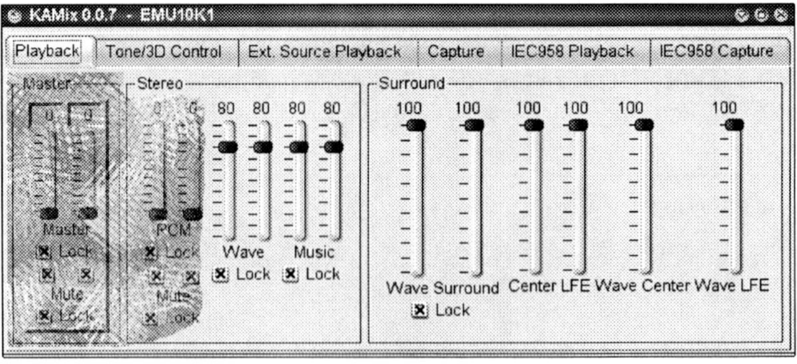

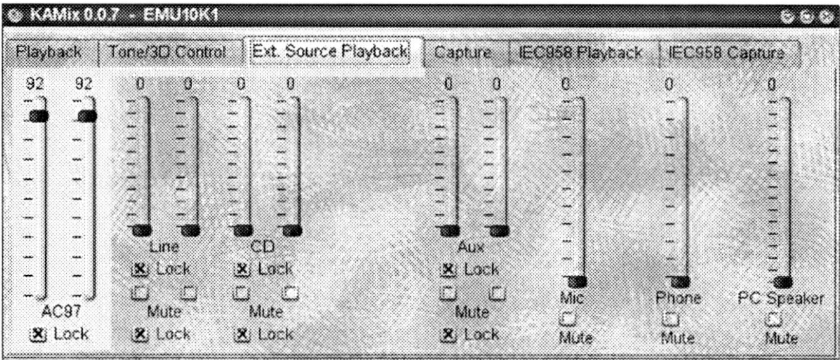

6.2.4 Avoid Clipping

One major concern when recording audio is clipping. In simple terms, clipping occurs when you record at too high a level and permanently clip the tops and bottoms off of the sampled wave form. In this example, the green saw wave in the middle is comfortably within bounds, and no clipping occurs. The red one has been clipped severely. Clipped wave forms sound terrible. In the real world, it's rare to find something as flat and even as this simple drawing, so it is quite easy to wind up with a sample where the quiet to moderate passage are perfectly fine, but the louder parts are grossly distorted.

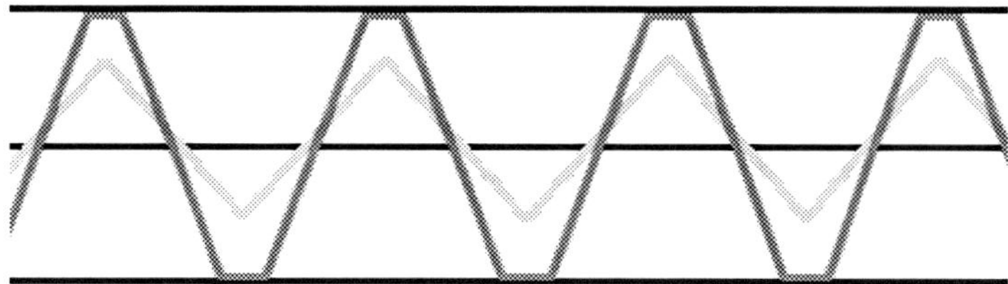

Rosegarden and JACK avoid clipping by converting data into an internal format with much more resolution than what can be stored on disk. If you set a level too high on an audio track, for example, and cause clipping, no permanent harm comes to the data until that data is physically written out into a *.wav* file. However, since the process of recording audio involves a continuous cycle of capturing a snippet of data into a buffer and then flushing it out to disk once that buffer is full, recording operations effectively involve an immediate conversion of the data to a *.wav* file, even though the Rosegarden interface insulates you from this fact.

What that means for you, is that it is very important to check your levels before you lay down your best licks. If your input gain is too high, permanent clipping can occur, and your recording will sound horrible. I suggest that you do a number of test recordings during each new session to verify that everything is in order before sitting down to do any serious playing. Try to play snippets at the same range of volume and intensity you will use for the real recording to ensure you will avoid clipping off your louder passages. If the level is too high, fiddle with everything until you have arrived at a satisfactory combination of mixer settings and, for example, guitar volume to get good results. A weak recording can be amplified, but a clipped recording is ruined forever.

6.3   *Important Configuration Considerations*

Rosegarden can provide a count-in to give you an opportunity to help you come in on the right beat. It defaults to two measures, but you can change it via *Settings -> Configure Rosegarden -> General -> Behavior.*

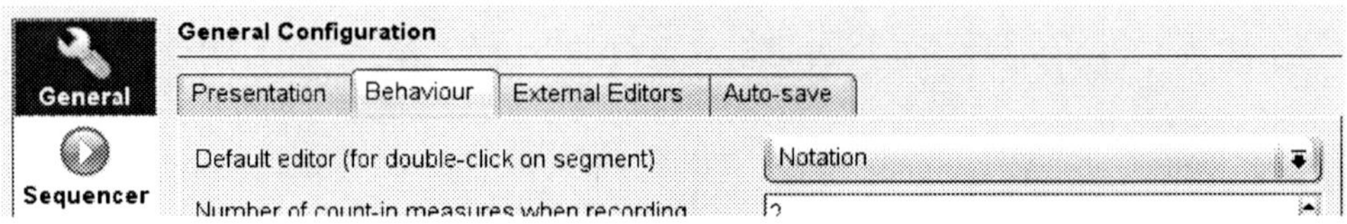

6.3.1 The Finite Composition

You should also be aware that Rosegarden compositions are of a finite length, and they do not expand to accommodate additional events if you attempt to record past the end of one. Once the transport reaches the end, everything comes to a screeching halt. This can be an extremely irritating buzz kill, and it has bitten me innumerable times. My best grooves always seem to be the ones I missed recording because I ran into the brick wall at the end of the ride. In order to cope with this unfortunate design flaw, you must anticipate how much room you need and expand the composition to a suitable size beforehand, via *Composition -> Change Composition Duration.*

> **NOTE**: The unstable branch of Rosegarden already has the infrastructure in place to bring an end to this hated "feature" very soon now, so rest assured that you will not have to live with it forever. Good riddance!

Audio Recording Time

If you are recording audio, your total recording time will be the greater of the composition duration, as determined by the tempo and total number of measures, or the audio recording time limit you set via *Settings -> Configure Rosegarden -> Sequencer -> Record and Mix.*

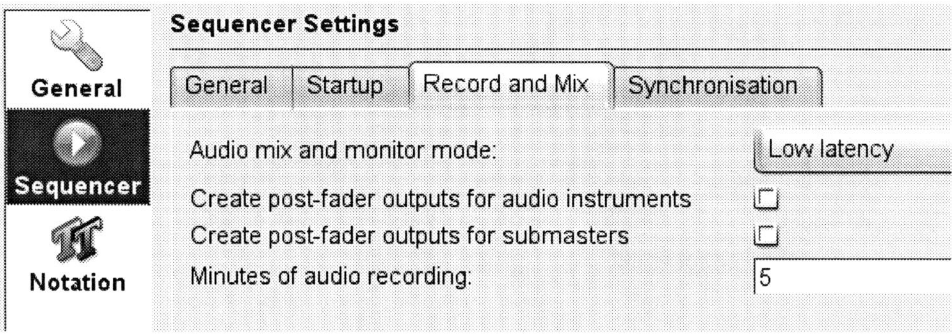

6.4 Normal Recording

From here, all you need to do to get started for a normal recording is hit a record button

on any of the various transports to start the transport rolling. (I will cover step recording in another chapter.)

A dialog will appear to inform you of how much time you have remaining from the point at which recording began until the end of the composition, or until the audio recording limit is reached. If the time is too short, see my notes in the previous section about adjusting the composition duration and audio recording limit.

In this recording mode, playback will jump back by the number of count-in measures you have configured. If the playback pointer was rewound to the beginning of the composition, recording will begin before the composition actually starts. If you have moved it to the start of measure 6, for example, the playback pointer will jump back to measure 4 (by default) and recording will actually begin at that location. This is done so that you have no danger of losing notes if you come in ahead of the selected start point.

6.4.1 Previews

As you play, a red segment will emerge for MIDI, and a blue one for audio, and it will expand as you go. If you are recording MIDI, and have segment previews turned on, you will see a running preview of what you are recording.

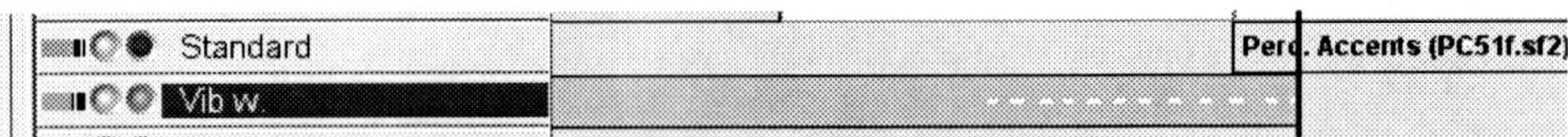

If you are recording audio, the preview won't appear until after the recording has ended, and the resulting waveform has been analyzed by Rosegarden.

6.5   Punch In Recording

In addition to normal recording, you can start the transport rolling and then punch in with the space bar.

> **NOTE**: It should be possible, in theory, to punch in and out multiple times while the transport rolls on. In practice, however, I have found that both Rosegarden 1.0 and the current unstable development branch (as of this writing) are prone to doing very bad things when I attempt this. The safest practice is to punch in, then stop the transport to end the recording. Punching in, then back out also works, but a subsequent attempt to punch in might wreak havoc, or even crash the application. Be careful!

7   A Different View

So far, we've only looked at the main window, and have not really edited anything. Rosegarden provides three different editors, each with its own unique view of the data. You can view the raw Rosegarden events with the Event List Editor, you can work with a piano roll metaphor with the matrix Editor, or you can see your data as notation with the Notation Editor. Each of these editors works on a segment level, so you must have at least one segment selected in order to open one. If you wish to start with an editor from scratch, you must first create an empty segment with the pencil tool, and then select it.

7.1   The Event List Editor

The event list editor is for editing the composition at the event level. This is the most raw of the three edit views, and the most difficult editor to use.

7.1.1 Events and Properties

Rosegarden is not a pure MIDI sequencer, and it does not store raw MIDI events; instead, it uses its own internal format, which is both more powerful and more flexible. There are many kinds of events in Rosegarden. As you would expect, MIDI notes, controllers and the like are events, but so are hairpins, dynamics, performance directions, clefs and key signatures, etc. Each class of event has its own set of unique properties.

Here are just a few examples of types of events with a few their properties. All of these can be edited from here in the event list editor, although you probably will find little occasion to tear an event apart and rearrange its insides.

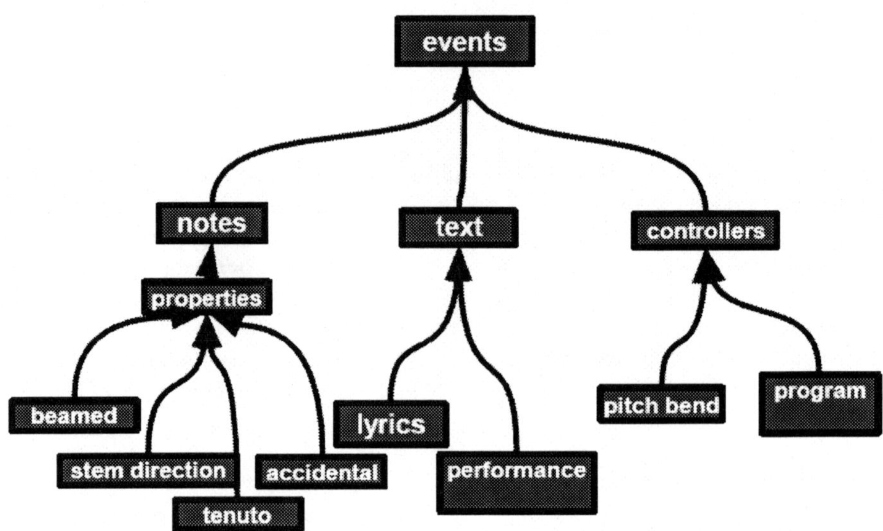

Opening and Event List View

Out of the box, the notation editor is the default, but that editor is a chapter unto itself. For the moment, let us begin with the simplest of the three. Pick a segment, and then right click on it. Choose "Open in Event List Editor" from the resulting context menu.

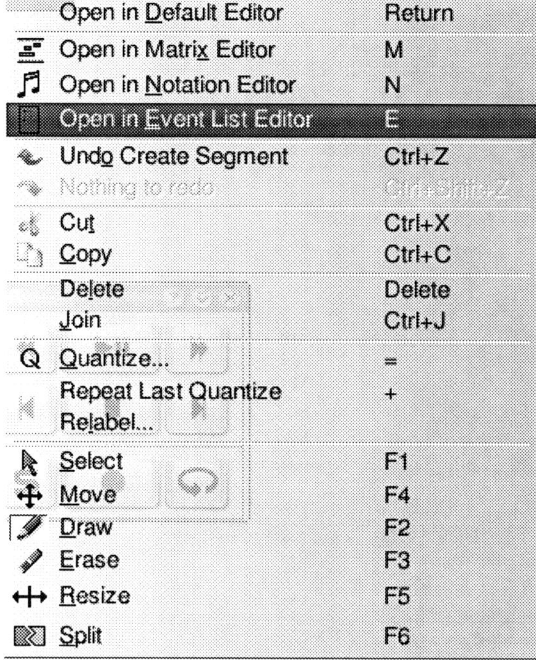

Here is one of the bendy guitar sections from Steve Conrad's "Bogus Surf Jam." You can see a variety of event types and properties:

Changing the Time Base

You can change the way Rosegarden displays the timing of events using the 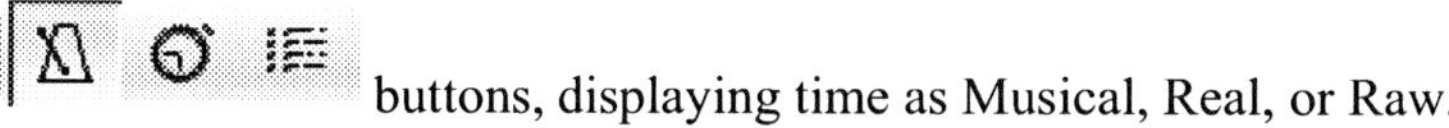 buttons, displaying time as Musical, Real, or Raw.

Filtering Events from View

You may wish to use filters to focus in on the classes of events that most interest you. Simply check or uncheck boxes from the *Event filters* box.

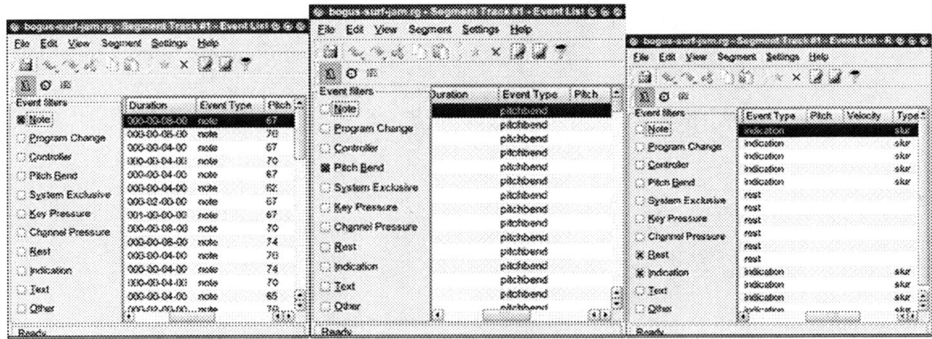

Creating a New Event

The truly brave among you might want to experiment with creating something entirely from scratch. If you click on the ✳ icon, you'll be presented with a dialog like this that allows you to make your own event out of whole cloth:

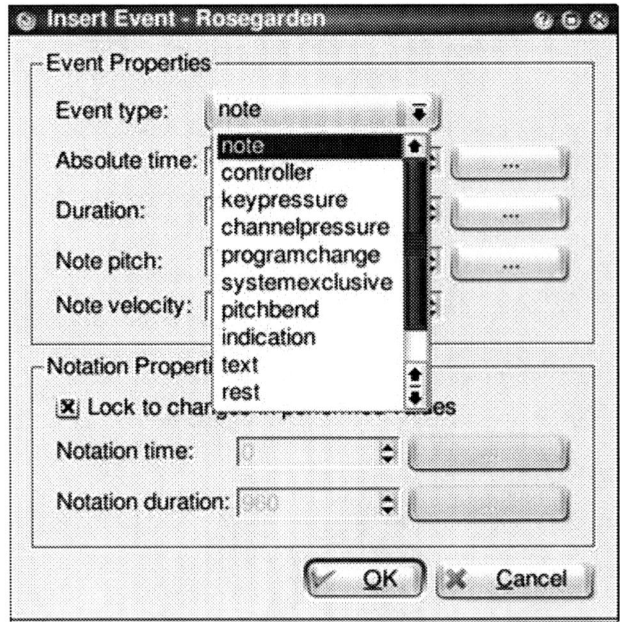

Editing Existing Events

You may edit existing events using either the simple ▱ editor...

..or the advanced  editor.

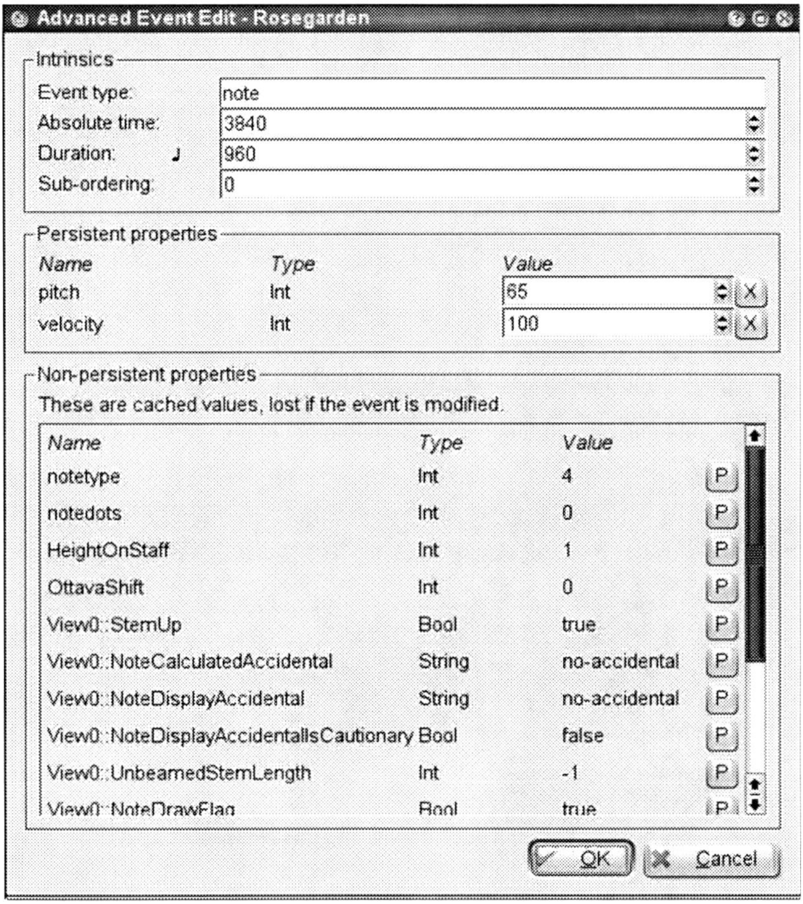

You may delete events using the  ✕ icon.

7.1.2 Example Use: Inserting a Program Change

One thing that can only be done from the event editor is the insertion of a mid-track program change. This might be useful, for example, if you wish to switch a string part from playing normally to playing pizzicato and back without having to write the parts on different tracks to assign them to different instruments.

The facility provided for this purpose is not terribly friendly. The only mechanism provided is the entry of program changes by number. There is no facility for changing the bank anywhere except at the instrument level, so any program changes you insert directly into segments will be done within the same bank the track's instrument uses. Looking at this from a GS perspective, for example, it means that you can change from "flute" to "piccolo" using this mechanism, but you cannot use it to change from "Piano 1" to "Piano 1w," because the variations involve bank changes. If you want to change a "strings" instrument to play using a "pizzicato" program at a particular point...

Determine the Insertion Point

The easiest thing to do is move the playback pointer to the desired insertion point. In this example, I've done it using the transport in beat:bar mode to ensure I'm in exactly the desired spot to insert a program change at bar 2, beat 1, tick 0.

Remember that the ⏸ button changes display modes on the transport.

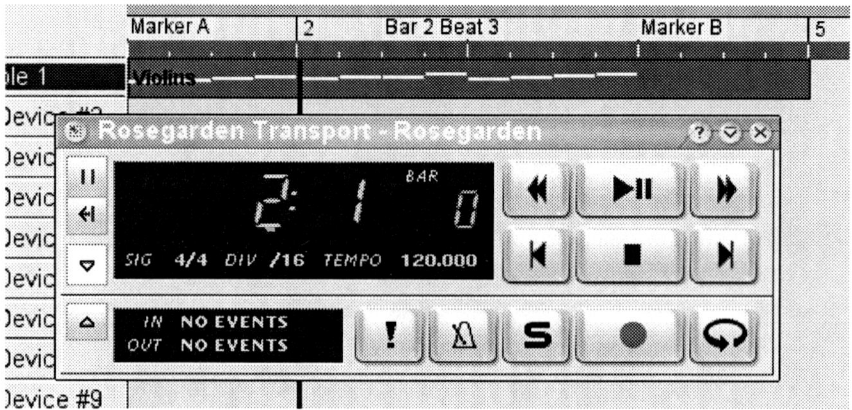

Open the Editor, Create an Event

If you right click on this segment and choose to open it in the event list view, your cursor should already be at the right spot to insert a program change at the desired time. In this sample, there happens to already be a note at that particular time, but that will not prevent you from inserting a program change event here at the same time. In fact, if you are inserting a program change into otherwise empty space, you will have to set its time manually.

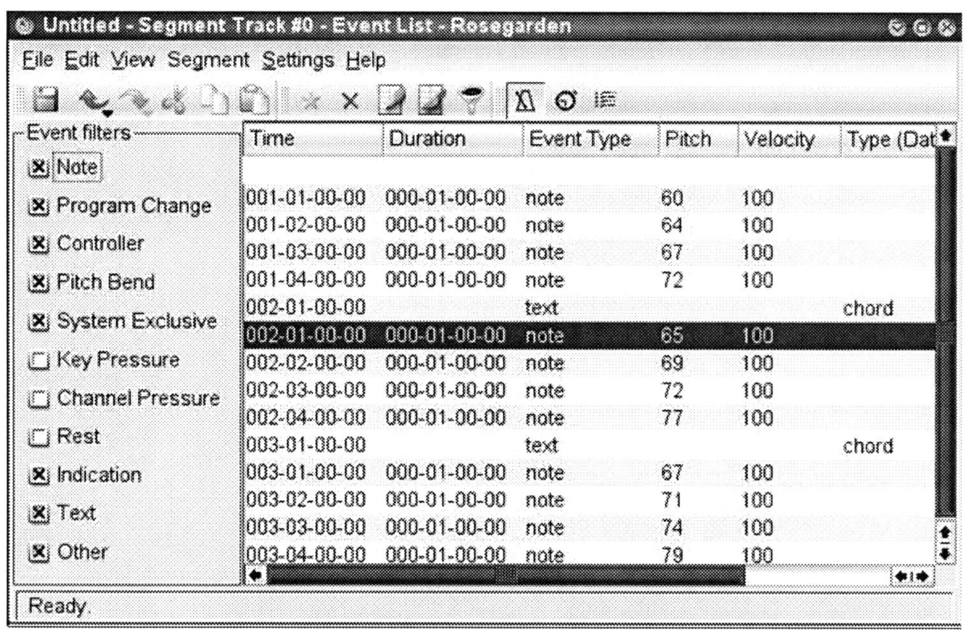

Click on the icon to insert a new event. The dialog will open out to a default event type of "note." You want to dial "programchange" into the "Event type" combo box to make this event into a program change.

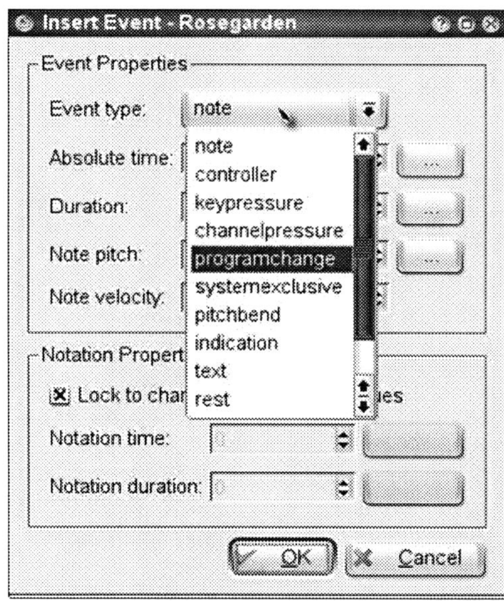

Create the Program Change

Now you should have a dialog like this (I have already twiddled the settings in this particular example).

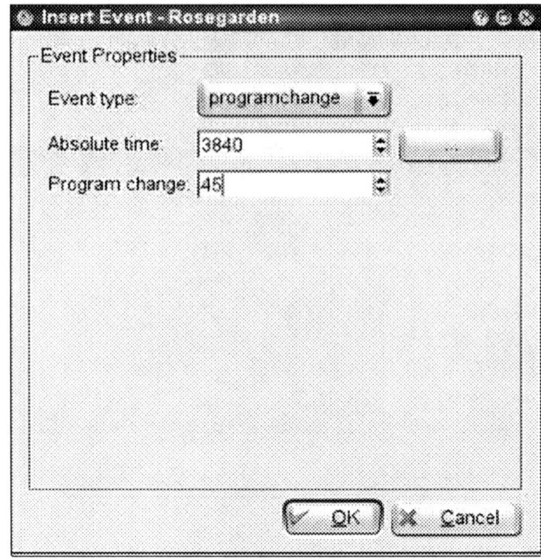

Now you need to dial in the program change by number. Unlike the numbers used elsewhere in Rosegarden (which appear out beside the name when changing programs in the *Instrument Parameters* box, for example), these are zero-based, rather than one-based. If the program "Acoustic Grand Piano" shows up as program 1 in your studio, you'll have to subtract one from that and use 0. I've included a specially-prepared, zero-based list of General MIDI program numbers in Appendix D for your convenience. In this case, "Pizzicato" is program number 45.

7.2   The Matrix Editor

The matrix editor is based around the familiar piano roll metaphor you have probably seen in other packages. It is useful for taking a hands-on approach to tweaking notes where their performance is more important than their visual appearance as notation. The matrix is my preferred method of sequencing percussion parts, and I use it whenever the notation editor is simply unable to cope with my data, and needs a bit of a brute force shove to get things to come out right. There hasn't been a quantizer written yet that can make consistently good decisions in the face of the kind of mistakes I tend to make while playing my keyboard (lots of accidental "grace notes" from where my clumsy fingers hit two keys at once by mistake), and I spend quite a lot of time flipping back and forth between matrix and notation views to clean things up.

7.2.1 Performance vs. Display

Every Rosegarden event maintains independent duration values for performance and display. This makes it possible to create a composition that looks good printed on paper, and yet preserves all of the slight human imperfections that give a performance its character.

The matrix can only edit *performance* attributes. This can create interesting challenges both for performance and notation. If you are working on a human performance, and you draw notes to their full length here in the matrix, you may damage the character of the performance slightly, and you will probably want to go into the notation editor to run an *Interpret* on the notes to "humanize" them. On the other hand, if you draw slightly long or short notes here, or knock the timing off the grid lines intentionally (such as when tweaking a strummed guitar chord to be more life-like), you will create ugly notation in the process, which you will want to *Quantize* back into shape in the notation editor.

One particularly noteworthy side effect of the way Rosegarden stores events is that tied notes are a series of discrete dashes here on the matrix. It is really not possible to determine whether a series of notes at the same pitch will sound as one note or several without looking at the affected area from the Notation Editor.

7.2.2 Overview

Let's start with an empty segment one measure long, and I'll show you the basics. Draw your segment, select it, and then right click on it and choose "Open in Matrix Editor" from the resulting context menu. You'll see something like this:

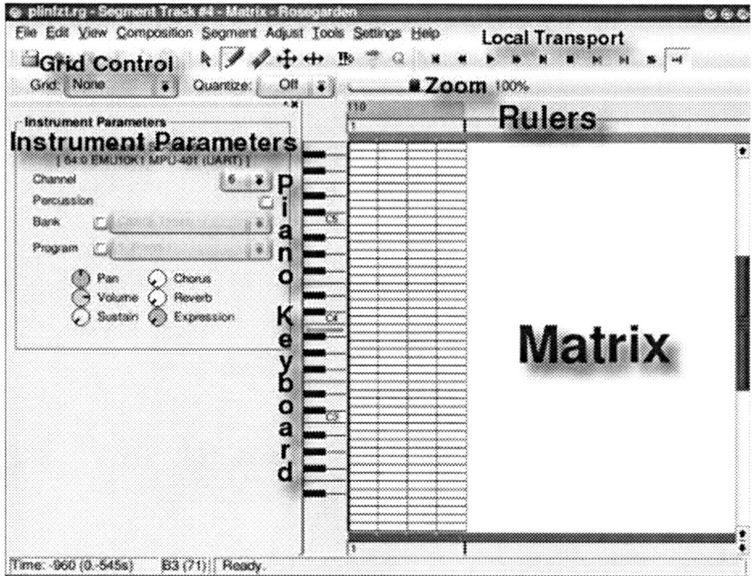

7.3   The Insertion Cursor

If you take a second look at the rulers, you should see that the one toward the top of the screen has a magenta cast. This ruler is for controlling the insertionl cursor, which is a magenta version of the playback pointer. You can set it in the same fashion you set the playback pointer, and the two cursors function independently of each other. The insertionl cursor sets the destination for certain operations. The bottom ruler controls the playback pointer and sets loops, just as both rulers do in the main window.

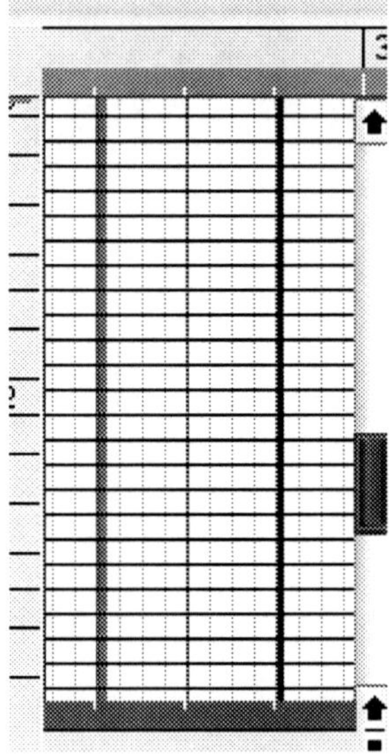

7.3.1 Entering New Notes

Now let's do a little one bar loop for demonstration purposes. Just like on the main window, the 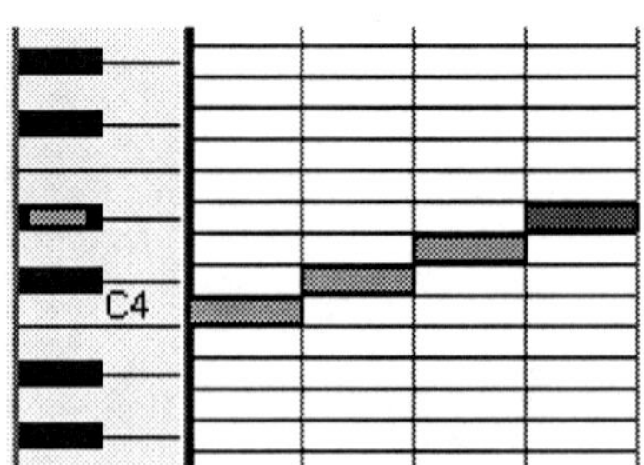 cursor is used to create something new from scratch. In this case, of course, we're entering notes.

You may have noticed that those came out as quarter notes. In order to control the default length of new notes, you must change the grid setting. Now let's enter eight 8th notes. First dial in the 8th note on the grid button:

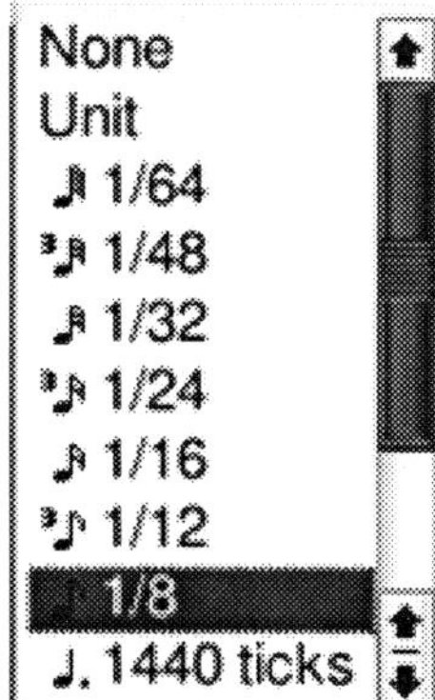

Now new notes you enter will take this duration by default:

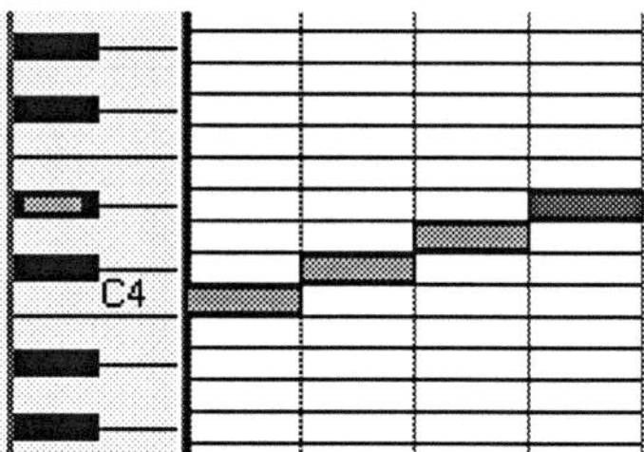

You can enter an entire composition this way if you desire, although I don't recommend it.

7.3.2 Adjusting Existing Notes

You can move notes around with the cursor.

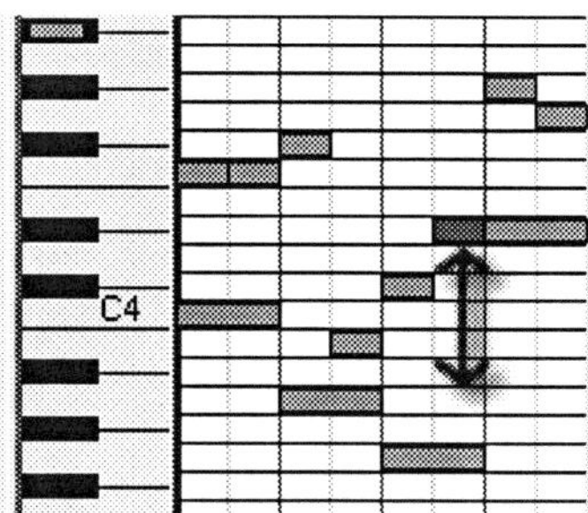

You can resize notes with the 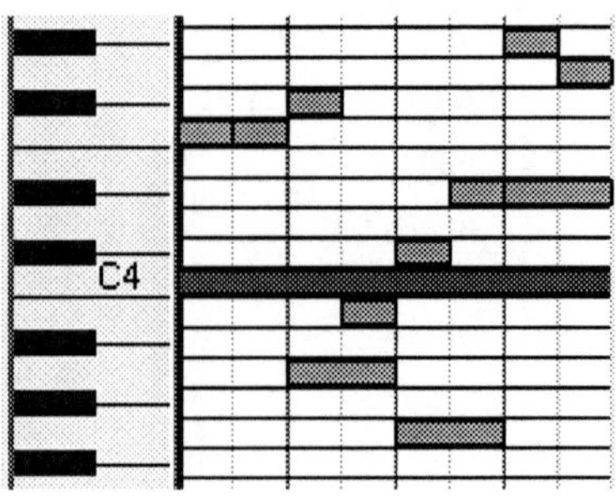 cursor, by clicking on a note and dragging it.

By default, resize operations snap to grid lines. If you wish to drag the note to some arbitrary length, do so by holding the shift key while dragging the note.

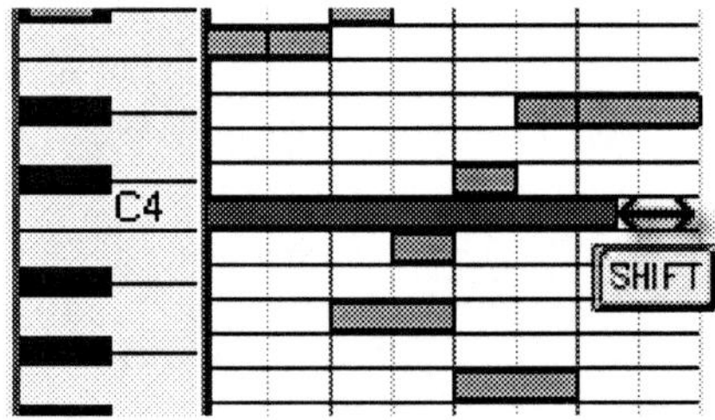

7.3.3 Selecting and Acting on Multiple Notes

All of these operations can be performed on more than one note at a time. In order to do so, you need to make a selection. You can use the cursor to select individual notes one by one while holding down the shift key.

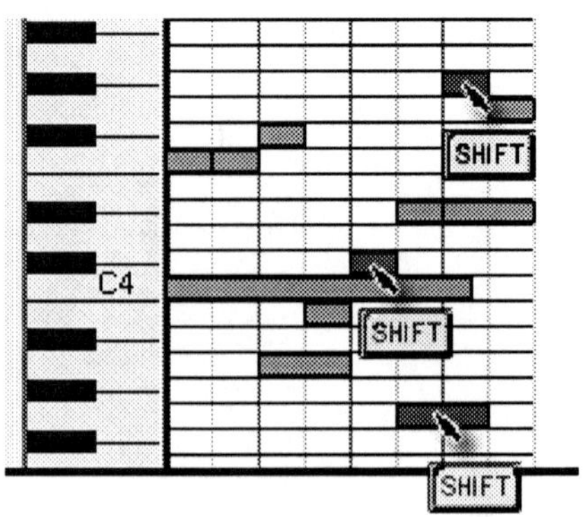

If you wish to select a broad range of notes, you can select every note of a given pitch by selecting the arrow cursor and shift clicking on the individual notes on the piano keyboard. Each click will select every note of the desired pitch, and you can select any number of pitches in this fashion.

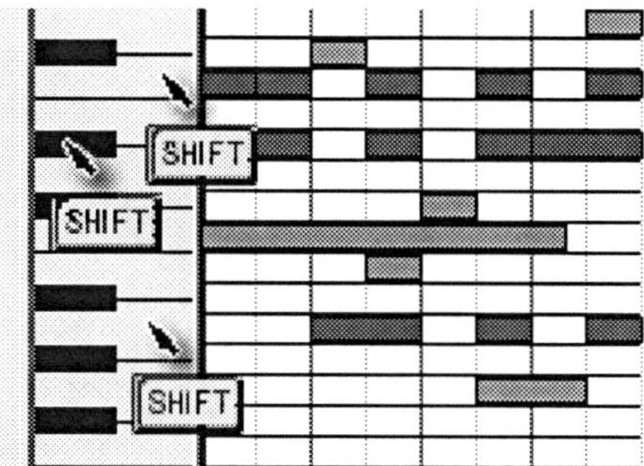

It is also possible to select a band or several bands of notes by sweeping the arrow cursor across the keys while holding shift.

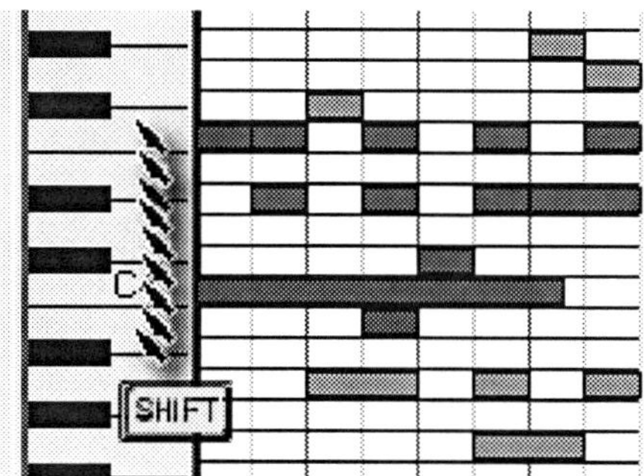

Finally, if you have some need to select ranges of notes within an area less than the entire segment, you can use the selection event filter. Start by making a broad selection, and then click on the filter icon to summon the dialog. You can then dial in various criteria for the notes you wish to remain selected after the filter is applied. I'll demonstrate one use for it later on in this chapter.

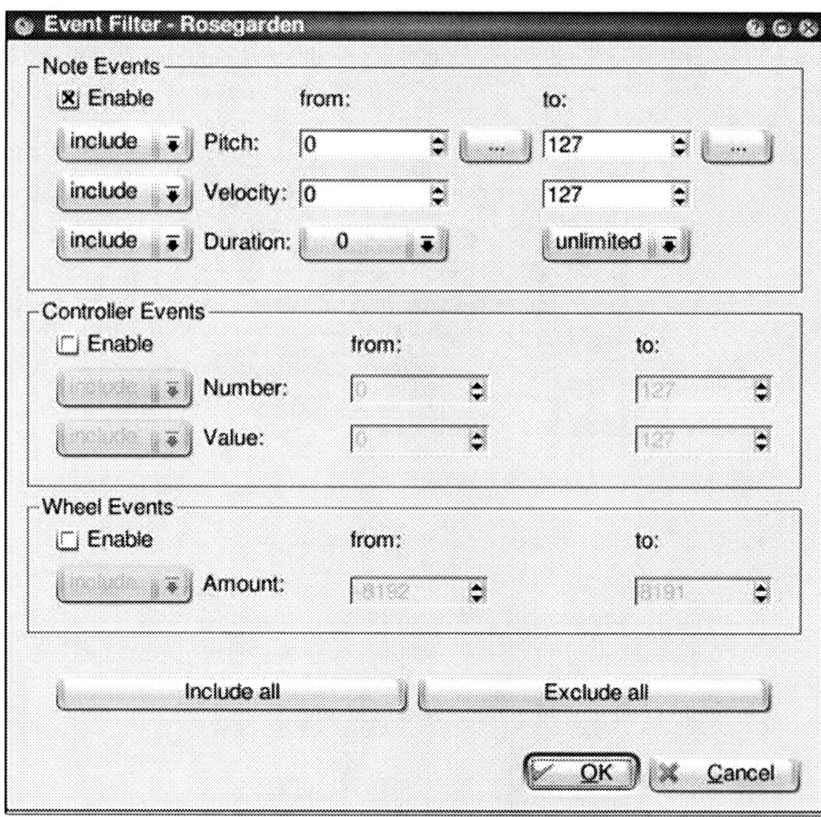

7.3.4 Velocity

Velocity is a MIDI parameter that describes how hard a note was hit on the keyboard or other device. It allows for finer expression of volume than what can be accomplished merely by adjusting the volume parameter for the MIDI channel. If you have a velocity sensitive keyboard, this parameter will be recorded as you play. Under certain other circumstances, you may end up with events that have no velocity property at all, or a default velocity of 100. Regardless of how it did (or didn't) get there, it's a simple matter to tweak it to suit your needs.

Showing the Velocity Ruler

If the events you're editing have velocity properties, you can edit them with the Velocity Ruler. If it's not visible, turn it on from the View menu with *View -> Show Velocity Property Ruler*. In this example, all the events have a velocity of 100, and they show up as orange bars on the ruler.

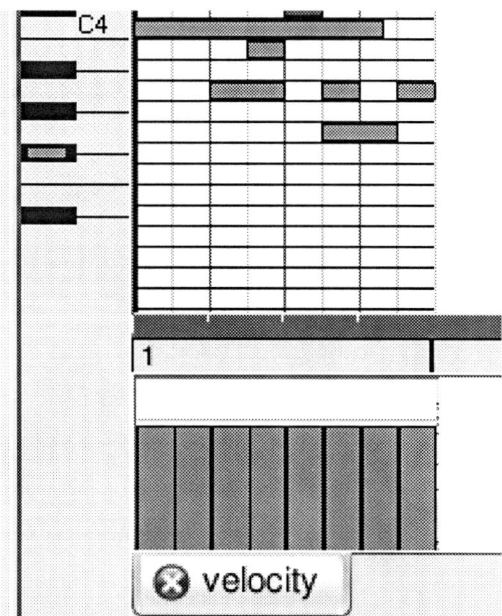

They can be changed by dragging them up and down, and the bars change colors to reflect their value. Here I've arranged them so that you can see each bar. Notice that the notes on the matrix itself change to reflect these same colors.

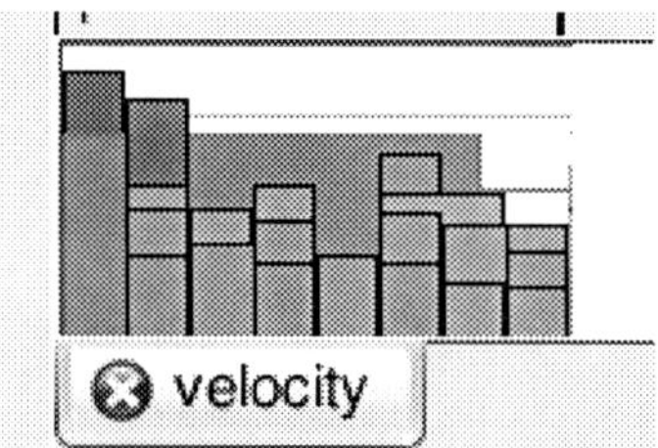

> **TIP**: It can be somewhat tricky to know which note you're adjusting if there are several notes of the same duration at the same time. When multiple notes occur at the same time, use the [and] keys to flip through the available choices, then watch the matrix above for the color change that reveals which note you are adjusting.

Setting Multiple Velocity Properties

It is possible to adjust the velocities for an entire selection of notes. *Adjust -> Velocity -> Set Event Velocities* presents you with a dialog box that allows you to choose from several different patterns. The Value ranges from 0, which is the softest possible key strike, to 127, which is the most forceful.

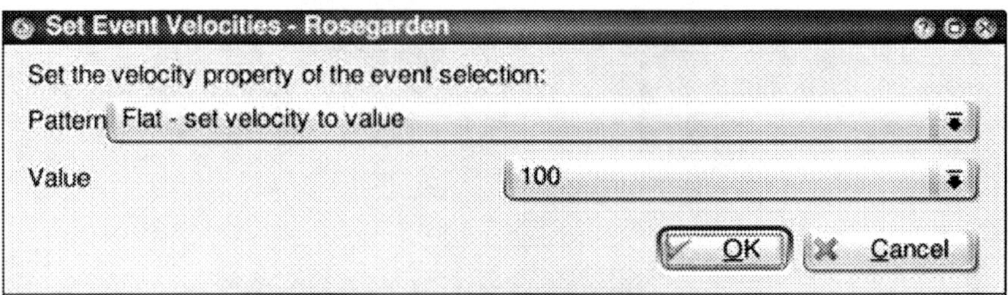

TIP: If you find that you have notes that don't have velocity properties for some reason (there are no bars on the velocity ruler for those notes), you can also use *Set Event Velocities* to create new ones.

7.3.5 Controllers

It's possible to transmit controllers from here in the matrix with the various control rulers. Let's add a Modulation ruler. *Choose View -> Add Event Ruler -> Modulation Controller* and you should now have a new tab at the bottom of your matrix.

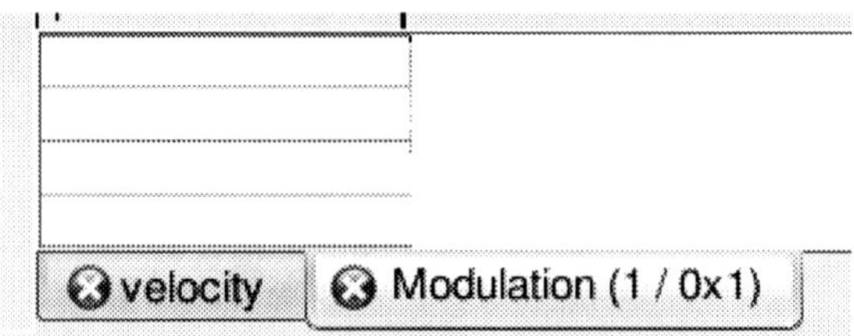

If you right click on the ruler you can insert a controller event, or even an entire line of them.

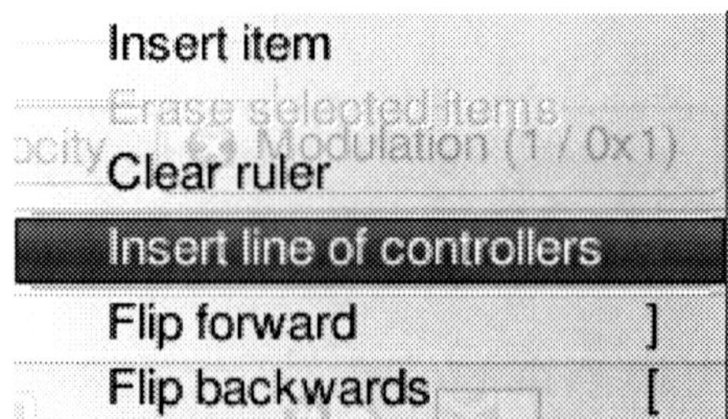

In this example, I have elected to insert a line of controllers. After making the selection from the menu, the cursor changed to a pointing finger. I picked a start point with this finger, and continued to hold the button down while dragging the resulting line up and to the right. After I released the button, it produced this line of controllers:

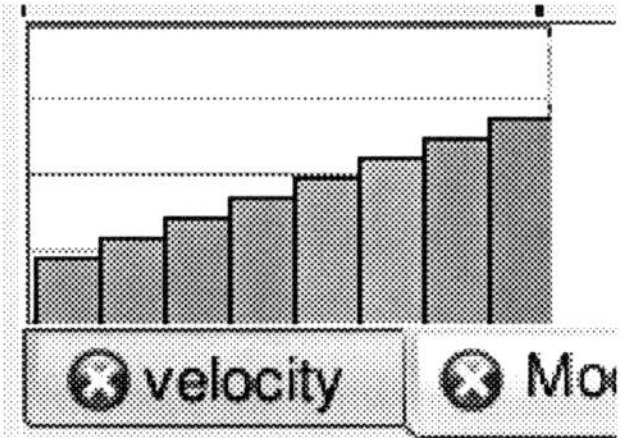

You can move individual controllers up and down, or you can select and move them in groups. It's rather less obvious than selections elsewhere, but if you look closely, you can see that selected controller bars are each outlined in red. If you hold down shift and drag these up and down as a group, they all move at once.

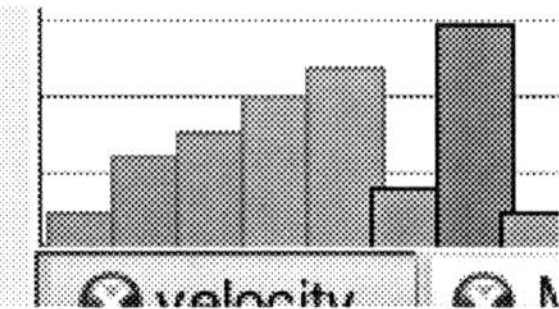

7.4 Example Uses

7.4.1 Sequencing a Drum Pattern

The matrix is arguably the best place to compose drum patterns. (Although the adventure some among you might want to check out is the brand spanking new Drum Matrix in the unstable development branch.)

Create a New Segment

In order to have some place to put the drums, create a new segment four bars long.

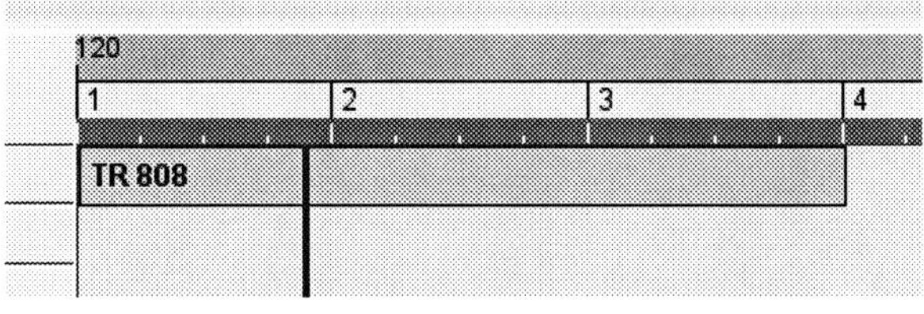

NOTE: I'm leaving this mistake in for the amusement value. I was about to submit a bug report documenting how I created a segment four bars long, opened it in the matrix, and could only edit three bars. Can you spot the reason why that happened? Oooops.

Route the Track to a Percussion Instrument

In order to hear drums, you need to route this track to a percussion instrument from the main window. If you have General MIDI-compliant equipment, all that should be necessary is to route this track to the instrument #10 belonging to a suitable device.

In this particular example, I want to use the TR-808 drum kit that's part of the soundfont I'm using on my Sound Blaster Live!, so I need to check the *[x] Percussion* box, then check *[x] Bank*, then *[x] Program* to get the Program box alive. Then I can simply dial in the correct kit by picking from the list.

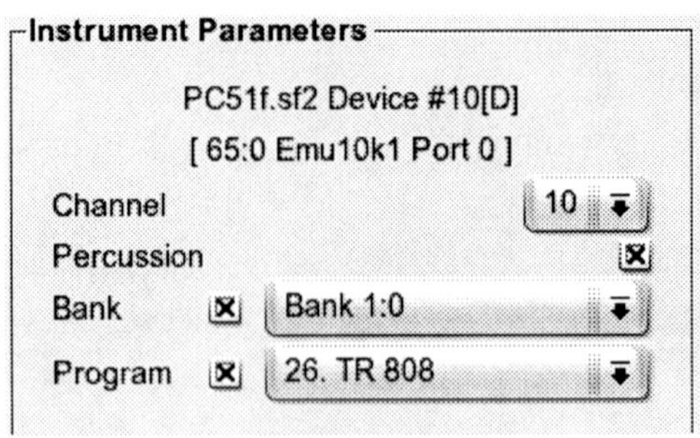

Set the Grid and Loop Points

Now that the track is routed to play using suitable sounds, head back to the matrix window. It's probably a good idea to pick a finer resolution than the standard quarter note for the matrix grid. For this part, 16th notes were convenient, so I dialed 1/16th into the *Grid* combo box.

To make it easier to get the pattern right, set the first bar to loop using the ruler on the bottom.

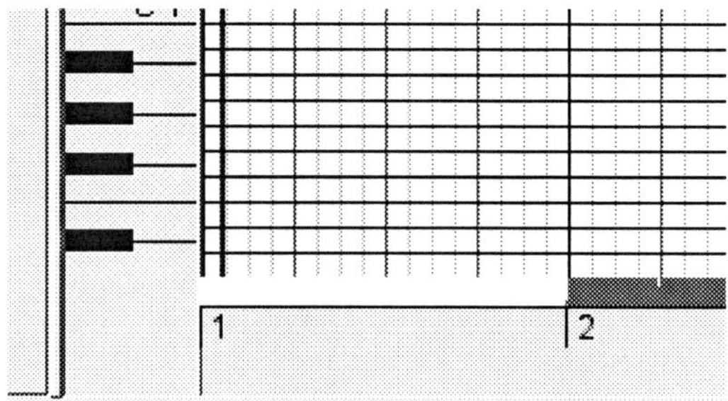

Sequence the Pattern

The rest is trial and error. Set the main transport window to loop mode 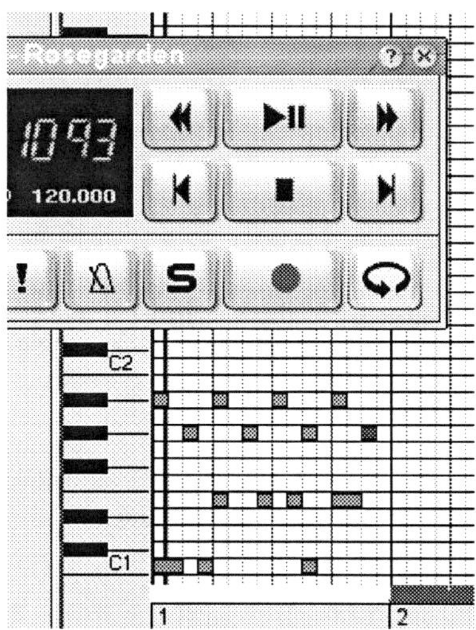 and hit play. Use the edit tools to insert, remove, and move notes until you get a pattern you like. Rosegarden provides no facility for labeling which keys play which drums, so you may need to putter around a bit before you figure out where they are. This example uses a bass, a snare, and a couple of hi-hats, and I have completed my pattern in this snapshot.

Copy the Pattern

Select all the events and paste them three times. Use the top ruler to set the local cursor to the destination for each paste operation. You should wind up with something like this:

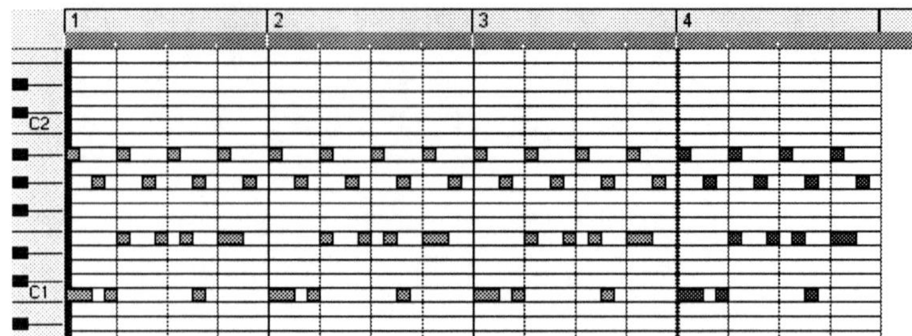

Finish with a Fill

Now set only the last bar to loop, then adjust the pattern to make a little fill.

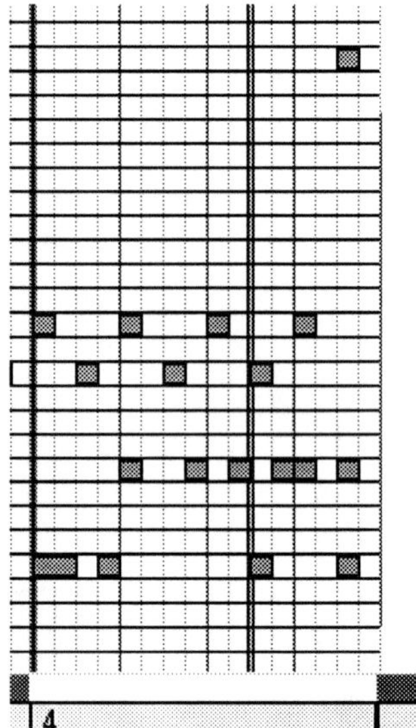

> **TIP**: I found it a trifle fiddly using copy and paste to make these copies. I didn't get the placement of the local cursor quite right, and I had to quantize the results. The next time I had to do this, I started with a segment one bar long, looped it, then when the time came to copy it three times, I marked it as repeating in the *Segment Parameters* box, then double clicked on three of the copies, selected all four segments, and used *Segments -> Splint and Join -> Join* to join them back into one; then I finished by un-checking repeat for the segment. It's a toss-up whether method B is faster, but it's definitely more precise.

7.4.2 Adjusting Velocities with the Selection Event Filter

One place where the selection event filter shines is in its ability to quickly focus in on a particular range of notes within a selection. In this example, I had an arpeggiated part that I entered with flat velocities, and I wanted to add some life to the performance by accenting the top and bottom notes, while bringing down the velocity in the middle. As the part cycled up and down through several chords, it was impossible to use the click-on-the-keyboard method I described earlier in this chapter to select only the events I wanted.

Make a Selection

The first step is to select all the events in the four bars of the first chord using the  tool.

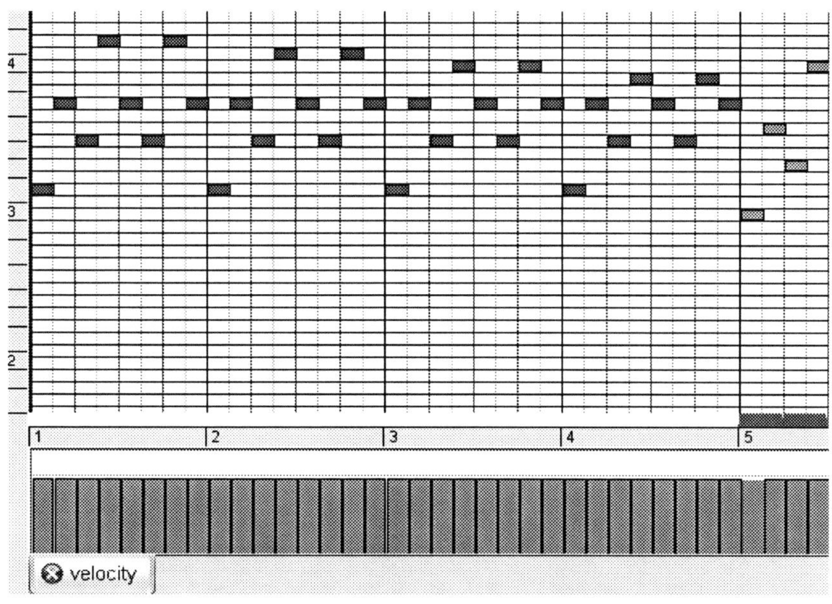

Configure the Selection Event Filter

Next, I wanted to catch the middle notes, so I used the icon to summon the event filter dialog. Then I used the icon to pop up the pitch chooser for the *from*: pitch. In this case, E3.

> **TIP**: I find it a bit tricky to use the pitch picker in this dialog from the matrix view because I'm comparing a constantly changing clef and staff to a pitch on a piano keyboard. I find it error prone, personally, and so I have taken to looking at the status bar at the bottom of the window as I hover over notes. It shows the absolute MIDI pitch, and makes it a breeze dialing the values I want straight in.

I repeated the process for the *to:* pitch, selecting B#3. Since I wanted to select the notes in between these two extremes first, I left the associated combo box set to "include." This caused it to include all the notes between E3 and B#3. Since I wanted to grab notes irrespective of duration or velocity, I left these filters at all-inclusive settings.

Adjust the Velocities

After clicking *OK* to apply the filter, the following selection resulted:

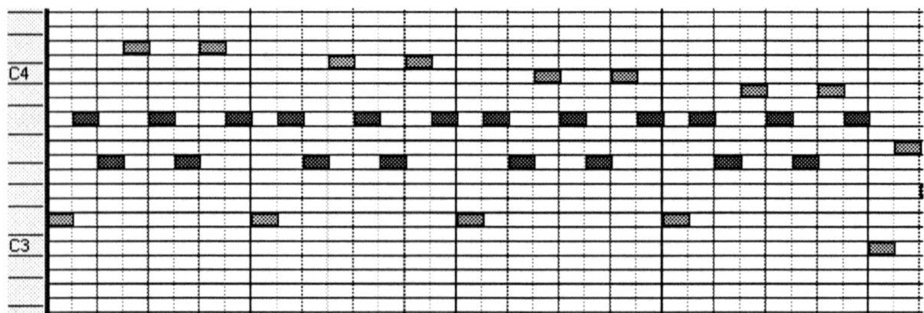

> TIP: If you didn't get quite what you were after, hit the filter again. It remembers the last settings you used, and you can fine tune it on subsequent runs until you get it just right.

Now that I had filtered the selection to the range of notes I wanted to affect, I used *Shift+Down* to lower all of these velocities at once, producing the following result:

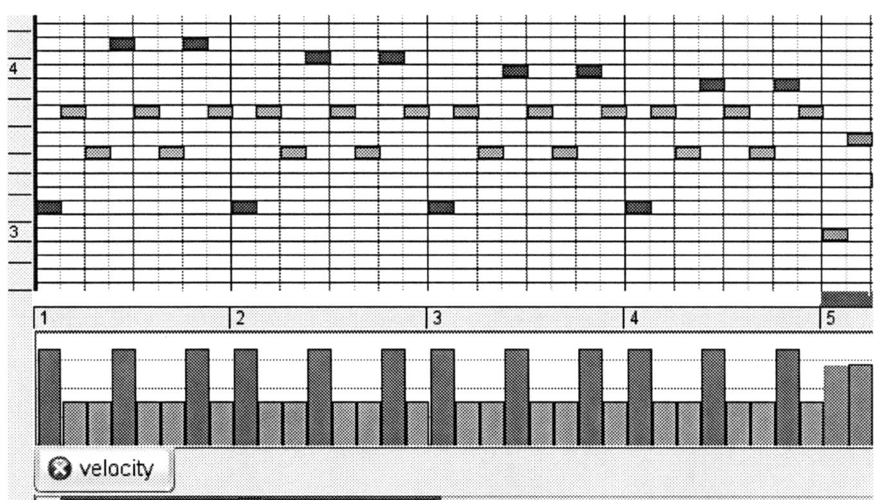

I could have used the filter the other way as well. By setting the combo box to "exclude" the range, I could have selected and adjusted the high and low notes to a higher velocity...

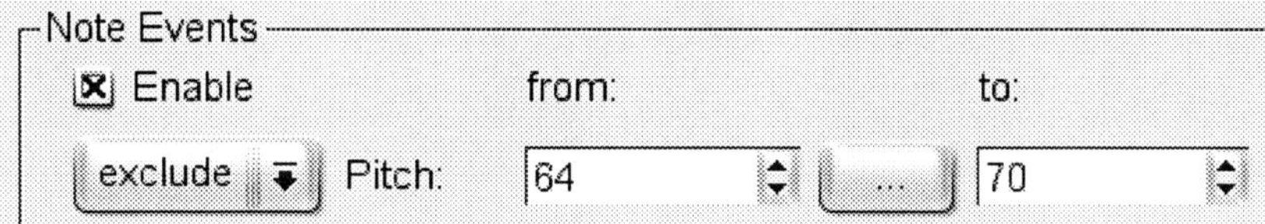

With the following result...

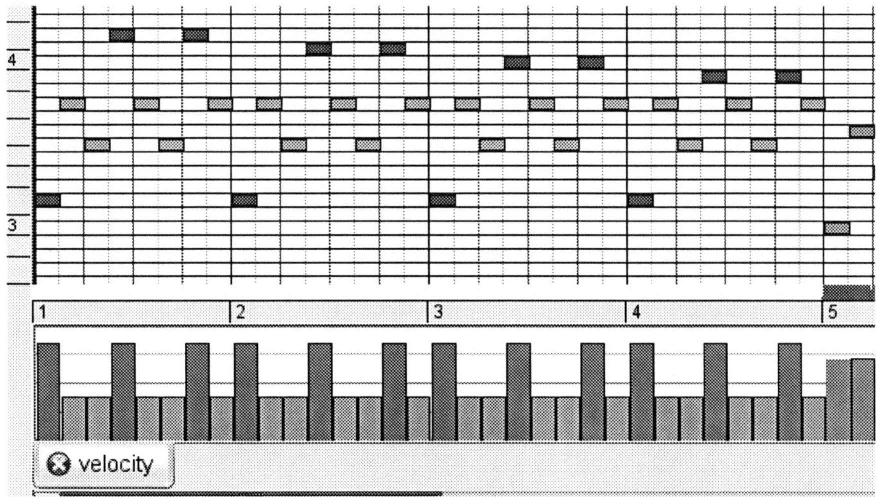

8   The Notation Editor

I have mentioned elsewhere that Rosegarden is not purely a MIDI sequencer, and that it is not possible to create or manage raw MIDI events directly. Neither is it purely a notation editor. Applications dedicated to notation typically work with notation internally, and any MIDI performance capability they have is the result of interpreting that notation and translating it into MIDI. These applications typically do a rudimentary job at best in the MIDI arena, and the results almost always sound very artificial and mechanical. At the other extreme, applications dedicated entirely to MIDI sequencing tend to have rudimentary notation capabilities, and it is often all but impossible to produce legible notation with these unless the MIDI data itself has been beaten into a state of mechanical purity that causes the results to sound just as artificial as that produced by dedicated notation packages.

Rosegarden sits squarely in the middle between these two extremes, possessing most of the features of both, with few compromises. In order to allow the richness of a human performance to coexist with legible notation, every note event, whether recorded, imported, or entered by hand, contains not one, but two different duration properties. One duration is used to determine how long the note will sound for MIDI performance, while the other is used for displaying clean, legible notation. This exciting feature allows you to have your cake and eat it too, so to speak.

8.1   Notation Editor Overview

In order to open the notation editor, you must have at least one segment available. You can open any number of segments on any number of tracks simultaneously by selecting the segment or segments you wish to edit, and then right clicking on one of them and choosing "Open in Notation Editor" from the context menu.

Additionally, the notation editor is the normal default, so you can also open it either by pressing *Enter*, or by double clicking on a segment (you can configure this behavior from *Settings -> Configure Rosegarden*).

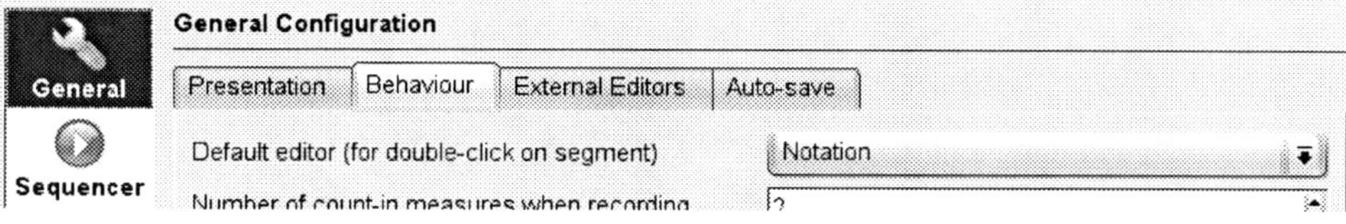

After you have opened it, you will see something a bit like this. Your screen will probably look somewhat different, because this particular example is in multiple page layout mode, which is not the default.

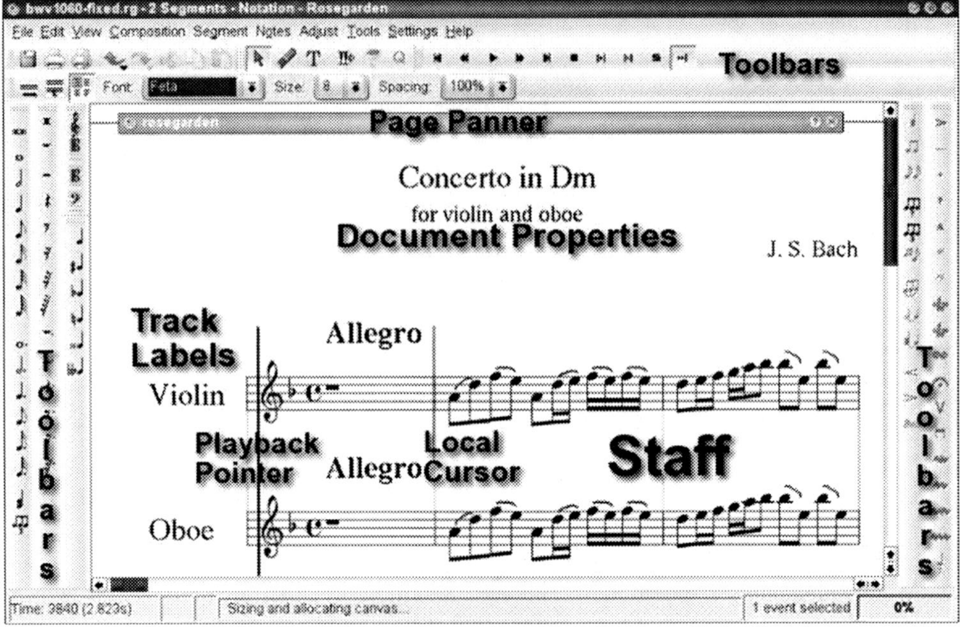

(I should have done this initial screenshot in the default, linear layout mode, but I chose this mode instead so I could showcase a small bit of my favorite piece of music.)

8.1.1 Notation Toolbars

The notation editor is just bristling with toolbars big and small. I will defer many of them until time to describe their function in more detail. The standard toolbar includes print and save icons, as well as the usual cut/copy/paste tools.

The tools toolbar has several of the same tools found in the main window, but it adds icons for step recording and the quantizer.

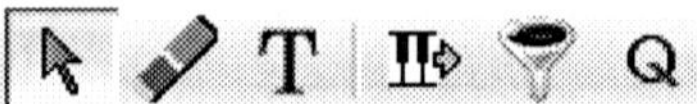

The transport toolbar is the same as the one found in the matrix.

The layout toolbar allows you to change the way notation is displayed in various ways. You can switch between linear layout mode, continuous page mode, and multiple page mode. The linear mode scrolls continuously off to the right, and it is the only mode that has rulers. The continuous page mode displays notation formatted as though it were a printed page, but it scrolls continuously toward the bottom. Multiple page mode breaks the notation into discrete pages, and provides a pager to allow you to get access to the portion of the wish to view or edit.

You can use the *Font:* combo box to choose among the standard Feta (courtesy of the Lilypond project), a bitmap version of Feta called "Feta Pixmaps," and the bitmap font used by a previous incarnation of Rosegarden, called "RG21." The *Size:* box functions somewhat like the zoom slider in the other views, allowing you to magnify or reduce your view (but not your printouts or exports.) The *Spacing:* box allows you tweak how much space Rosegarden uses when laying out the notation horizontally.

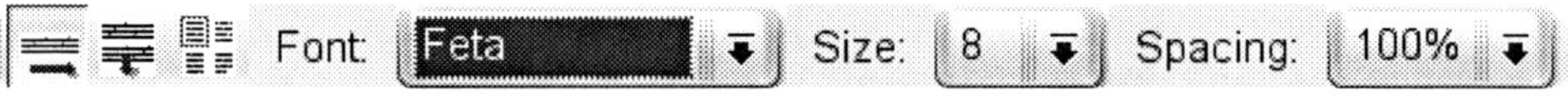

> **NOTE**: To change the size of fonts for printing, use *Settings -> Configure Rosegarden -> Notation -> Font -> Font size* for printing (pt) (It is not possible to print using more than one size, currently, and this setting affects everything you print until you change it.) To change the size of fonts *on-screen* in the notation editor, use the *Size:* box.

> **TIP**: It is also possible to use fonts from packages like Finale if you prefer. See the "Note Fonts" (*help:/rosegarden/nv-note-fonts.html*) and "Customizing Rosegarden" (*help:/rosegarden/developers.html*) topics in the Rosegarden Handbook for more details.

The meta toolbar (not enabled by default) toggles the other toolbars.

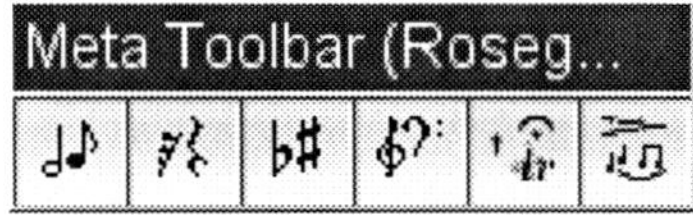

The remaining toolbars need more than casual treatment, and will be mentioned in due course.

8.2   Opening Multiple Staffs

Many posters on the rosegarden-user mailing list use Rosegarden to work with piano notation, so I have chosen a simple flute with piano accompaniment arrangement as the place in which to demonstrate various entry and editing features.

I mentioned in the introduction to this chapter that Rosegarden has made few compromises in order to be able to do a bang up job as both a notation editor and a MIDI sequencer. This example also serves to highlight one of those compromises. It is not possible to display an entire piano part on one grand staff. Neither is it possible to do a good, clear job of writing multiple parts or voices on the same staff. Due to both of these limitations, you will probably want to write the bass and treble parts in different segments, and thus on separate staffs. These segments can be in the same track, but if they are exactly the same length, and they overlap each other exactly, it will be impossible to select whichever segment lies on the bottom. For this reason, I recommend putting the right and left hand parts on different tracks as well.

For this example, I have created three segments on three tracks. I've labeled the top one "flute" and have assigned it to a device and instrument that will play a flute program on channel 1. The remaining two tracks are labeled by right or left hand, and they are both assigned to the same piano instrument, which will play using a piano program on channel 2. I have selected all three of these segments in order to open them in a combined notation view:

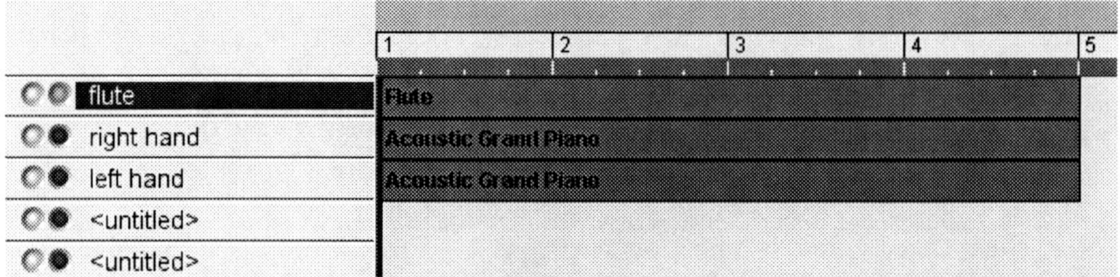

8.3   Notation Basics

Unless you have changed the default notation display mode, the notation view should open in its default linear layout mode, like this:

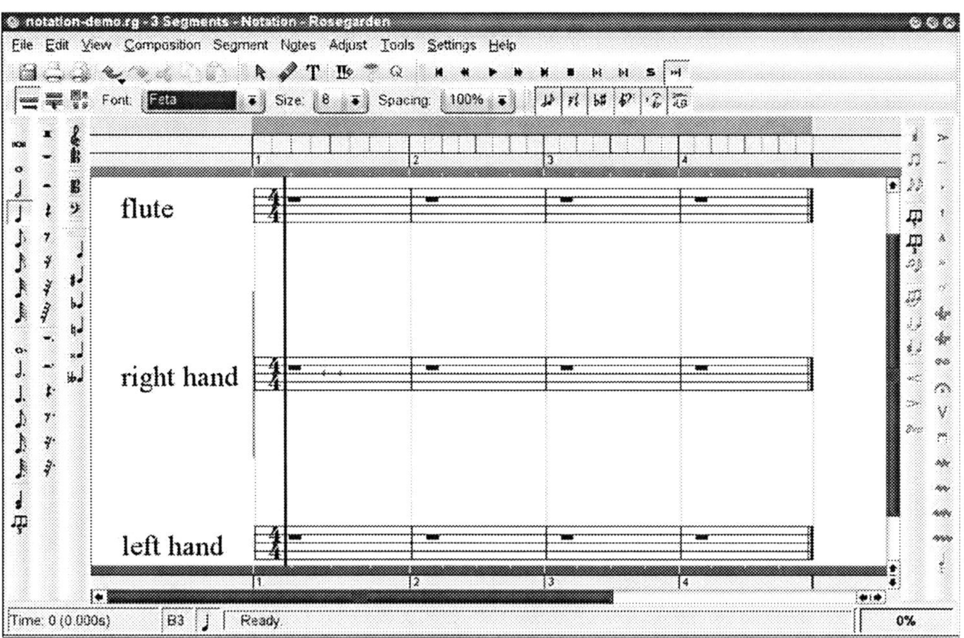

8.3.1 Notation Rulers

Just like the matrix view, there are two distinct sets of rulers here. At the top of the window you will find a tempo ruler, a special raw note ruler, which I will describe later on, and an insertion ruler for manipulating the insertion cursor. As in the matrix, the insertion cursor determines the point at which notation elements are inserted or pasted.

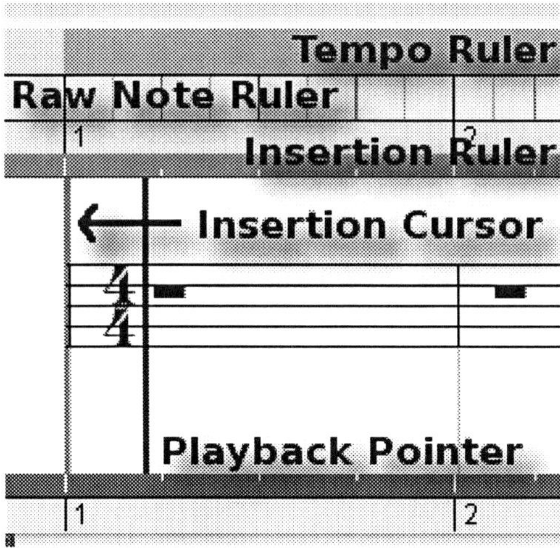

In a multiple staff situation such as this, you will notice that the insertion cursor only spans a single staff. This lets you know which staff is the active target for various operations.

8.3.2 Clefs

There are at least two ways to enter a clef. Regardless of which you use, you first need to position the insertion cursor at the correct insertion point, if it isn't there already. Select the target staff by double clicking on it. Then you can use *Segment -> Add Clef Change* from the menu. A clef chooser dialog will appear, allowing you to choose from a variety of different clefs in different 8va configurations by clicking on the various arrows. The up/down arrows change between 8va and 15ma up or down, respectively, and the left/right arrows cycle through the various available clefs. The dialog will remember the clef you used last time, making it more convenient to insert multiple clefs. (There is no option to insert a clef in more than one place at once, so you will have to add a clef to each staff manually.)

The *Existing notes following clef change* portion of this dialog is particularly useful in a situation where you began entering notation before choosing a clef. Rosegarden thinks in treble, and treble is the default if no clef is present. If *[x] Transpose into appropriate octave* is selected, Rosegarden will attempt to find the best transposition of any existing notation relative to the new clef. (If this has undesired consequences, as it sometimes does, then you can transpose again by hand, as I will discuss in due course.)

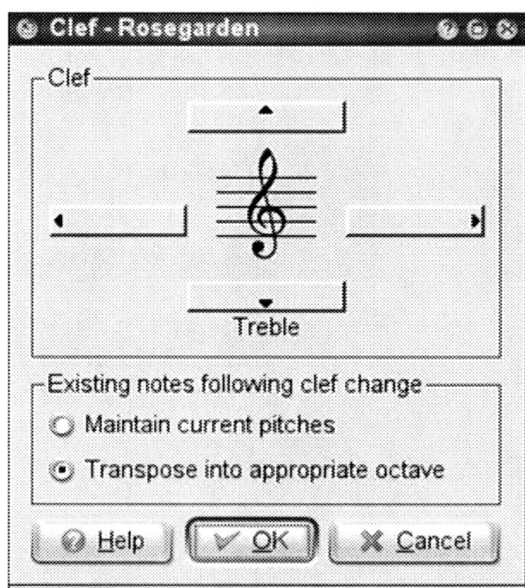

If you prefer, you can use the Clefs toolbar. (The Clefs toolbar is not toggled on by default.)

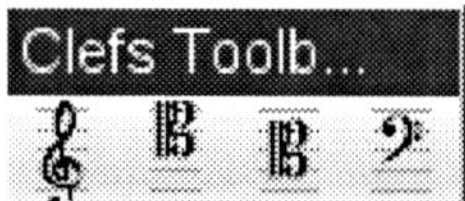

To use the toolbar, first switch to the cursor, then select one of the clefs from the Clefs toolbar. Click in one of the staffs, and the selected clef should be inserted. If you find a dead zone near the time signature, you may need to click around a bit until you find the magic spot.

Key Signatures

Key signatures are added in a similar fashion to clefs. Position the insertion cursor as appropriate, select the target staff, and then use *Segment -> Add Key Change* from the menu. You will be presented with a dialog that allows you to choose from all major and minor keys up through seven accidentals.

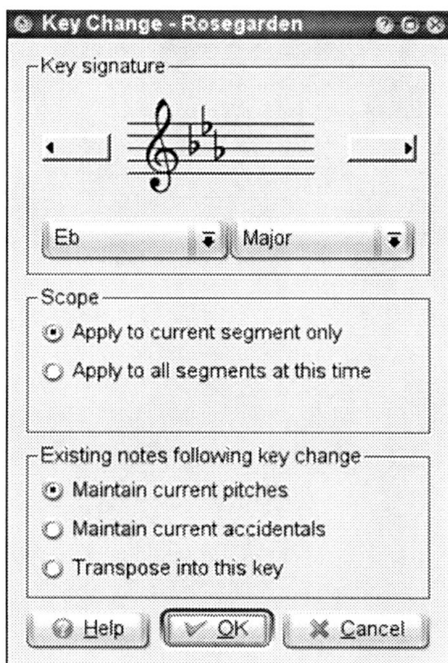

In addition to changing the key signature itself, you can use the *Scope* controls to change whether Rosegarden will insert the new key signature only in the target staff, or in all staffs (segments) at this point in time. You may also decide whether Rosegarden should favor the existing pitches, possibly creating new accidentals in the new key, or favor the current accidentals, which might change the pitches in the new key. Rosegarden can also attempt to transpose the notation into the new key.

8.3.3 Tempo and Time Signature

Both of these are attributes of the composition as a whole, and when they change, they affect all segments and, accordingly, all staffs at the same time. It is not possible to have different time signatures or different tempi in different segments at the same time. These attributes can be controlled from the main window, but they can also be edited from the notation view for convenience.

I already discussed the associated dialogs for both of these in an earlier chapter. To open the tempo and time signature editor, double click on the tempo ruler, or on a time signature. If you wish, for example, to insert a time signature change from 4/4 to 12/8 at bar 3, move the insertion cursor (by clicking on the top ruler) to the appropriate time, then use *Composition -> Add Time Signature Change* to open the time signature editor dialog.

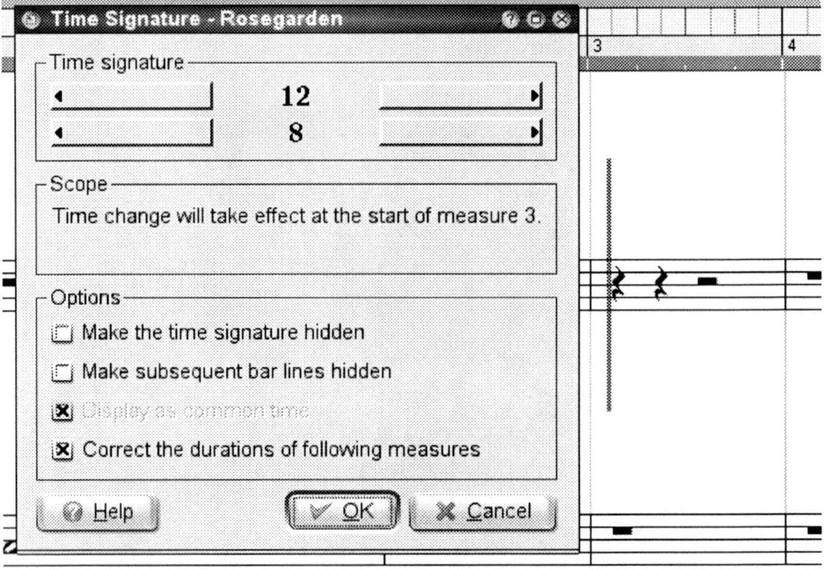

The time signature will appear in accordance with the various options that have been chosen.

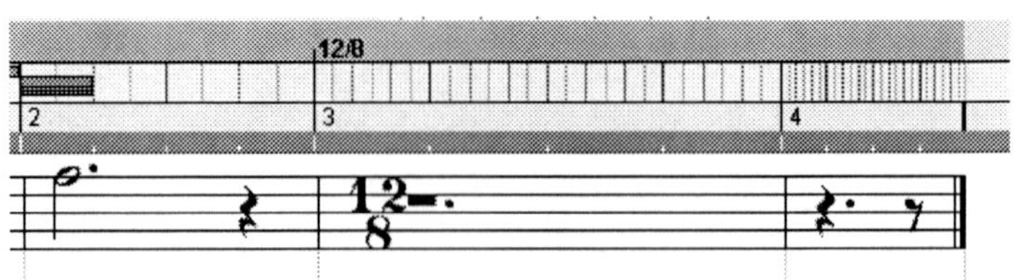

Notice in this particular example that the measure following this one did not expand to become full after this change. Time signature adjustments will not resize segments. Instead, the beats are reallocated as required, as is perhaps better illustrated by this 4/4 to 5/4 example. Instead of two measures with four beats, it has become one with five and one with three.

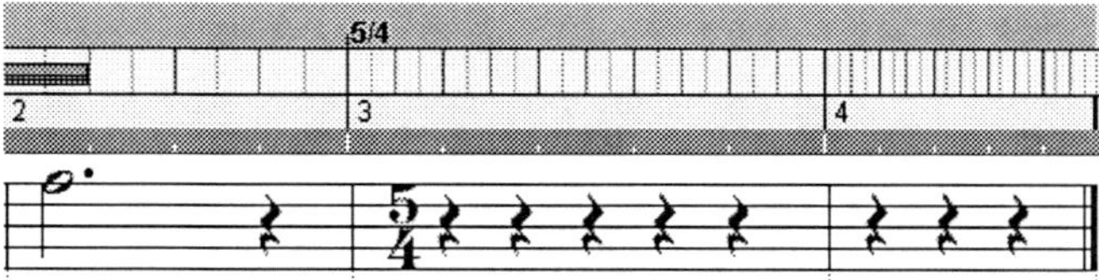

8.3.4 Entering Notes and Rests

Rosegarden provides a variety of ways to enter notes, providing tools for both mouse- and keyboard-oriented composers. Perhaps the quickest way to get started is to use the several associated toolbars and point and click a few notes into existence. (I will cover the other methods a bit later on.)

Notes

Switch to the ___ tool, which puts the editor into insert mode. To enter a note, choose either standard or a dotted duration from the Notes toolbar. Then click in one of the staffs to insert a note at that location.

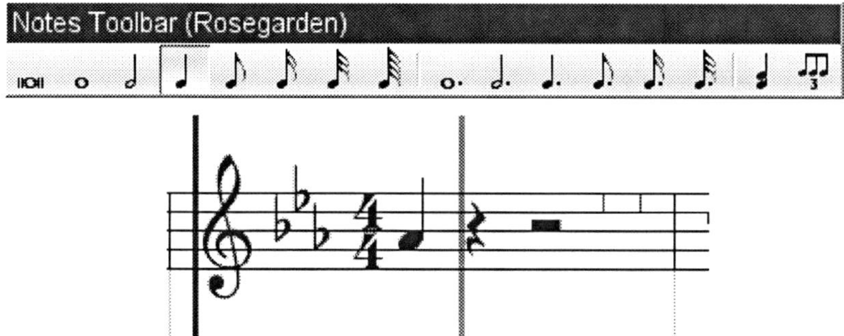

Rests

Rests are treated as negative space, and Rosegarden attempts to pad out the measure with rests automatically. However, it is often useful, even necessary, to enter them manually. For example, switch to the 8th note duration and then try to enter an 8th note on the far side of that quarter rest, leaving an 8th rest in between. It's impossible. You'll wind up with a result like this every time:

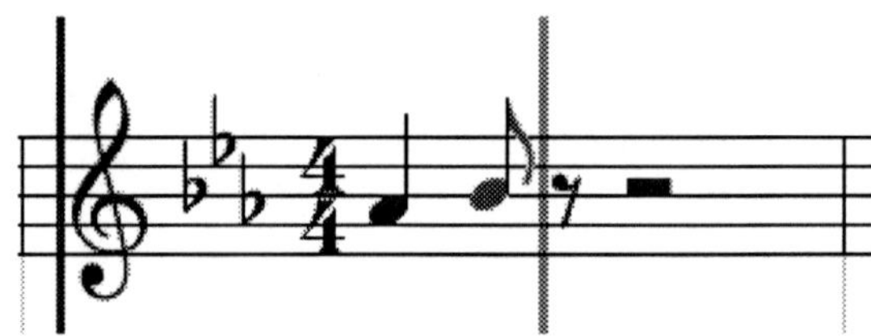

The trick to this is to manually insert a rest, which causes Rosegarden to subdivide the beat; giving you a place to insert your new note. To change this note into a rest, select an appropriate duration from the Rests toolbar, then click on the note head to replace it with a rest.

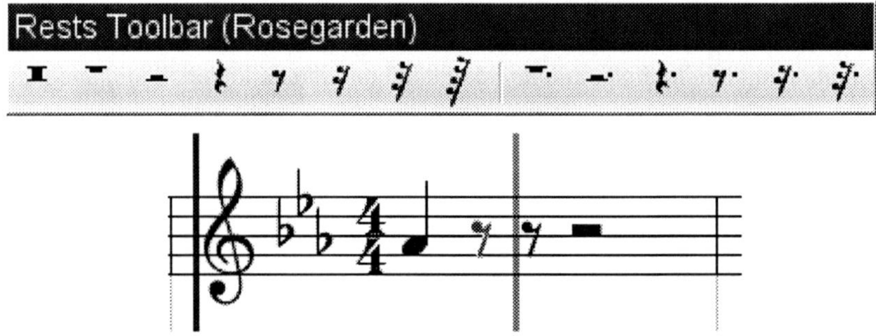

Now you can change to an 8th note on the Notes toolbar and enter the remaining note in the correct location.

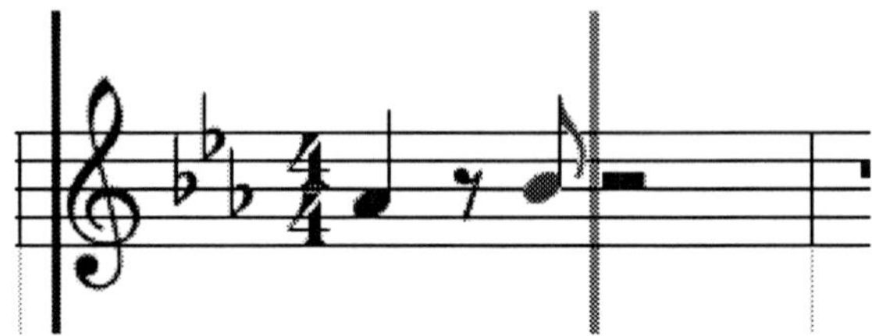

Notice as you do this that the insertion cursor advances to the next beat division. Remember that you can reposition it using the insertion ruler. What you cannot do, however, is move it to an arbitrary point in time. It always snaps along beat divisions, depending on how the measure is divided, and it can sometimes be a bit fiddly getting a note just where you want it. Particularly if you're adding a new note to existing notation, as when turning a single note into a chord, for example.

Chords

When using the toolbars and other graphical tools to insert notes, creating chords is as simple as clicking in a new note above or below an existing one.

You can also select a series of notes spaced out over time,

then use the  icon...

to pull them into a chord.

Nudging an Incorrect Pitch

In the preceding example, I entered what was trying to be an F major chord in the key of Eb. The easiest way to fix the errant Ab from here is to nudge it with the Up/Down arrow keys on the keyboard. First select the note in question, then raise it a halfstep by hitting the Up arrow key once (I could also have avoided writing the note incorrectly in the first place, as I will explain later on).

You can transpose individual notes or entire selections in this fashion, one semitone at a time. The accidentals along the way will be based on the key signature. Flats in a flat key, sharps in a sharp key. If you want to write a sharp in a flat key, you'll have to change it manually, as I will explain further on. You can also raise or lower pitches an octave at a time with *Ctrl+Up/Down*.

Erasing Notes

In order to pave the way for the next example, this is a good time to introduce the  cursor. Select it and then click on individual notes to erase them. To follow along at home, remove the F major chord and step back to a time when there was just an Ab here.

Avoiding Multiple Voices

Rosegarden cannot yet handle situations involving multiple musical lines written on the same staff very well at all. From a MIDI performance perspective, there is no reason why you cannot have an entire violin concerto in a single segment, and you can manipulate this data to your heart's content with the other editors, but the notation editor will never produce good results attempting to interpret data like this into legible notation. It attempts to display the notation as a single line, and this can lead to a great deal of awkwardness. For example, select a dotted 8th note duration from the Notes toolbar and then add a note above the first quarter note. Rosegarden splits and ties the quarter note and displays the whole mess as a chord.

You can undo this if you do so immediately, but if you wish to go back later on and erase the top note, the bottom note will remain a split-and-tied pair permanently, because it has become two separate events.

If you erase both of these notes, you wind up with some unwieldy looking rests.

All of these problems can be solved, and no permanent harm has been done, but the fact remains that Rosegarden simply is not able to cope with this kind of situation elegantly.

NOTE: Part writing is one of the most often-requested features, and is almost certain to be implemented in some fashion at some point in the future.

Making Selections

Just like in the other views, you can select groups of notes to isolate them from the rest

of a staff. Each note will sound as you select it. Switch back to the [cursor] tool. You can select individual notes by shift clicking them, or you can make a sweep selection by clicking and dragging the blue selection box until it includes the notes you want. You can select an entire measure at once by double clicking it, or you can select an entire staff by triple clicking. As elsewhere, you can also hold down *Shift* while clicking on notes to make a non-contiguous selection of scattered, individual notes.

Collapsing Rests

If you find yourself in an ugly situation such as the preceding example, you can instruct Rosegarden to recalculate and collapse the rests. First you will need to make a selection, then use *Adjust -> Rests...* to tidy things up. If you choose *Normalize Rests*, (or use the *Ctrl+N* shortcut) Rosegarden will attempt to reduce the rests along beat divisions.

If you choose Collapse Rests, Rosegarden will squeeze them down into the smallest possible space, irrespective of beat divisions.

> **TIP**: I find I have to normalize rests quite often after erasing notes or otherwise rearranging rhythms. Rosegarden can come up with some pretty strange looking results sometimes, but a select-and-Ctrl+N usually fixes it right up.

Accidentals

I already mentioned that you can nudge an errant note into place with the arrow keys, but what if you need to enter an accidental intentionally? The Accidentals toolbar allows you to control the accidental state of entered notes.

The default "No accidental" mode will enter notation that follows the key signature. You can override this with any of the other choices.

Of particular note is the "Follow previous accidental" mode, which will enter the note with the same accidental as was last used for this particular line or space. If you enter an F# in bar 3, then click on the F line in bar 6, it will be sharp if the Accidentals toolbar is in this mode.

To enter this phrase from J. S. Bach's Concerto in Dm, first enter a half rest to divide the measure in half. Switch to the 16th note duration to enter the E. Select the sharp from the Accidentals toolbar to enter the F# and G#, then switch back to the "No accidental" state to enter the A. Choose the natural to enter the B natural, then switch back to "No accidental" once more to enter the C. Finally, switch to the 8th note duration to enter the D.

Respelling

In Bach, I often encounter situations where a passage is written in a different key without a key change. Rosegarden will use flats in a flat key, and sharps in a sharp key, but this sometimes reads poorly. Take this passage for example (in the key of Dm):

The second measure here could read better if the Db were respelled as a C#. To correct this, *Notes -> Adjust -> Respell with Sharp* is just the trick. (Otherwise you would have to arrow the note down to C, transposing it in the process, choose sharp from *Accidentals* toolbar, then click on it to sharpen it. Or else erase the Db and put a new C# in its place, and lose any human performance duration in the process.)

Cautionary Accidentals

To make the passage I just demonstrated resemble the score I have in front of me, it is necessary to adjust the way Rosegarden handles accidental changes. The original score notates a flat on both Es, and puts a natural sign on the first E natural in the following measure. Producing this result requires changing two of the default behaviors and then closing and reopening the notation view to see the new options in action.

Accidental behavior is configured via various controls on the *Settings -> Configure Rosegarden -> Notation -> Accidentals* page. To achieve the particular results I want in this case, I need to make accidentals only affect the octave in which they are written, and I need to require explicit cancellations in the following bars. (There are also options to use cautionary accidentals in parentheses in these cases, as opposed to explicit accidentals.)

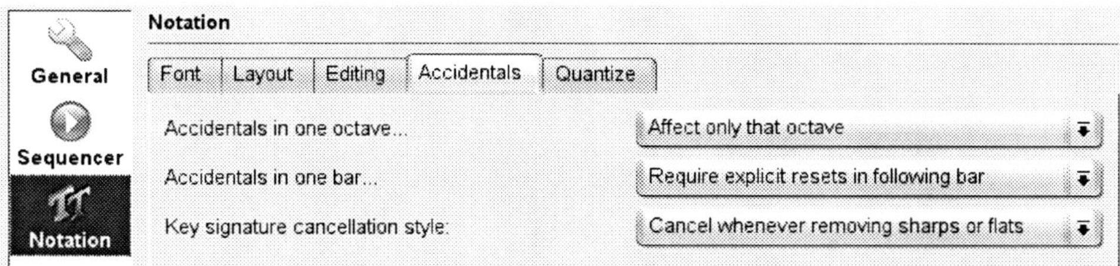

Making these changes, then opening a new notation view yields just what I want to match the score in front of me:

Triplets and Tuplets

There are several ways to enter triplets and tuplets. One choice is to enter some number of ordinary notes, then select them...

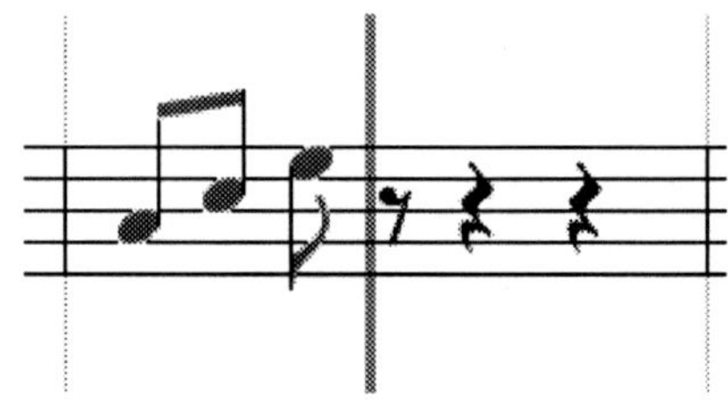

Then use the icon (or *Ctrl+R*) to transform them into a triplet...

It is also possible to do tuplets of, say, 5 in the time of 3 in similar fashion...

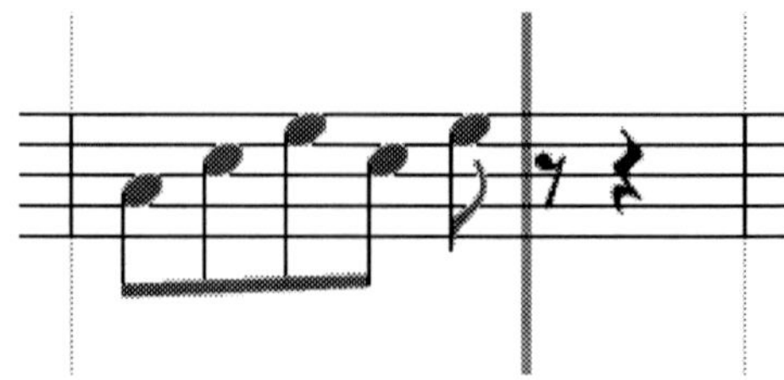

Enter five notes... then use the 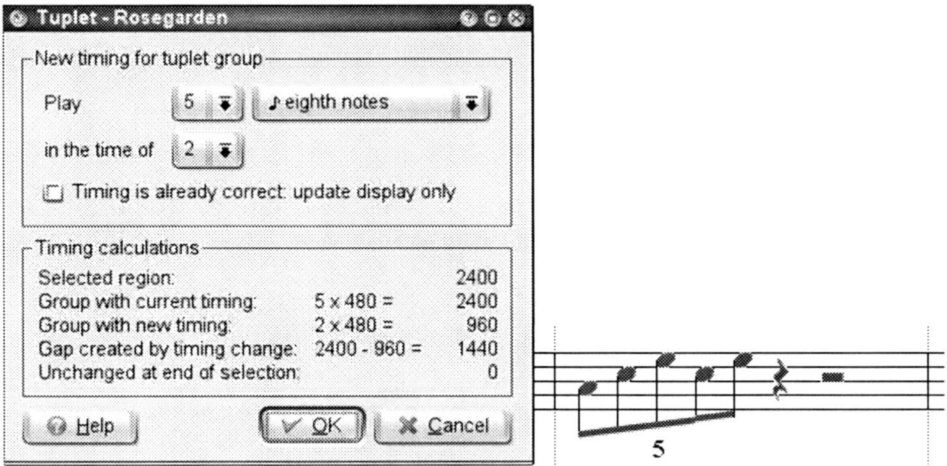 icon or (*Ctrl+T*) to generate a tuplet dialog allowing you to specify just what sort of tuplet you wish to create.

Keyboard Entry

For those with a lot of notation to enter, it is probably worth learning the keyboard shortcuts to speed all of the actions I have described thus far.

First, ensure a notation tool is selected to indicate the duration of note (or rest) you wish to insert. You can avoid the toolbar, and select the various note types using the number keys.

Keyboard Key	American Duration	British Duration
5	Double Whole Note	Breve
1	Whole Note	Semibreve
2	Half Note	Minim
4	Quarter Note	Crotchet
8	Eighth Note	Quaver
6	Sixteenth Note	Semiquaver
3	Thirty-second Note	Demisemiquaver
0	Sixty-fourth Note	Hemidemisemiquaver

Dots and Double Dots

After you have entered a note, you can use *Ctrl+.* to cycle through the stages of "dottedness" and add one, two, or zero dots to the duration. This is actually the only way to generate double-dotted notes from scratch, as there are no double-dotted duration icons on the Notes toolbar.

Quicker Triplets

As a shortcut to entering the notes as normal durations and then tripletizing them, you toggle in and out of triplet insert mode using the G key.

You can also toggle this using the ![triplet icon] icon if you prefer. Both this icon and the status bar will change to reflect the fact that you are in triplet entry mode, and the duration you have selected will effectively be 1/3 of the normal duration. If you enter 8 G then you will be inserting triplet 8th notes, and so forth.

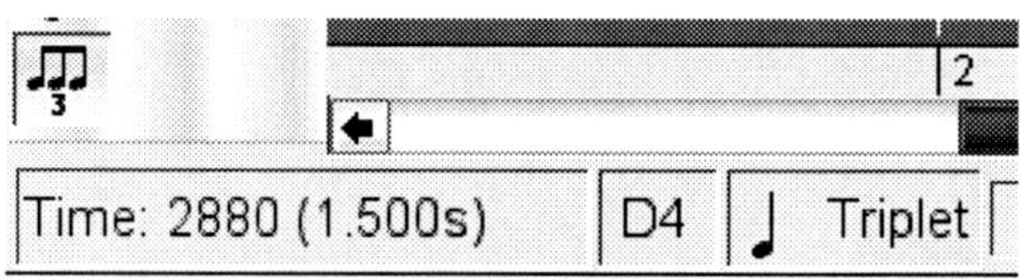

> **NOTE**: For tuplets other than triplets, you will have to use the icon (or Ctrl+T) and associated dialog box.

Chord Mode

You can toggle into chord mode using the H key or the ![chord icon] icon. The insertion position will not advance, and each new note you enter will be added to the chord until you turn this mode off.

Quick Pitch (Do Re Mi) Mode

The translators will have a hard time with this part. In the English-speaking world, we have names for the relative pitches of a scale. Anyone who has ever seen the film "The Sound of Music" knows the "Do a deer, a female deer" song. You can enter pitches in this fashion in Rosegarden, providing a quick way to enter notes relative to the tonic note of the key you happen to be in. (Unfortunately for non-English readers, most other languages ascribe absolute pitches to these words, so "do" = C. In the English speaking world, "do" is only C in the key of C major. In D minor, do = D, and so on.)

Keyboard Key	English Interval	International Interval
A	do	tonic (I)
S	re	super tonic; second (II)
D	mi	mediant; third (III)
F	fa	sub-dominant; fourth (IV)
J	so	dominant; fifth (V)
K	la	sub-mediant; sixth (VI)
L	ti	leading tone; seventh (VII)

To raise the pitch by an octave, move an row higher on the keyboard, *Q W E R U I O*. To lower the pitch by an octave, move a row lower on the keyboard, *Z X C V B N M*.

NOTE: This was designed for standard QWERTY layouts, and it is almost unusable on German QWERTZ, and other international variations. Unfortunately, the mapping is hard coded, and is not configurable without editing and rebuilding the application's source code.

Holding *Shift* or *Shift+Ctrl* before pressing a letter will sharpen or flatten the pitch as appropriate. (Some intervals already involve a halfstep, so you can't sharpen mi and ti, or flatten fa and do.)

Rest Mode

You can quickly switch between note and rest mode using the *T* and *Y* keys. Or else press *P* before inserting a note to make it a rest instead.

Step Recording Mode

You can also enter the pitches using a MIDI keyboard in step recording mode. Use the above keys to select a note duration and other factors such as triplet or chord mode, then...

Toggle step recording mode via the  mode. In this mode, pitch will be recorded, but notes will take a default velocity as configured elsewhere.

Changing Incorrect Note Durations

If you have entered with the wrong duration, you can replace it by selecting the new duration, then clicking exactly on the note head. Alternatively, you can use *Ctrl+number* to change it on the fly. For example, you've entered a quarter note that should have been a dotted 8th note.

Select the quarter note (or catch it while it is still selected, just having been entered)...

Then use *Ctrl+8* to change it to an 8th note, then *Ctrl+.* to give it a dot.

NOTE: By default, this *Ctrl+number* behavior affects both notation and performance duration. To change only the notation duration without affecting performance, add the *Alt* key. *Ctrl+Alt+8* for example.

8.3.5 Ties, Slurs, and Other Groups

Ties, slurs, other groupings, and a few miscellaneous actions are accomplished using the Group toolbar. As these actions are designed to affect groups of notes, most of them will be disabled until you have made a selection.

Slurs

To slur a pair or a group of notes...

Select the notes to be slurred...

Then click on the  icon to slur them... You can also use the) key to create a slur, or *Ctrl+)* to create a phrasing slur if you prefer.

As you can see from this example, sometimes the layout algorithm doesn't quite know what to make of a given situation. One solution is to adjust the beam directions, as I will mention in just a moment. Another thing to try is to flip the slur up or down with *Notes -> Indications -> Slur Position...* which allows you to specify the desired orientation, or restore the computed position.

In this case, the results might still be improved.

Stem Direction

If you need to change the computed stem direction, use *Ctrl+PageUp/PageDown* or *Adjust -> Stem Direction -> Stems Up/Stems Down*. Going back to the slur example, sometimes results of a badly-positioned slur can be improved by changing the stem directions around. I flipped the first four notes stems down, and the slur came out much better this way.

If you wish to restore the computed direction, use *Adjust -> Stem Direction -> Restore Computed Stems*.

Micro-Positioning of Notation Elements

If you have some particular reason why you would prefer not to change the stem or slur directions around, it is still possible to improve our badly-rendered sample slur. You can re-position virtually any notation element to take matters into your own hands and give things a nudge when required. Simply select the element or elements you wish to reposition, hold down the shift key, then drag them wherever you want. Their new positions will be remembered, stored with the composition, and printed, although this micro-positioning is not exportable to external notation formats like Lilypond.

You can take this to ridiculous extremes if you wish. I'll show you one example of a way to work around one of Rosegarden's limitations by taking advantage of the no-holds-barred nature of this feature later on, but it is not usually terribly useful to abuse your power to this degree:

However, when used in a reasonable fashion, this gives Rosegarden the ability to produce quite satisfying results. In this case I have gone back to the original stem and slur directions as computed, and have moved the wayward slur just a trifle.

From this...   to this...

If you find you've made a complete mess of things, you can use *Adjust -> Fine Positioning -> Restore Computed Positions* to revert the position of the selected element, or elements to normal.

Moving Notes

Now that I have mentioned micro-positioning, I should point out that you can also move notes and some other notation elements in time as well as space by dragging and dropping them. Notes can be moved to any visible staff, and to any point in time. If you are dragging a selection, only the "root" element will move, and the remaining notes will fill in on either side of it, as appropriate. For example, I entered a bit of notation in the first staff, then selected alternating notes.

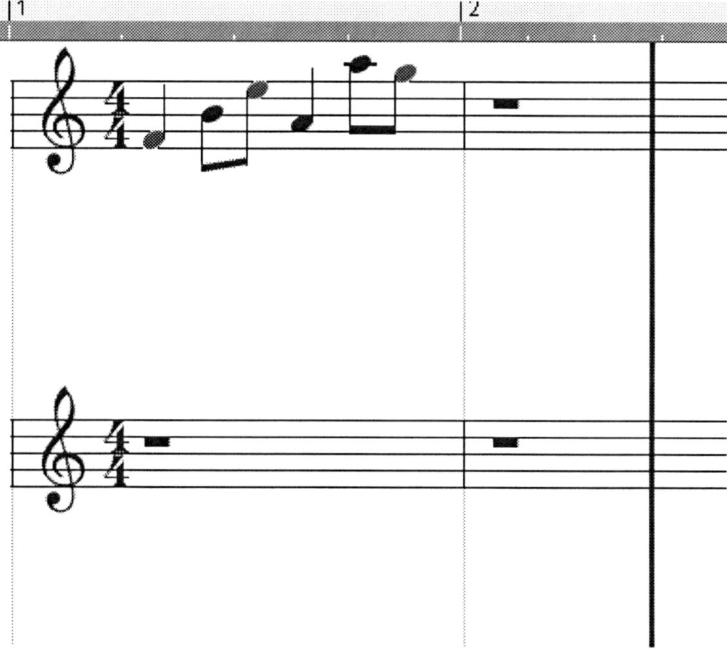

Then I dragged the center note and dropped it in the next staff down, right over the bar line. The remaining notes took their places on either side of it.

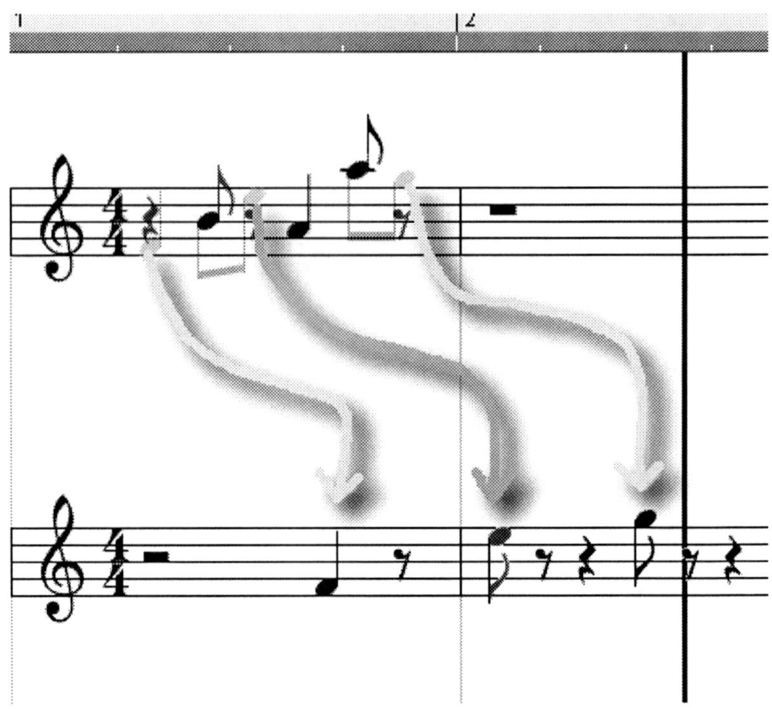

Ties

Ties work just like slurs, except that they must occur between two notes of the same pitch. If you attempt to tie two notes at different pitches, this will fail silently. No tie will appear, although the first note will actually have a "tied forward" property, and if you subsequently drag it in line with another note, the invisible tie will spring to life. This can be a source of confusion if you forget what you did.

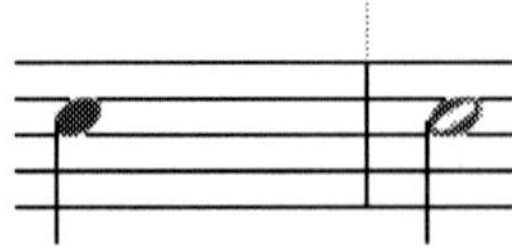

Select two notes...

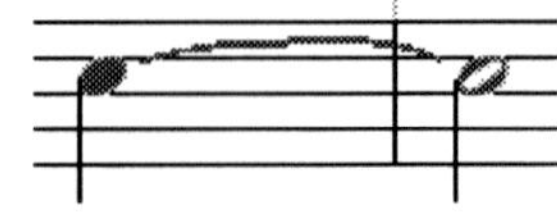

Use the ♩♩ icon (or the ~ key) to tie them....

Beaming

You can beam or un-beam notes as required using the icons, or *Ctrl+B/U*.

For example, Rosegarden's automatic beaming doesn't quite match the score I'm copying.

I need to fix it.

I select the first group to beam...

Then use *Ctrl+B* to beam them...

Then I finish the job by selecting and beaming the remaining pairs...

It is sometimes be a bit fiddly to achieve the desired results. If ugly things happen when you beam manually, you may need to break up an entire group (select them, and use *Ctrl+U*) before you can rearrange its beaming successfully.

> **TIP**: Changing the beaming of slurred notes causes the slur to be re-computed. If you have micro-positioned the slur, your manual adjustment will be destroyed, and you will have to reposition the new slur. As a consequence, it would probably be best to get the beaming straight before adding slurs.

8.3.6 Marks, Slashes and Fingerings

The Marks toolbar contains too many icons for me to possibly describe each in detail.

Rosegarden does not try to be your mother, and it will let you add an absolutely insane number of marks in ridiculous combinations to a note.

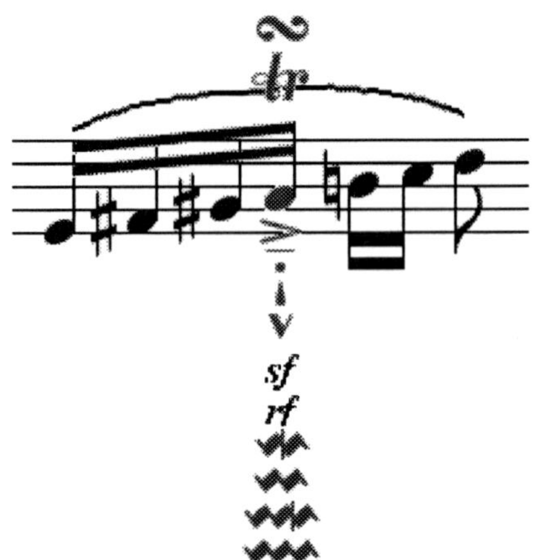

To undo a mess like I've created above, use *Notes -> Marks -> Remove All Marks*. There is also a text mark ♩ that can be used to stick any arbitrary text onto a note.

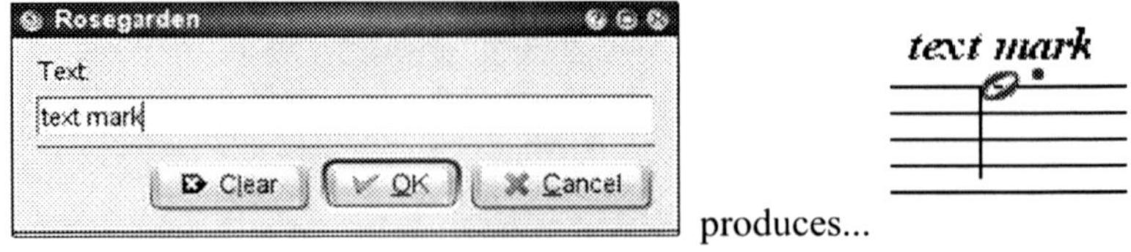

produces...

Slashes

Although it functions a bit differently, a logically-related idea is to add slashes to note stems. Notes can have up to five slashes. Select the notes, then use *Notes -> Slashes...* to add an appropriate number, or to cancel them.

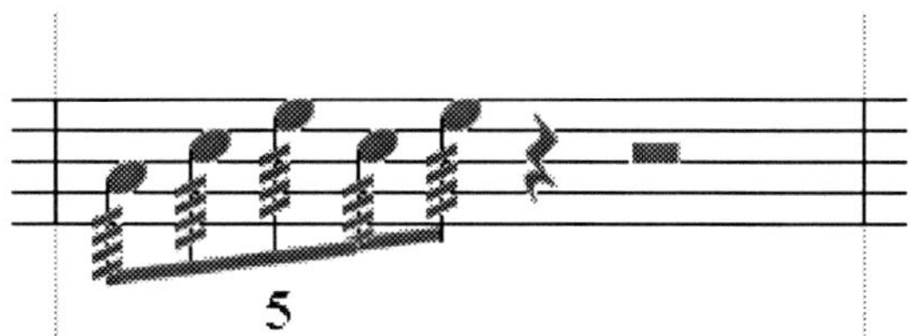

Piano Fingerings

You can add piano fingering marks to notes by selecting them, and then using *Notes -> Fingerings...* to pick the desired fingering notation (or to remove all fingerings.)

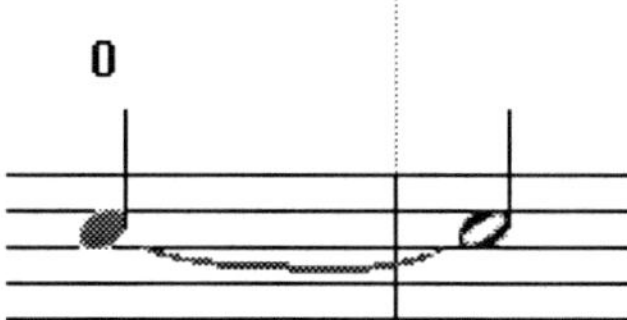

You can use the *Alt+0* through *9* shortcuts to make quicker work of this, or you can use *Fingerings -> Add Other Fingering* to do something from scratch.

> **TIP**: When reminding myself how to play the trumpet, I found it useful to use this feature to indicate the valve combinations right on the notes:
>
> 

8.3.7 Hairpins

To create hairpins to indicate crescendos or decrescendos (diminuendos), select a note at either end of (or the entire) range...

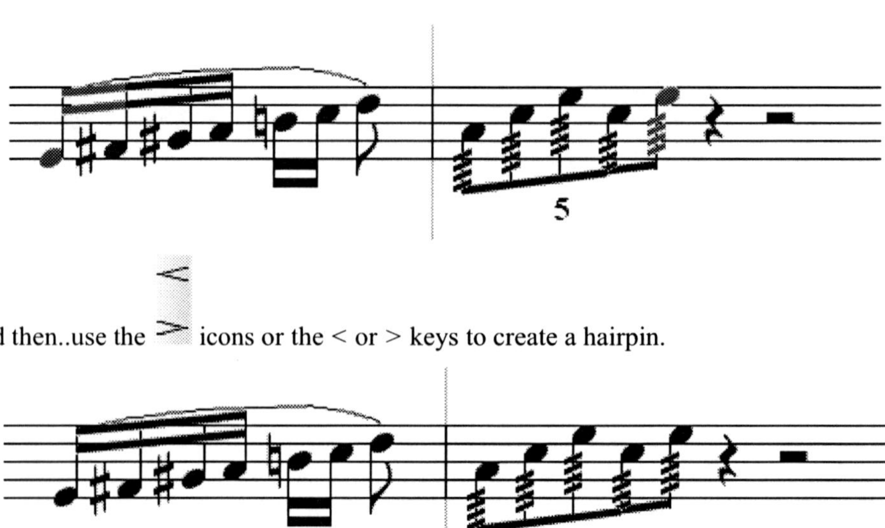

and then..use the $\gtrless$ icons or the < or > keys to create a hairpin.

8.3.8 Text Events

Rosegarden allows you to insert a variety of text events into your composition. All of these behave in basically the same way. For example, to insert dynamics on either side of the hairpin we just created...

Switch to the **T** tool and click on the first E in the series. A text insertion dialog like this appears:

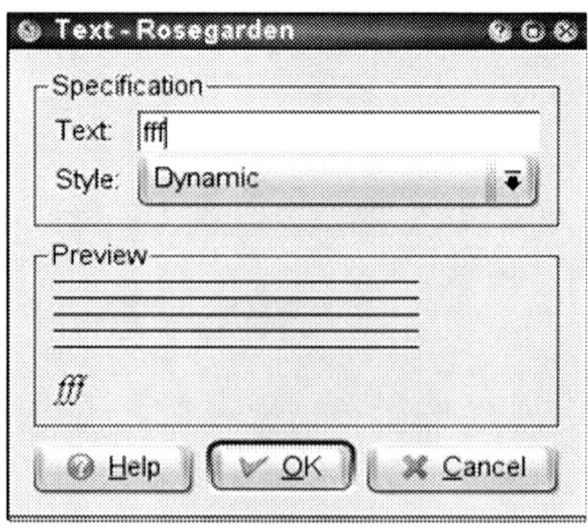

Since we are inserting a dynamic here, we'll use the default style. After inserting the dynamic on either end (the second one inserted on the rest after the last E) the hairpin shrinks up a bit to accommodate these, and the result looks like this:

TIP: If you wish to interpret the hairpins later on, the procedure I have documented here is not quite reliable. I can obtain better results by putting a dynamic under the first E, then another dynamic under the last E, then selecting the range from the F# to the C and applying the hairpin to that selection.

Text Styles

There are a variety of text styles for various purposes. While all of them are intended to serve different musical functions, they are really just text of a particular style and size oriented either above or below the staff, depending on the type.

TIP: To get the example above, I had to make heavy use of the micro-positioning feature to smooth things along a bit. If text overlaps something else, hold down *Shift* while clicking and dragging it.

Annotations

Annotations are a special type of text event meant to resemble little post-it notes. They can be toggled via *Settings -> Show Annotations* if they are not already visible.

Lyrics

At their heart, lyrics are just text events of type "Lyric," and you can add them one by one in this fashion if you wish. Rosegarden also provides a simple lyric editor that allows you to write down all the lyrics for a segment in one place. Unfortunately, Rosegarden is not capable of handling multiple verses, so there is only one set of lyrics per segment.

Start with a segment that has some notation to which you wish to add lyrics, then open the lyric editor via *View -> Open Lyric Editor*. You will see something a bit like this:

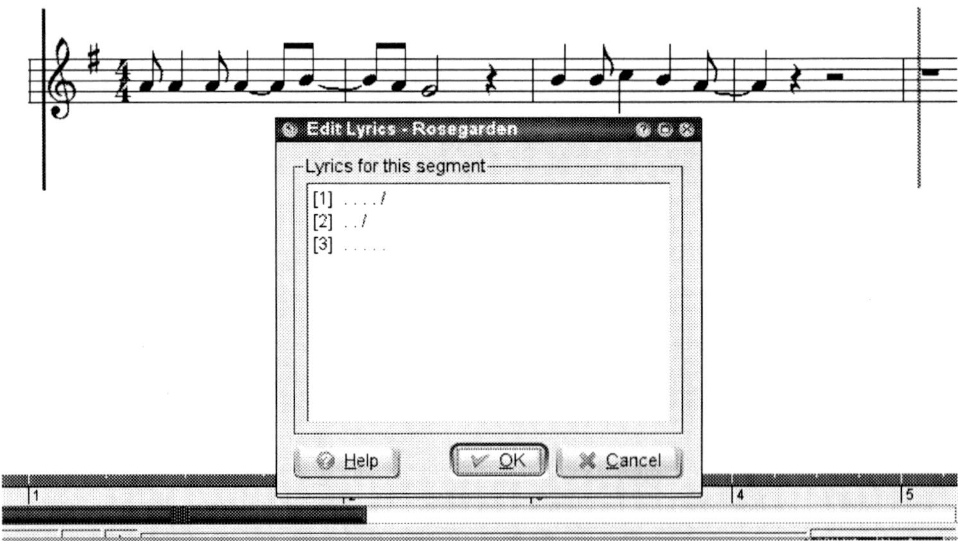

Rather than reinvent the wheel, here is what the Rosegarden Handbook has to say about the lyric editor:

> The lyrics you enter should follow a particular format. Bar lines are vital to avoid the editor getting confused, and are represented with a slash ("/"). Within each bar the individual syllables are separated by spaces (at least one space: the editor doesn't care about any extra whitespace). Each syllable in turn will be attached to the next subsequent note or chord within that bar (although at the moment the editor can get quite confused by chords that are not exact, i.e. that requires smoothing or quantizing).

> If you want a note to have no syllable attached to it, you need to provide a dot (".") as the syllable for that note. (This is why the default lyric text for a segment is usually full of dots.) Remember to separate the dots with spaces, so that they are clearly separate syllables.

If you want more than one syllable on the same note, with a space between them, use a tilde ("~") instead of the space. It will be shown as a space on the score.

If you want to split a syllable across two notes, with a hyphen, you need to enter a space following the hyphen so the editor knows to treat it as two syllables. (Hyphens get no special treatment within syllables.)

Syllables consisting only of numbers surrounded by square brackets (like "[29]") will be ignored; this is the format used for the automatically-generated bar numbers shown in the editor.

As an example of actual practice, I have entered a bit of my song "Autumn Rain" here.

I ii iii IV

Someone asked me how he could use Rosegarden to notate Roman numerals to indicate intervals or chord progressions. While there is no facility specifically for this purpose, chord names work perfectly well, as they are just mid-sized Roman text printed above the staff. Here I have marked off the I IV V of a typical rock chord progression.

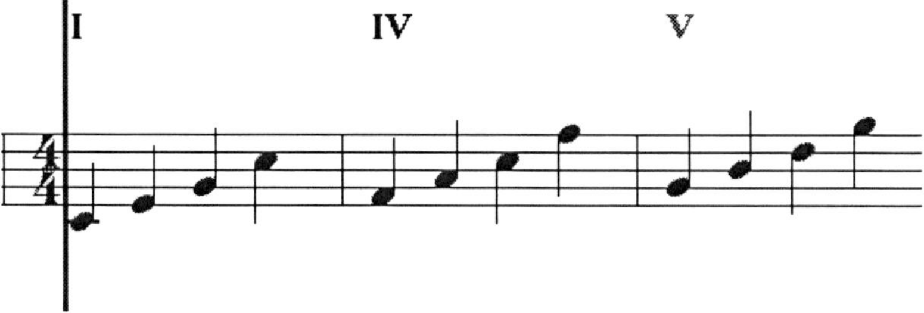

8.4   Legible Notation from Performance Data

You should have a solid understanding how the notation editor works by now, but there are a number of more complicated issues I have held back along the way, and reserved until now. The largest challenge most people face in using the notation editor is making good looking notation out of a MIDI recording or an imported MIDI file. Good performances almost always make for notation that is almost impossible to read. Human beings rarely play notes exactly on the beat boundaries, and unless a slur or tenuto is involved, notes are seldom held for their full written duration. A notation editor that draws notes with mechanical precision will render such a performance as a completely insane mess full of bizarre short notes, punctuating a sea of bizarre, short rests.

Here is a MIDI file imported with no quantization. Most of the bar lines are red, indicating that the events inside the measure do not fit correctly, and that the measure contains too many beats.

Here is the same file after a reasonable notation quantization has been done. It still has problems, but it requires much less manual intervention than the original.

buglers.mid

use event filter to select all 1/32 notes and make them 1/16 for vast improvement

8.4.1 The Quantizer

Rosegarden's quantizer can be quite a complicated animal to understand. "Quantization" is the process of combing through a series of note events, comparing their start times and durations to logical beat boundaries on a grid, and nudging them around to tidy them up. It can move early or late notes back on center, it can stretch or squash notes that are too long or too short into a more logical and legible pattern. It is particularly useful for rendering readable notation from an imperfect human performance, and, as I have mentioned, it can perform these operations on the visible notation, leaving the original human performance untouched.

8.4.2 Triggered Segments and Ornaments

Another way that Rosegarden lets you have your cake and eat it too is in its ability to make use of triggered segments to provide ornaments. The ornament is stored in a special segment apart from the main body of the composition, and is triggered by a special trigger note that can have marks indicating the type of ornament represented by the triggered segment. These ornaments can be recycled as well, because it is possible to have more than one trigger note pointing to the same triggered segment.

One place where this is particularly useful is when trying to clean up a nice MIDI performance in order to produce a readable score from it. My test score has ornaments that really can't be used directly if I want to reproduce the score exactly, so I will kill two birds with one stone here, demonstrating how to replace a bunch of ugly gibberish with an ornament made from scratch. Unfortunately, yes, this will alter the human performance somewhat, so there is some compromise here between an authentic performance and an exact score.

Before

This is a typical example of an ornament in an imported MIDI file. The quantizer really can't really do much to improve the look of this, and it would be awkward to read even if all the short notes were written out neatly. It is a prime candidate for conversion into a triggered segment and a trigger note.

The First Try

To start, I needed to change the first 8th note into a dotted version. I accomplished this by selecting it, and using *Ctrl+.* and then I selected the body of the ornament...

Next, I used *Notes -> Ornaments -> Make Ornament*, which presented the following dialog. Since this ornament is a trill up from E to F, I chose E as the base note. I left the suggested name at its default.

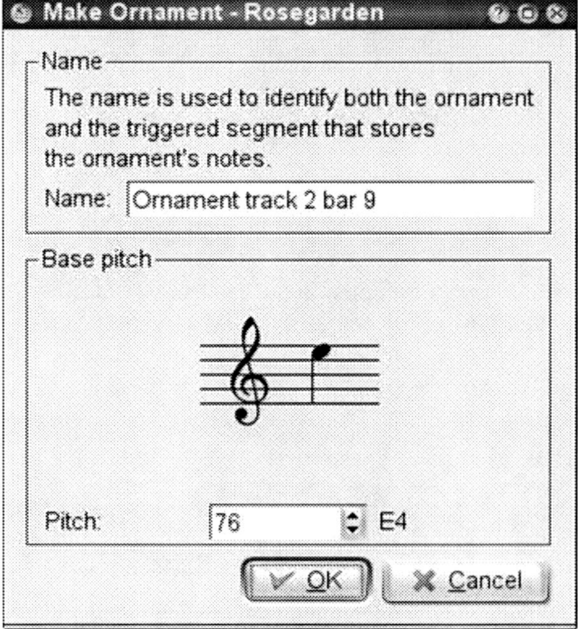

The resulting ornament wasn't quite what I was after. There were several distinct notes with fairly long durations bound up in that jumble, which couldn't readily be extracted. I could have set the ornament to play in a shorter duration by selecting this trigger note and changing it to a dotted 8th note, and could have added extra notes to make up the difference on the page, but those extra notes would have been extra. I wanted to preserve the accuracy of the performance while cleaning up this trill, and this didn't quite work in this case...

...so I hit undo (*Ctrl+Z*) until I got back to the point before making the ornament, and then I re-selected the events, and then deleted them (*Ctrl+X*).

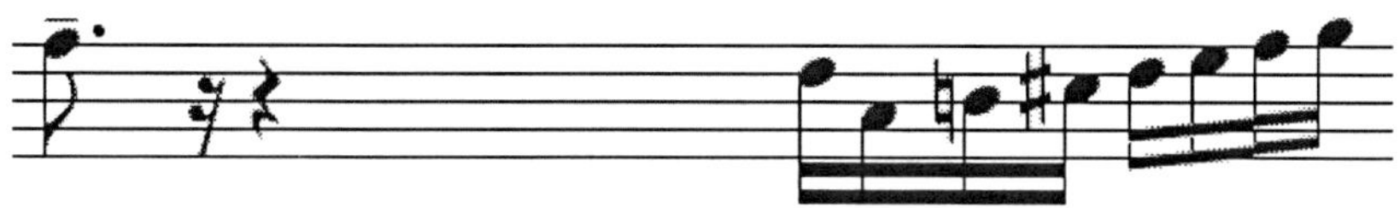

The Second Try

Next, I inserted the untrilled notes that were bound up with that ornament, and left a rest where the new ornament needed to go...

Then I notated a trill using 32nd notes, selected it...

...and used *Notes -> Ornaments -> Make Ornament* again, then I followed up by beaming the trigger note to the note after it, and adding a *tr* with a wavy line. (The wavy line was not actually part of the original score if there are any purists in the audience. You caught me.) The result is much improved compared to the part that has not yet been similarly doctored:

Reusing Ornaments

The bottom part in this example is the same as the top, except transposed for trumpet. Having just gone to all the effort documented so far, it sure would be nice if I could avoid having to go to that much trouble a second time. Indeed, I can, and Rosegarden does most of the work for me automagically.

First I paved the way in the same fashion as before, except I filled in the spot for the ornament with an ordinary note, then selected that note:

Next, I used *Notes -> Ornaments -> Trigger Ornament*, which presented this dialog:

Perform using triggered segment allows you to choose which ornament to use in the event that you have more than one. That is why you are able to name each triggered segment as you create it. *Perform with timing* isn't really needed in this case because the duration of the two notes is the same, but it can be used to stretch or squash an ornament to fit into a different space of time, or to force the fit in various other ways:

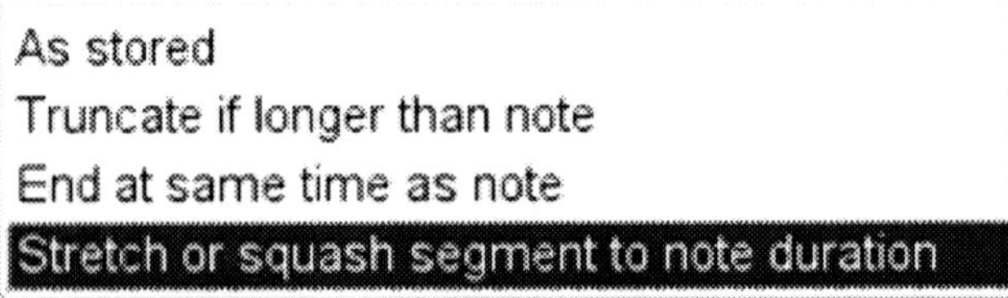

Then finally, I moved the note up to the correct pitch. (Oops.) The trill followed along, and I got another trill without having to re-enter all the 32nd notes.

8.5   Tweaking Parts with the Selection Filter

I have demonstrated the selection event filter in other places, and I usually use it from the matrix view myself, but it has its uses here in the notation editor as well.

8.5.1 Bringing Parts into Range

One of the best uses I have found for the event selection filter is for cleaning up parts that were written without respect to the practical playable ranges of actual instruments. For example, I have an oboe part in a short piece I wrote for inclusion with a computer game. I knew little about the oboe at the time, and did not particularly care about writing a playable part, because I was writing music for a computer and synthesizer to perform. My handy dandy pocket guide to arranging indicates that the useful range of the oboe is from the D below the staff to the D above, so in order to make this part playable, I have to do something with the notes outside that range.

As I have demonstrated elsewhere, the selection event filter works by filtering events out of a selection. You must first make a selection to filter. So, make an appropriate selection (or *Edit -> Select Whole Staff*) and then...

click on the  icon...

...then dial up the appropriate filter range (the Db below the staff to the D# above)... and set the first box to "exclude" this range...

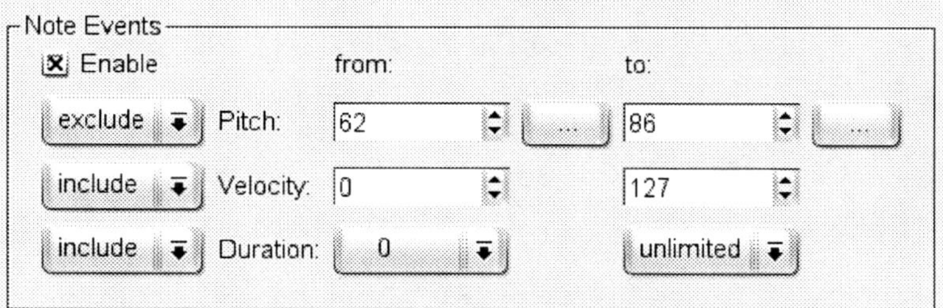

(Yes, if you are paying close attention, I took a screenshot that displays incorrect numbers. That should be from 61 to 87 so that the low and high extremes will be excluded from the selection. I goofed. Oops.)

...leaving you with the out-of-range notes selected, so you can rearrange them as you deem appropriate.

In the preceding example, it happened that all the notes I needed to adjust fell toward the bottom of the playable range. What I encounter most often in arranging is the case where I have notes both too high and too low. In that case, I transpose the selected notes in the direction that pushes the fewest notes even further out of range, then I repeat the process of making a selection and filtering it to pick off those notes and transpose them down a couple of octaves.

8.5.2 Correcting Odd Durations

Another good notation use for my filter is to change the duration of notes en masse. For example, I found a MIDI file that imported and quantized with consistently awkward pairs of 32nd notes with 32nd rests that were probably trying to be 16th notes. I selected the notes...

...then I set the selection filter to leave me with all 32nd notes selected...

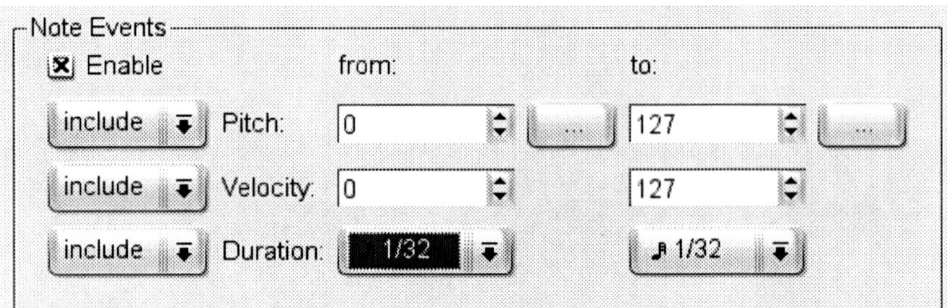

Leaving me with this:

Then I simply used *Ctrl+6* to change all of these into 16th notes, leaving me with this:

Then, of course, I had to select everything again and *Notes -> Beams -> Auto Beam* to correct the beaming:

8.5.3 Interpreting Notation

Rosegarden can interpret hand-edited notation to give it a more human performance. This feature is useful for making an entirely hand-entered composition sound more natural, and it is also useful for blending hand-corrected parts back into a notation quantized performance. Here is a short demonstration segment that I entered manually:

The Raw Note Ruler

The Raw Note Ruler shows you the difference between the notation duration visible on the screen, and the actual performance duration of the notes. If it is not on, toggle it via *Tools -> Rulers -> Show Raw Note Ruler*. The ruler in the preceding example reveals that the notes I entered by hand all have the exact duration I selected from the toolbar. This results in a most un-natural performance.

The Interpret Dialog

I have gone back to add some marks, a dynamic, and have selected all the notes in this segment. I have also turned on the Velocity Property Ruler to show that the hand-entered notes were all created with a default velocity of 100.

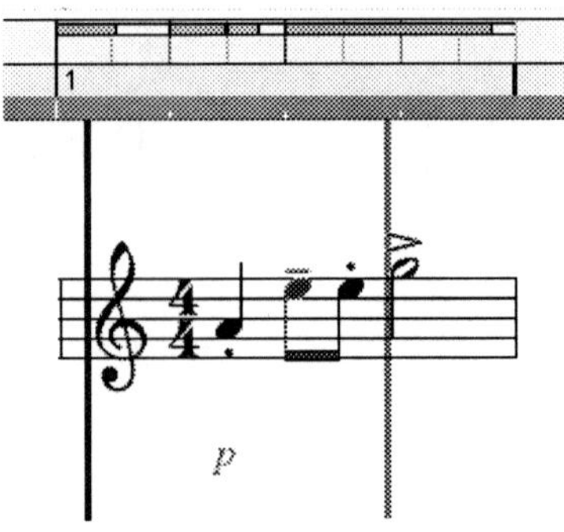

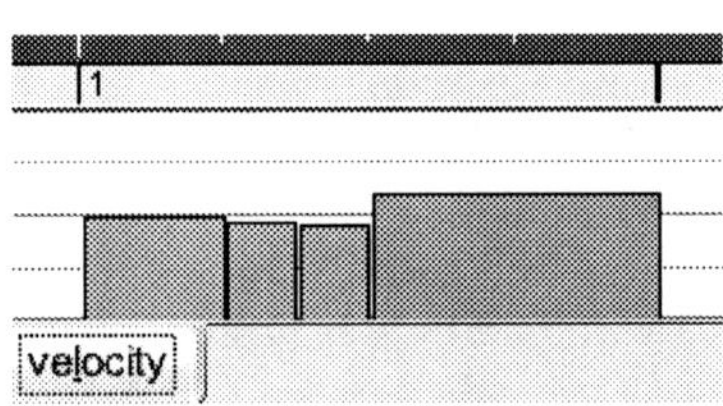

Now I am ready to interpret this with *Adjust -> Notes -> Interpret*. A dialog appears, offering several interpretation options.

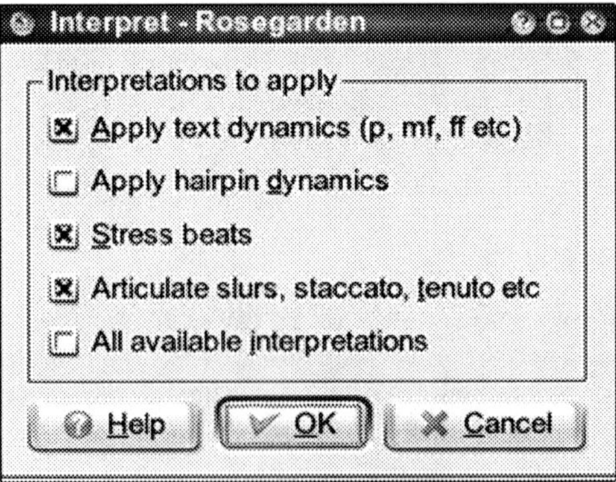

Now we see the results. Rosegarden interpreted the p dynamic by lowering the velocity, then increased this velocity slightly to accent the first beat. It cut the staccato quarter note and 8th note quite short, and left the tenuto 8th note at full value, while it only cut a little off the end of the half note. Finally, it increased the velocity on the accented note even more than the accented first beat.

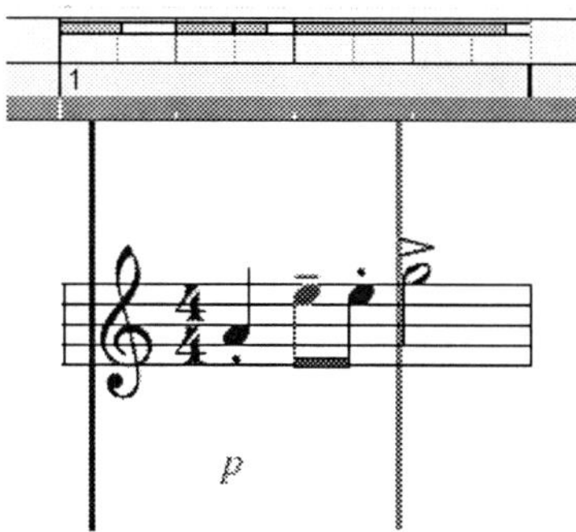

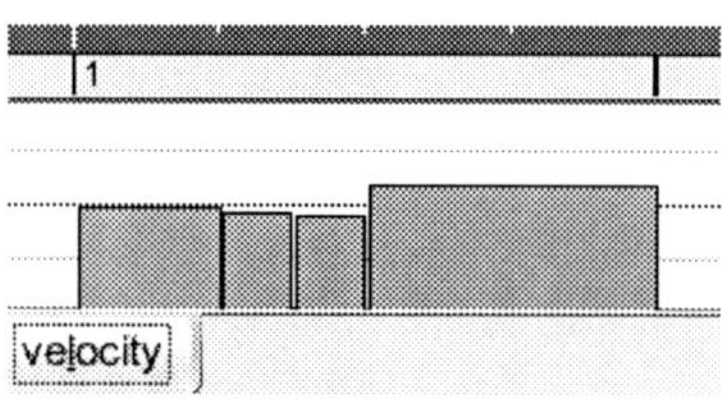

8.5.4 Pedal Notation

You can insert pedal down and pedal release events in the notation, and these will automatically manage the sustain controller for you. Position the insertion cursor as desired, then use *Segment -> Add Pedal Press/Add Pedal Release* as appropriate. The sustain control ruler visible in this snapshot shows that these notation elements have indeed inserted the requisite controller events.

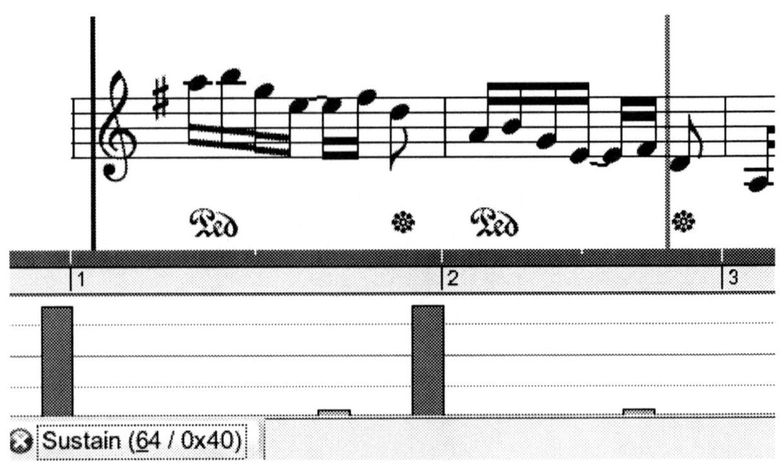

Removing a notation element will remove the associated sustain controller...

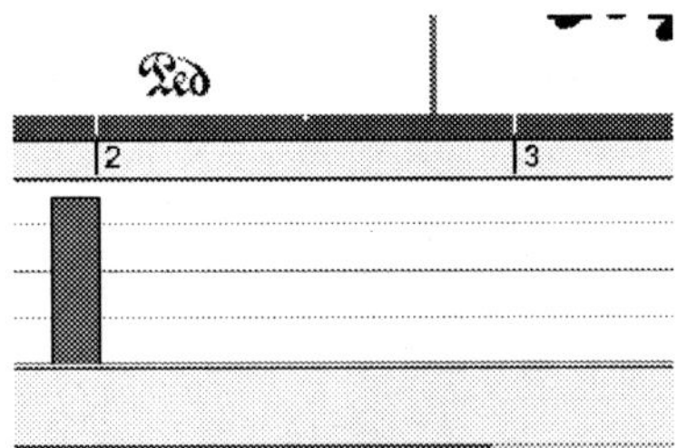

... and inserting a new controller event with the control ruler's context menu *Insert Item* function will also generate appropriate elements in the notation...

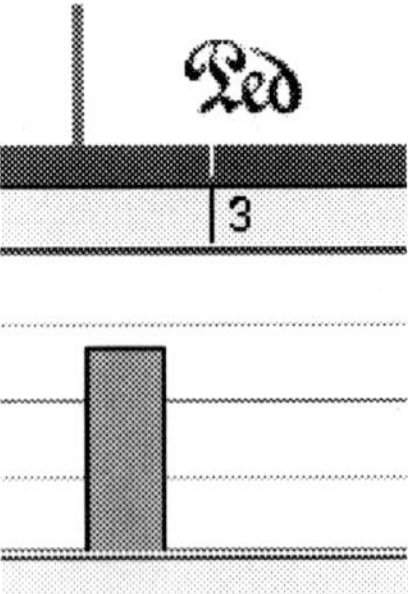

8.5.5 Repeats and Double Barlines

Rosegarden is not yet capable of any complex notation involving repeats and other flow control, although this is planned for the future. If your piece involves multiple endings, multiple verses, D.C. or D.S., segno, or fine directives, or a coda, you will not be able to notate any of this within Rosegarden. You can reproduce the musical performance, just like you could with any other MIDI sequencer, but you will have to string all of the events together in a straight line, and the resulting score will have to contain whatever combination of redundant notes the flow control in the original was meant to reduce into more compact form.

Currently, the only sort of compaction you can perform on a score is to make use of the most rudimentary sort of repeats. As I mentioned earlier, while describing *Segment Parameters*, segments can be set to repeat until they bump into another segment. These repeating segments are displayed between repeat signs here in the notation editor.

Double Barlines

To pave the way for a repeat, you need two segments with a gap between them. Select both segments, and open them in a combined view. A double barline separates the two segments.

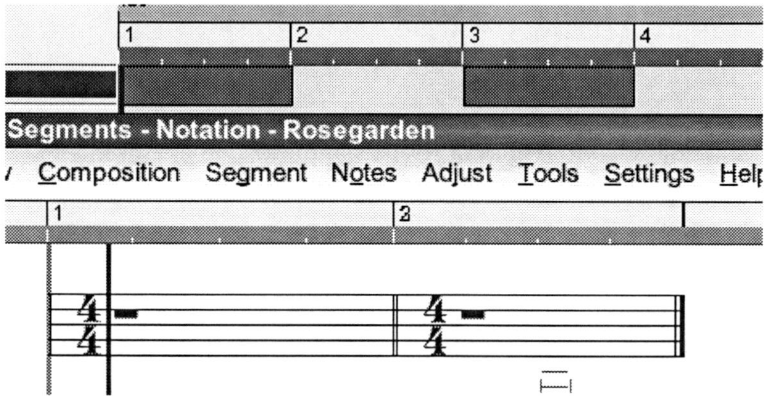

Repeats

Go back to the segment canvas, select only the first segment, and then toggle its repeat parameter on.

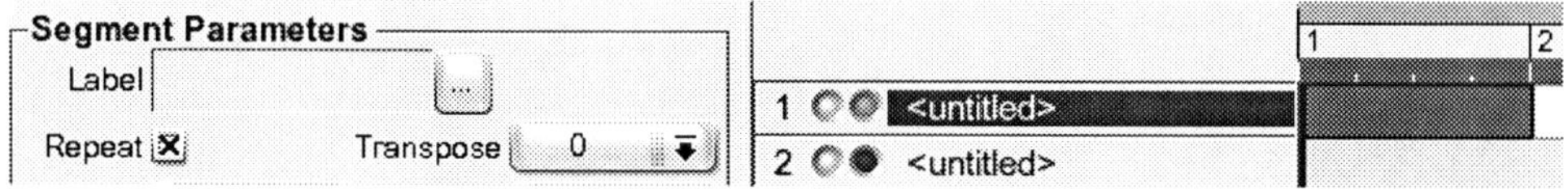

A repeat of this segment is drawn in at bar 2, and the repeats cut off once they bump into bar 3. (You will have to close the notation view and re-open it in order to see this change take place).

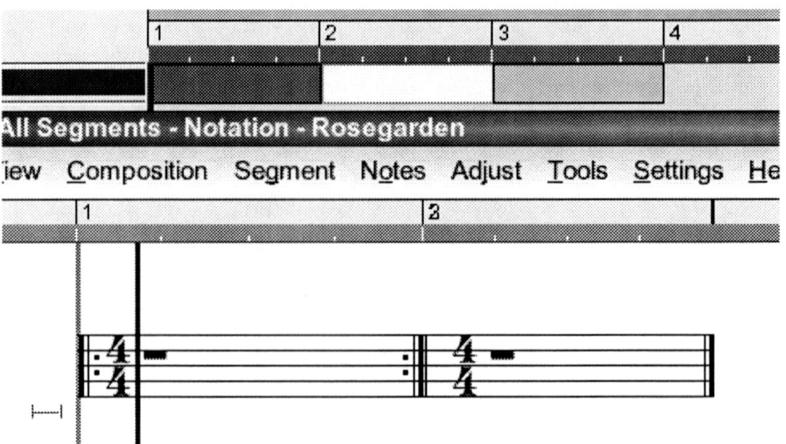
All Segments - Notation - Rosegarden
iew Composition Segment Notes Adjust Tools Settings He

9   Mastering to Disk

You have polished off your composition, and now you want to share it with the world. If you wish to reach the largest possible audience, the best way to distribute your finished product is as an audio file that can be played by anyone, regardless of the platform and software they have available. This is a particularly good approach if your composition uses any audio, or makes use of any unusual MIDI equipment you might have.

Many packages similar to Rosegarden call this feature "bounce to disk". Rosegarden does not have a bounce to disk feature per se. It is possible to use Rosegarden to record its own output back into itself to produce such a file, but I do not like to do this because I find it tedious to go fish out the RG-AUDIO-00??.wav file from the composition's audio path and then rename it. Instead, I prefer to do this phase of the work using external applications.

9.1   Built-In Mastering Tools

While it lacks a bounce to disk feature for the final step of the process, Rosegarden does provide several tools which are particularly useful at mastering time. It has a mixer for MIDI, a mixer for audio, and an audio submaster architecture which can be used to route audio from various sources through the same set of controls. These tools make it easy to survey the whole of your composition from one convenient place, and to make adjustments to the instrument parameters for all the tracks in your composition.

9.1.1 The MIDI Mixer

Click on the icon to open the MIDI mixer. It will appear with the tab representing your first MIDI playback device in focus:

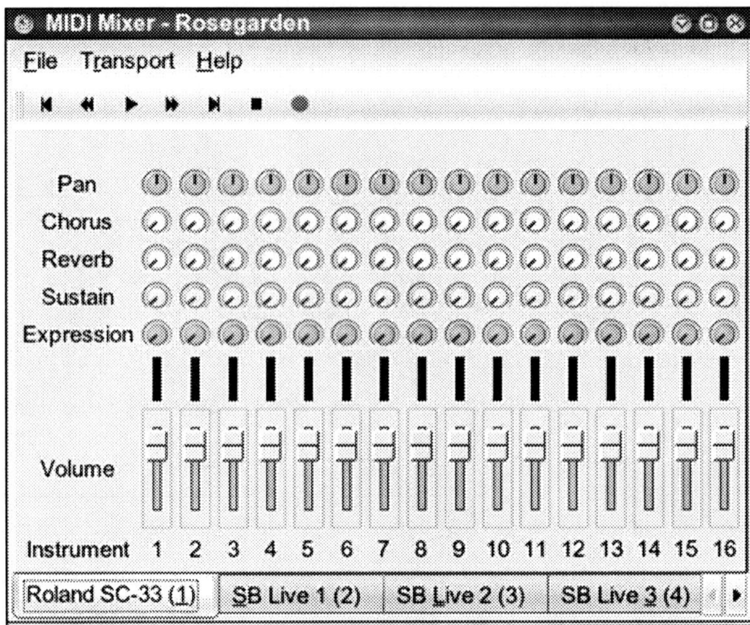

There is a handy transport toolbar at the top. Each of the 16 instruments has knobs for any controllers you have defined (and which are configured to have a slot in the Instrument Parameters box; refer back to the Studio chapter for details), VU meters to show output levels during playback, and a volume slider for controlling channel volume. Remember that these instruments are associated with MIDI channels, but there is not necessarily a one to one correspondence between instrument numbers and channel numbers, depending on how you have assigned everything elsewhere.

Across the bottom, each of your available playback devices has its own tab. In this case, all the MIDI in this particular composition is played via my "SB Live 1" device, so I want to bring that into focus instead. Next, I hit the play button on the transport to watch the VU meters, and to verify that I'm on the right tab. Notice that I only have three controllers defined for this device, so only three knobs are available.

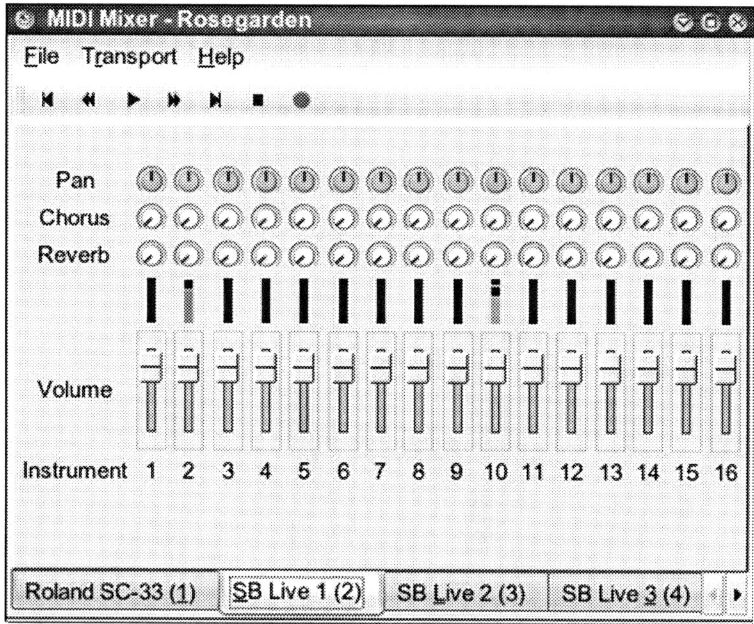

Now I have played with the mix a little, and I also added a custom controller in the studio, just to demonstrate that it would show up here.

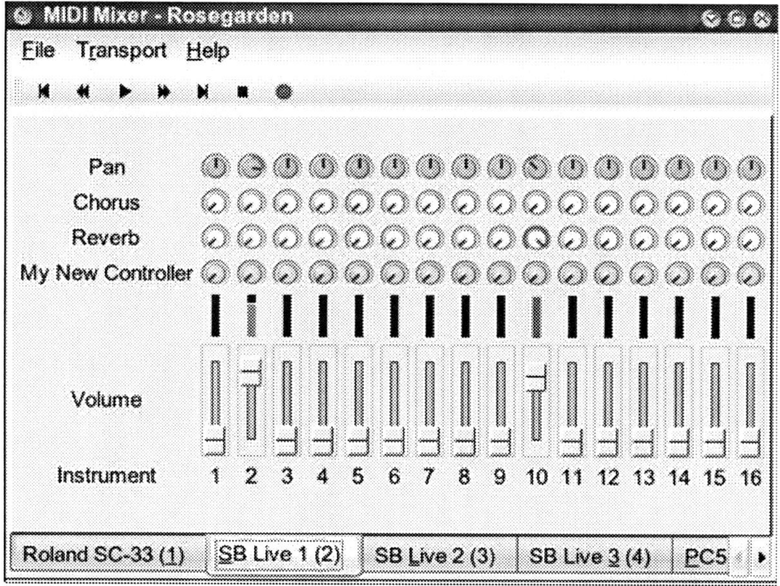

9.1.2 The Audio Mixer

The audio mixer contains banks of controls for each synth plugin and each audio instrument that is assigned to a track, along with sliders for master output volume and master recording level, and any submasters you have created. Unlike the MIDI mixer, which always displays 16 instruments per tab, the audio mixer only shows you instruments that are actually assigned to tracks by default. If you find the mixer window is too large for comfort, you might want to go delete any unused audio and synth plugin tracks before opening it. This will keep it as small as possible.

Click on the 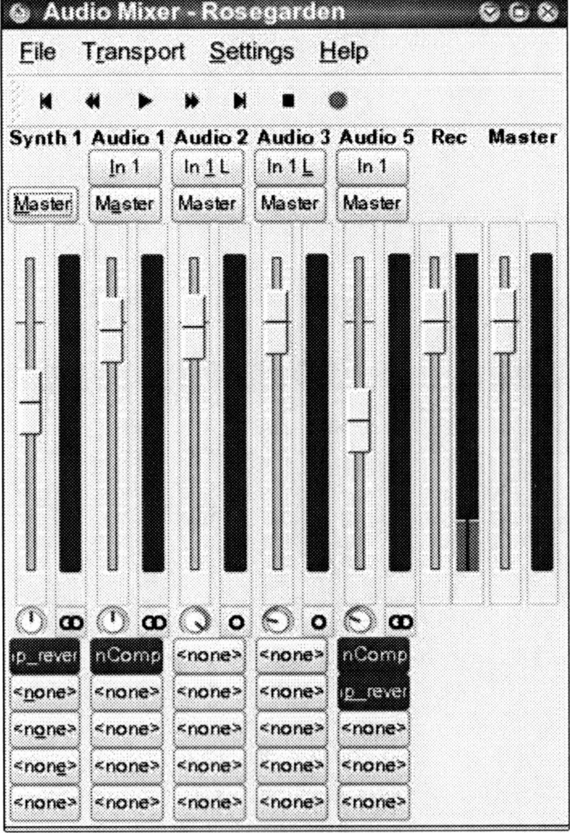 icon to open the audio mixer.

The audio mixer, just like its MIDI counterpart, provides a combined view of all the individual *Instrument Parameters* boxes for the various instruments. However, unlike the MIDI mixer, this one has some important functionality that isn't available anywhere else within Rosegarden.

The Audio Mixer Settings Menu

In addition to the rather obvious toggles that allow you to switch off various mixer elements as desired, you will also find two important things hiding here on the *Settings* menu.

Number of Stereo Inputs

The first is the control for the number of stereo inputs. By default, Rosegarden creates two inputs. If configured to create default JACK connections automatically, it connects one pair of these inputs to "alsa-pcm" and leaves a free pair for whatever other purpose you might dream up. In this first screenshot, you can see this setting left at its default, and you can see the standard default state of affairs in QJackCtl's audio connection manager.

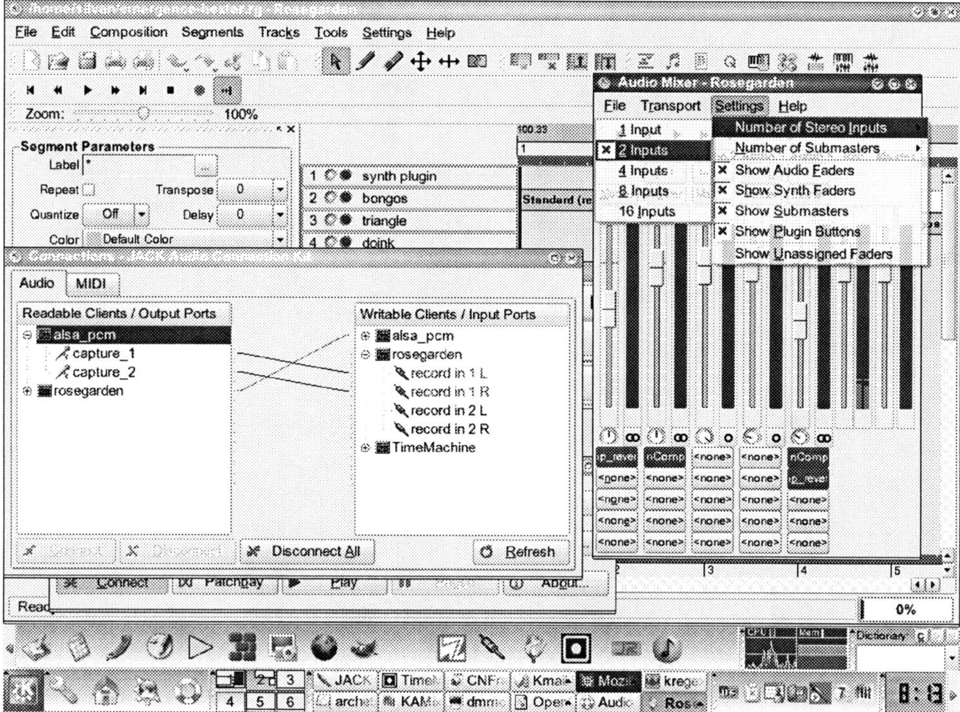

If you need more inputs for some reason, create them here, then go hook them up as required. For example, navigate to *Settings -> Number of Stereo Inputs -> 8 Inputs*, then go check out QJackCtl's connection manager again. Now there are eight pairs of inputs, numbered 1 through 8 available for routing in various ways among other JACK applications.

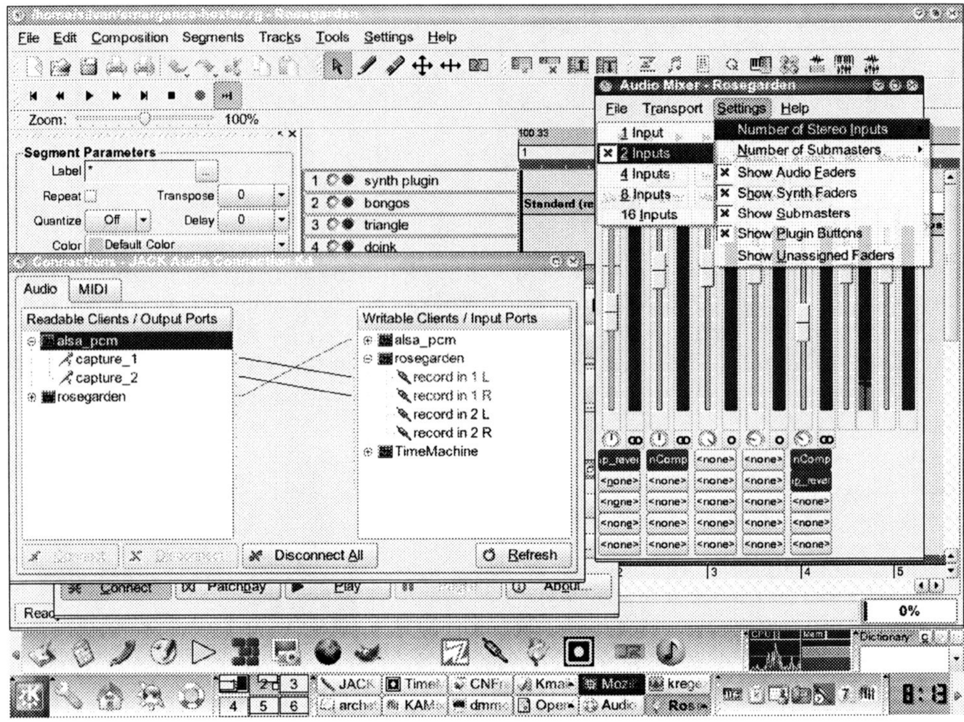

Number of Submasters

You might have noticed that both the synth plugin and audio *Instrument Parameters* boxes have mysterious controls called Out:, and that the audio box also has an *In:* control.

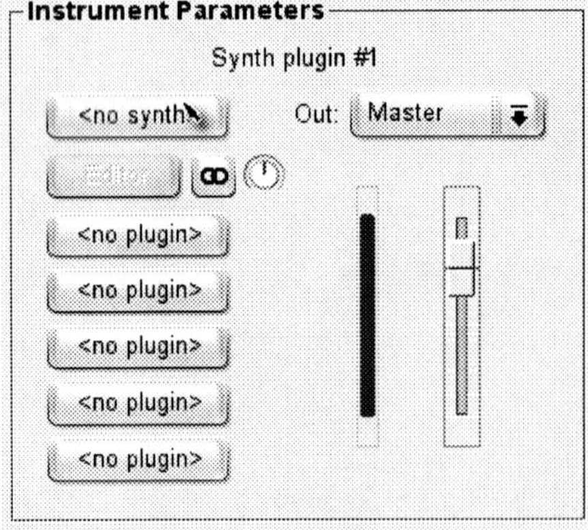

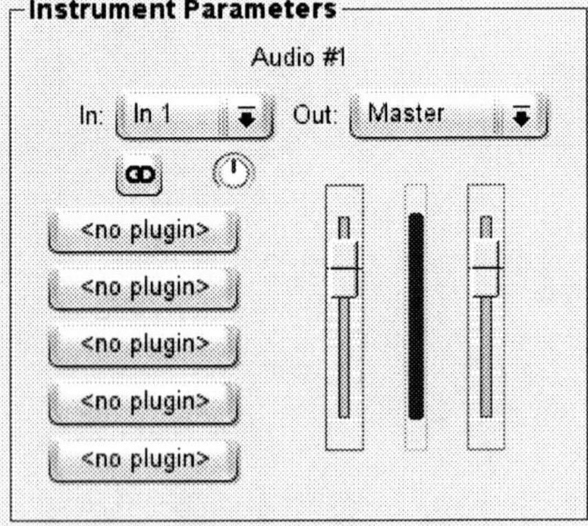

Up until now, these controls have not been particularly useful, because you have only had the default of one single master audio bus. If you go to *Settings -> Number of Submasters -> 2 Submasters*, you can create a pair of submasters, and give those mysterious controls some reason to exist. After doing so, the mixer changes slightly. Now you can see *Sub 1* and *Sub 2* added at the right side of the panel.

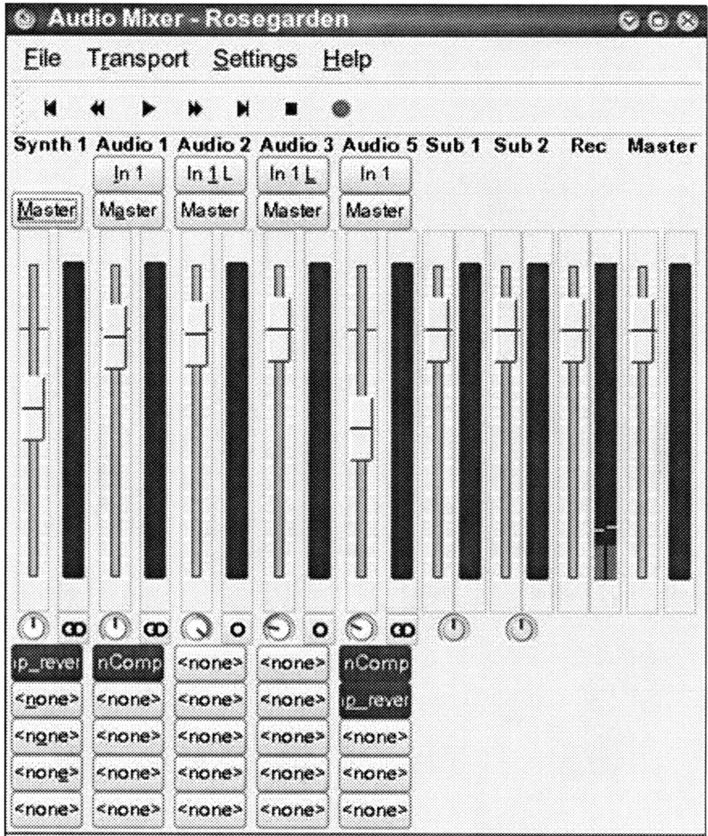

Sub-masters are secondary audio buses that can be used to route more than one instrument through a shared bank of controls, and then on out through the master. The sub-masters are useful for grouping similar instruments together, so that you can control them as one unit.

Mixing Down

Now that you understand the tools available, you can play with the mixers until you achieve just the right sound you are looking for. If you have external audio sources coming in through the soundcard in real time, as is the case, for example, with my Sound Canvas, then you may need to adjust your soundcard's mixer as well to achieve the best overall effect.

One thing to pay particular attention to at this stage is the VU meters on the audio mixer. In the next shot, you can see that both *Audio #5* and the *Master* are spiking out badly. No harm comes from this while playing everything in real-time, and I hear no clipping, thanks to the magic of JACK. However, if I were to record this to disk in this state, the results would be horrible. I need to play with this mix to bring everything back out of the red before the final recording.

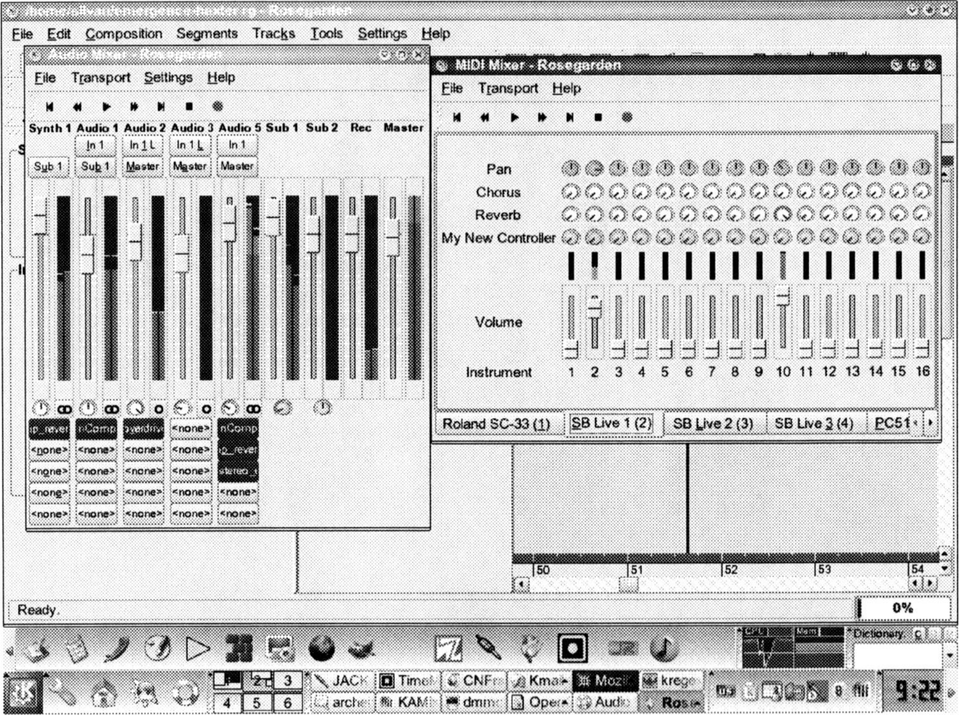

9.2 *Bouncing to Disk*

Now that the mixdown is complete, you can capture the final result to disk, and can then go on to do post-processing if desired. My utility of choice for this purpose is Time Machine. It is simple, and it just works.

TIP: I have borrowed an idea from Studio..to go!, and have configured my Time Machine to run out of my *~/Desktop* directory. That way I can just click on, click off from my desktop environment, without having to bother fooling with the command line. Using KDE, I created a menu item as depicted here. I had to go fish out the icon by hand, from */usr/share/timemachine/pixmaps* Be sure not to omit the "-f wav" command line arguments. Otherwise Time Machine will record in a strange format that few applications are able to handle properly. Now when I run Time Machine, it deposits its recordings directly on my desktop for easy handling. Thank you Chris Cannam of Fervent Software for the good idea.

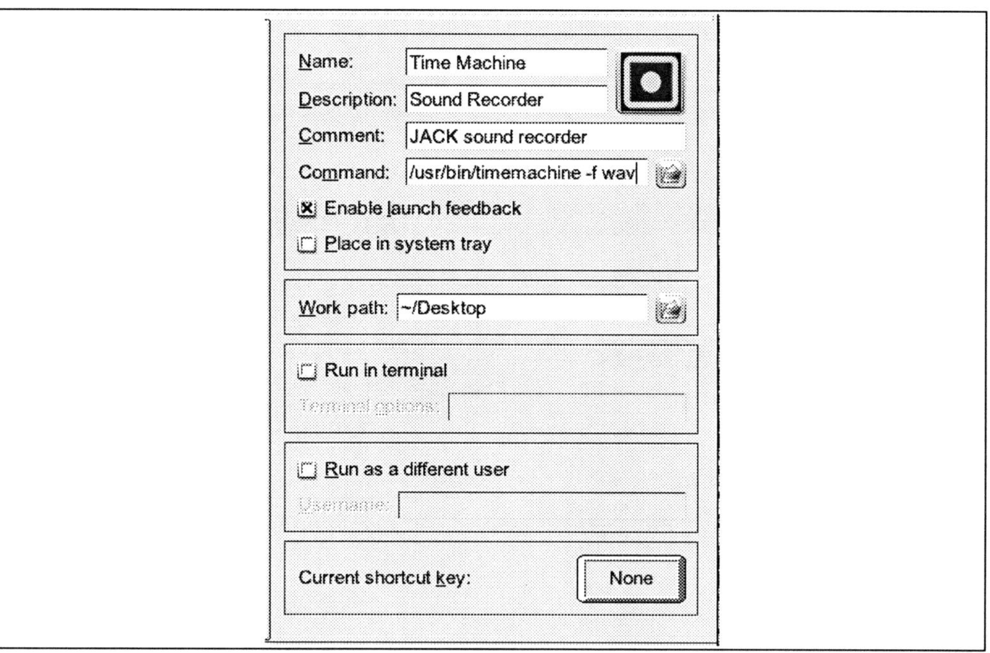

9.2.1 Recording with Time Machine

If you have gotten everything else in line, and have created a handy wrapper for Time Machine as suggested above, then these last steps really couldn't be easier. Start Time Machine. A window appears with a sort of green bullseye shape in it, like this:

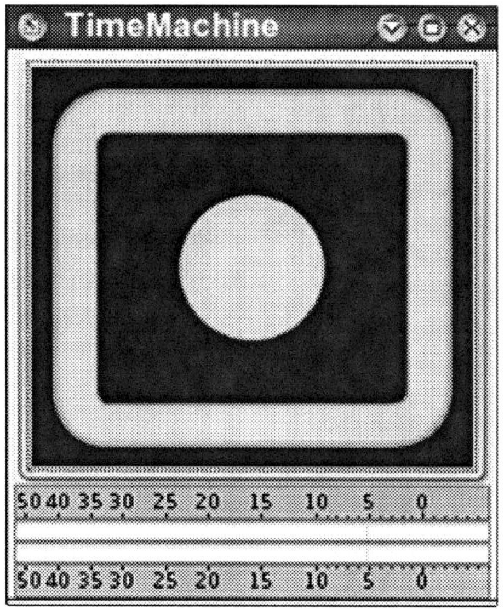

Making Connections

There are VU meters across the bottom, so you can see what Time Machine is hearing. If you hit play on the Rosegarden transport, you will see that it isn't hearing anything yet. Unlike some of the other applications I have featured so far, Time Machine does not set up any JACK connections by default. You need to go hook up its outputs with QJackCtl.

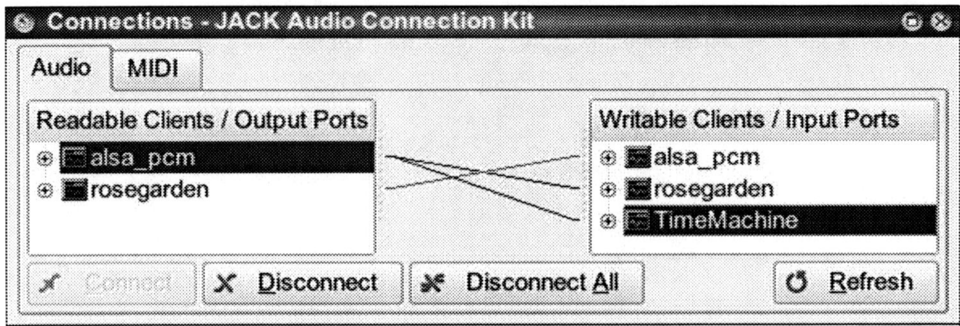

Checking for Signs of Life

Now you should be all set to record as far as Time Machine and Rosegarden are concerned. Hit play on the transport and watch the VU meters to see if there are any unexpected surprises. If it still does not hear anything, then perhaps you need to adjust your soundcard's mixer configuration as well. I just found that I did not have my soundcard's mixer configured to capture the *Wave* channel. I corrected this, then hit play on the transport, then had another look at Time Machine. It's alive!

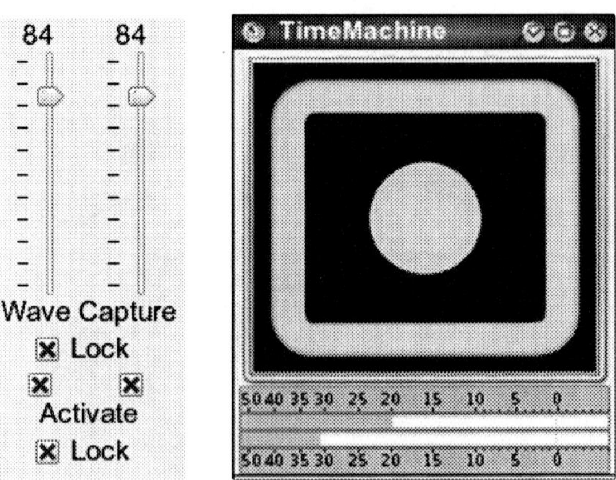

Tweaking the Final Level

Time Machine's VU meter has the final word in determining what sort of recording you're going to get. First I cranked everything up through the roof. Notice how the VU meter is spiked at 0 dB.

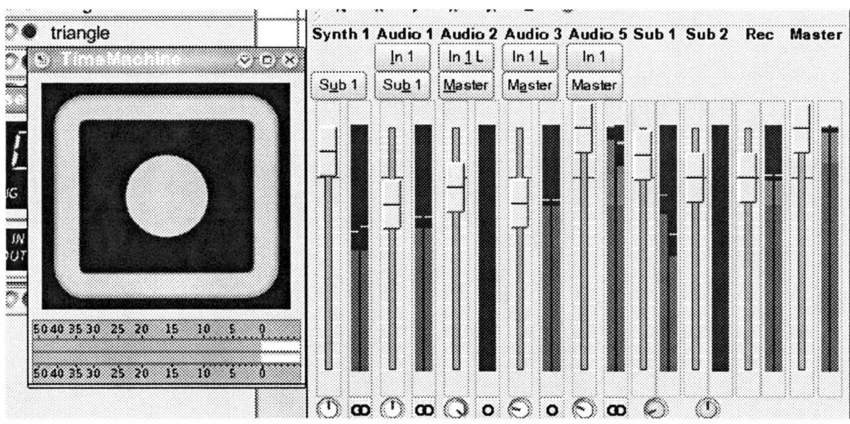

Recording

Click the big green button, and Time Machine will do its thing, and turn into a big orange button. If you're looking at your desktop, you should see a file pop up immediately. These files have rather awkward names based on the date and time of the recording, which is yet another reason why I prefer to run Time Machine off of my desktop. I find it convenient to rename this gibberish to something more meaningful immediately, so I don't lose track of which recording is which.

Click the big orange button to turn it back into a big green button again, and stop the recording. I realize that Time Machine is terribly complex when compared to a simple application like Rosegarden, so I apologize for not being able to find an audio recorder that's easier to use.

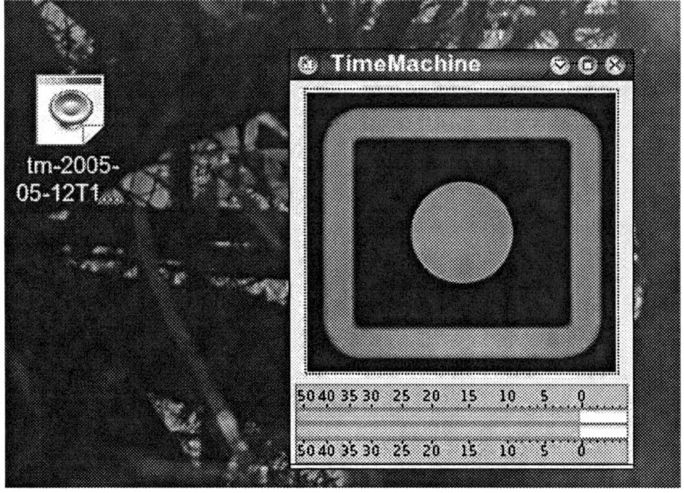

Tweaking

I will come back to using a wave editor just a bit later, but here is what that capture looked like. This recording is severely clipped. There is no salvaging this complete garbage, and it makes me glad I didn't have my speakers turned on throughout this little demonstration.

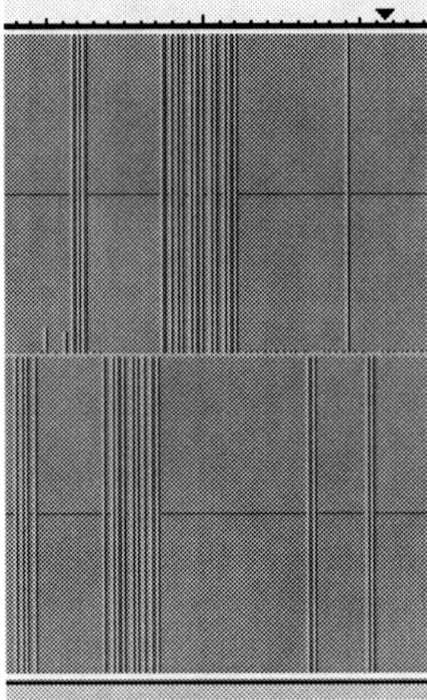

If you wind up in a situation like this, you need to play with your mix in Rosegarden and in your soundcard's mixer as well, and bring the levels down off the ceiling. I find I usually obtain good results if I shoot for the sound centering around -10 dB, with no peaks higher than -5 dB, but it is sometimes necessary to aim even lower.

I obtained a much better recording this time, although I still need to play with the overall mix to bring the low passages and the high passages into better proportion with each other, and to improve the left-heavy balance.

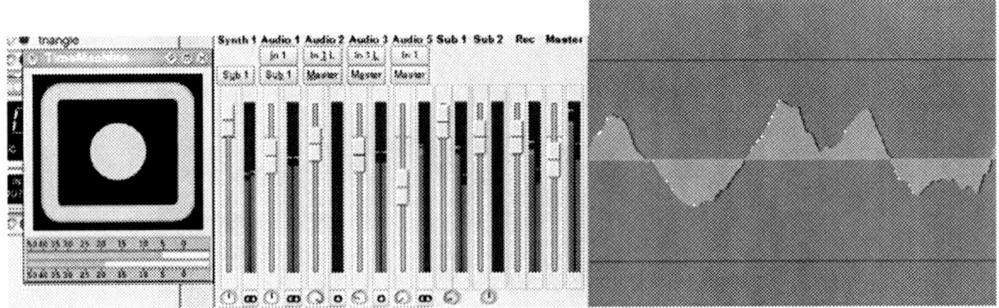

9.2.2 Post Production

Now that you have a recording on your desktop, you will need to do some post-production work on it. Time Machine actually records the five seconds preceding your pressing the big green button, and you will have to cut this lead-in off the front. You may also wish to add a fade out, or run the results through a dedicated mastering application like JAMin. (I had intended to demonstrate JAMin, because it looks useful, but if you are even capable of understanding what to do with that, you probably use Ardour for your audio work, and you probably aren't reading this book anyway. I really can't make heads or tails of it, in truth).

Choosing an Audio Editor

What editor to use is a somewhat complicated question. There are a number of good editors available, all with different strengths and weaknesses. Chief among them are Sweep, Audacity and ReZound. As of this writing, however, I can only find one editor, ReZound, that is properly JACK-aware. Depending on your hardware, you may find that you cannot run non-JACK audio applications while JACK is running, so you may have to stop JACK before editing audio with Sweep or Audacity.

ReZound

Even though it is JACK aware, my reZound package did not know how to cope with JACK out of the box. I found it necessary to intervene manually, and pass it a command line option to steer it in the right direction. If you find yourself in a similar situation (as will be obvious by having a look in QJackCtl's connection manager to see if ReZound appears there) the quickest way to get there is to use an *Alt+F2* Run Command box, and enter "rezound –audio-method=jack" into the box.

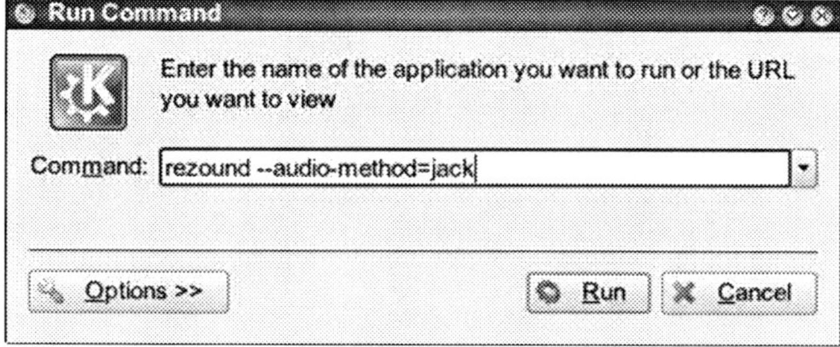

The first time you run it this way, it asks you how you want it to make JACK connections. The defaults are probably fine.

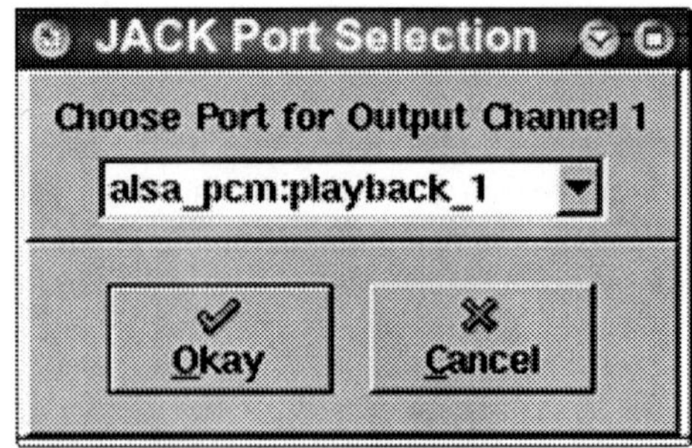

Verify that the connections were made by having a look at QJackCtrl's connection manager:

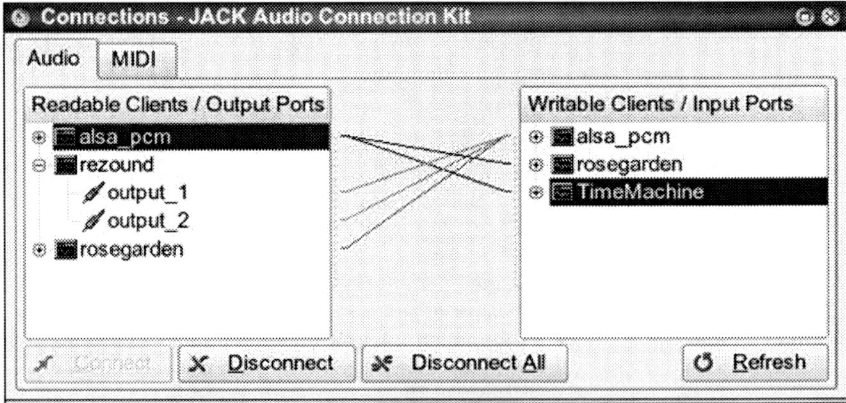

Now start ReZound, load the file off your desktop, and highlight the extra bit of silence at the beginning, use *Edit -> Cut* to get rid of it, and you're well on your way. Unfortunately, showing you how to do more than this with ReZound is well beyond the scope of this book.

Sweep

Sweep is my favorite editor for doing fade outs. I cannot find a way to accomplish the same thing with ReZound. To do a fade out with Sweep, grab some suitable length of squiggle on the right side of the sample...

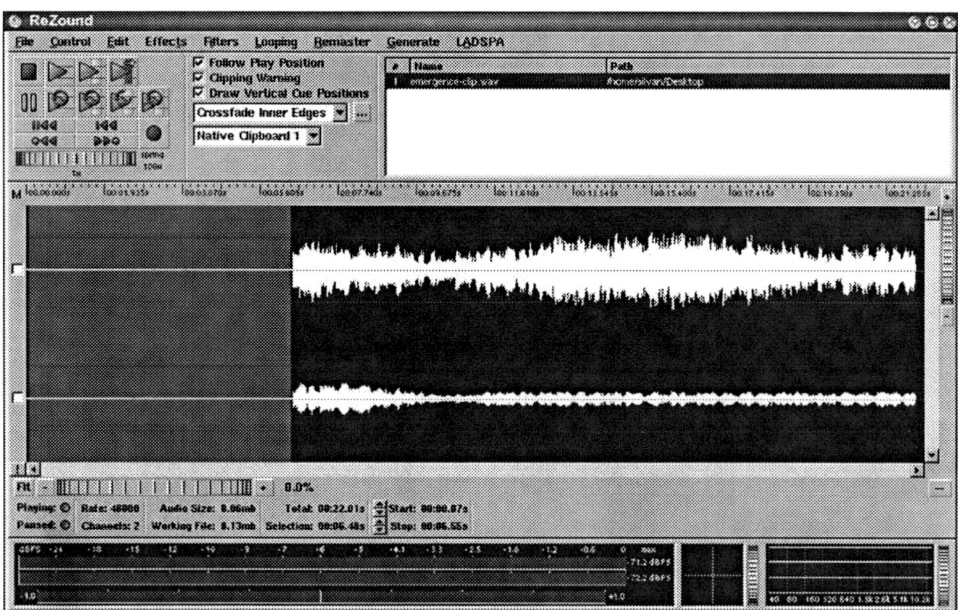

Then use *Process -> Echo ... Feedback -> Fade Out* to apply a LADSPA plugin...

...and presto, the volume fades off quietly into the sunset, just like this book is about to do.

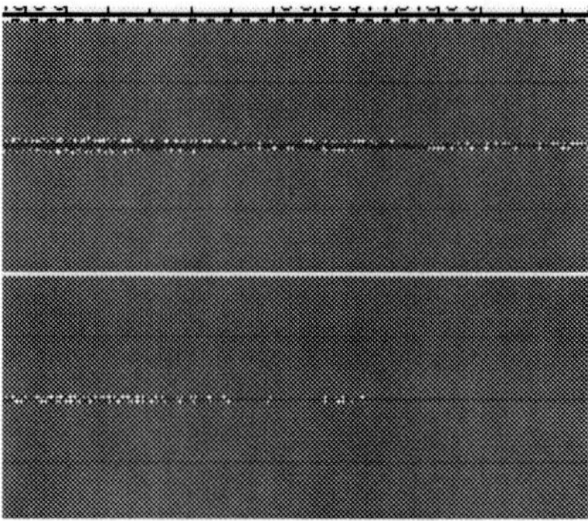

I will leave it at that, and leave you to go on to play with this for yourself from here. Now, before I wrap this up completely, I want to make some important announcements concerning good housekeeping lessons I have learned the hard way.

9.3   Recommended Housekeeping

I tend to forget that hitting *Ctrl+Z* to undo a botched audio recording does not actually make the associated audio file go away, and neither does deleting an audio segment. The segment disappears, but the file remains loaded in the audio file manager, and it remains on disk. I have found it quite tedious trying to clean up this mess, so I have developed a recipe for my own use, which I now share with you.

9.3.1 Unload Unused Audio Files

Unloading the audio files from the audio file manager is the first step in the makeshift housekeeping solution I have come up with. Click on the icon to open the audio file manager.

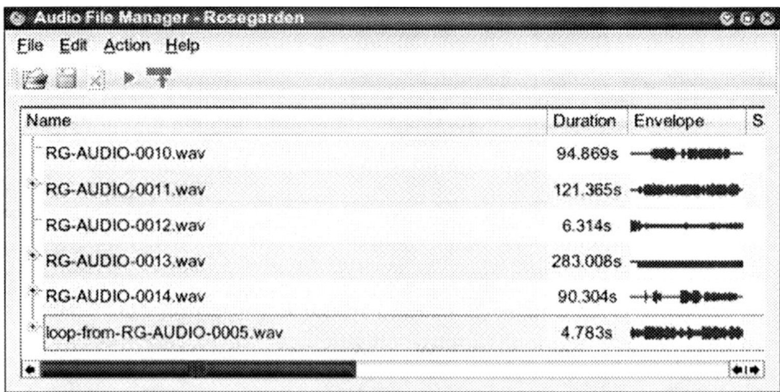

Now use *Edit -> Unload All Unused Audio Files* to unload the files that are no longer associated with audio segments on the segment canvas.

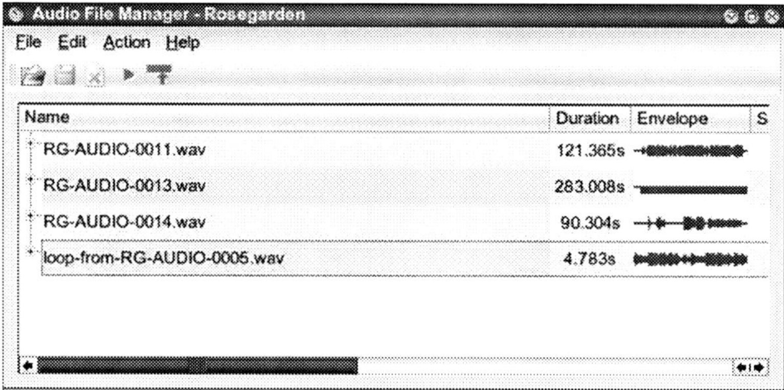

9.3.2 Remove Files Not Contained in the Composition

Now that you have removed the unused audio files from the file manager, save your file. Get the rg-clean-audio script from *http://rosegarden.sourceforge.net/tutorial/scripts/rg-clean-audio/* and save it to disk. **Use the script carefully, and only if you dare!! I cranked it out expressly for this book, and I only tested it once!** Go to a command line (I'm sorry). Make it executable by running:

```
chmod +x rg clean audio
```

Then run the script against the *.rgd* file you just saved. I am running this against emergence.rg but you should of course substitue the name of your own file:

```
./rg clean audio ~/emergence.rg
```

A sample run of the script looks like this:

```
Performing analysis of /home/silvan/emergence.rg...

File        refers        to        audio        path:
/home/silvan/rosegarden/emergence/

I have determined that the following files are not used by
the

Rosegarden composition named /home/silvan/emergence.rg...

Size    Filename
```

```
824K                /home/silvan/rosegarden/emergence//RG-AUDIO-
0009.wav

3.7M                /home/silvan/rosegarden/emergence//RG-AUDIO-
0008.wav

3.2M                /home/silvan/rosegarden/emergence//RG-AUDIO-
0007.wav

4.0M                /home/silvan/rosegarden/emergence//RG-AUDIO-
0006.wav

3.0M                /home/silvan/rosegarden/emergence//RG-AUDIO-
0004.wav

11M                 /home/silvan/rosegarden/emergence//RG-AUDIO-
0003.wav

6.1M                /home/silvan/rosegarden/emergence//RG-AUDIO-
0002.wav

2.8M                /home/silvan/rosegarden/emergence//RG-AUDIO-
0001.wav...


Do you want to delete these files PERMANENTLY? (y/N)y
```

9.3.3 Farewell

And on that note, I bid you farewell. I am glad I finally finished this book. I have been working on it for more than two years. I started this back when Rosegarden was just barely bordering on useful, in the hope that I could help people understand how to use the thing on its own terms, and in so doing, make it a more viable contender as a replacement for equivalent software on other platforms. Along the way, I became a reluctant developer, a technical support provider, and now, a published author. What a trip!

I hope it was all worth the effort. Thank you for buying this book.

D. Michael McIntyre

Christiansburg, VA, USA

May 15, 2005

Appendix A: Useful Web Resources

Here are some useful resources on the web which are of interest to the Rosegarden user. (All of these should be entered into your web browser as one line, without spaces.)

Description	URL
Rosegarden's home	http://rosegardenmusic.com
Studio..to go!, a music-oriented live CD put out by the developers of Rosegarden	http://ferventsoftware.com
The AGNULA project, distributors of DeMuDi, a music-oriented live CD	http://www.agnula.org
Planet CCRMA, music packages for Red Hat	http://ccrma.stanford.edu/planetccrma/software/
Alsa Project, information about supported soundcards and other driver issues.	http://www.alsa-project.org
Linux Sound, an extremely useful site with a host of mostly current information.	http://linux-sound.org
Home of QAMix and ALSA Modular Synth, among others	http://alsamodular.sourceforge.net
The MIDI Manufacturer's Association	http://www.midi.org
Sweep audio editor	http://www.metadecks.org/software/sweep/
reZound audio editor	http://rezound.sourceforge.net/

Appendix B: MIDI Primer

I have found, somewhat to my surprise, that many new Rosegarden users are completely unfamiliar with MIDI. This is by no means a comprehensive treatise on the subject, but it should serve as a satisfactory introduction for those who are new to these concepts.

MIDI stands for Musical Instrument Digital Interface. It is a simple serial protocol that electronic instruments and computers can use to talk to each other. MIDI-capable instruments vary enormously in their capabilities and complexity, ranging from simple analog synthesizers to pipe organs to electronic guitars, and even to electronic woodwinds and brass instruments. Traditional MIDI equipment is connected using standard 5-pin MIDI cables, which are readily obtainable from any music store. These cables run in one direction only, so it is necessary to have two of them, OUT to IN, IN to OUT, if you wish to play and record from a keyboard simultaneously. Newer equipment is moving to USB, the Universal Serial Bus, and it is changing these traditional rules somewhat. I am speaking primarily of traditional MIDI equipment here, although the underlying fundamentals apply to everything.

MIDI-capable instruments aren't required to have much in common, but there are a several categories of characteristics that most of them share.

Channels

If you have a cable TV, you can receive more than one television channel over the same wire. MIDI channels behave in a similar fashion. Any one MIDI cable can be used to carry up to 16 channels of information. Most common modern equipment is capable of receiving on all 16 of these channels simultaneously, and many types of equipment can also transmit on more than one channel.

These channels work something like the tracks in Rosegarden, which is why channel assignment is done at the track level (through Rosegarden's instruments mechanism). If you set the reverb level for channel 3, this setting will (typically) only affect notes that are transmitted on channel 3. Channels are similarly useful for playing different instruments at the same time, over the same cable, or for playing using different voices on a single instrument.

Programs

Most common MIDI instruments are polyphonic and multitimbral. This means that they can play more than one note at the same time, and they can play notes using different voices. Many instruments try to simulate a proverbial band-in-a-box by offering a range of sounds ranging from piano through the orchestra into synthesized and ethnic sounds. These simulated instruments are called either "programs" or "patches."

In the most common MIDI standard, General MIDI (GM), instruments must be able to play using any of 128 different programs. Music written to be performed on one GM instrument should sound similar on any other. The GM specification dictates that channel 10 will play drum sounds, and it defines a standard arrangement of keys on the keyboard to represent different drums.

Banks

Beyond the GM standard, many MIDI instruments have banks of additional programs. Each bank can contain an additional 128 programs, and it is theoretically possible for a single piece of equipment to have more than 16,000 different programs available. Most MIDI instruments arrange these banks in one of two ways. Roland's GS and Yamaha's XG are both supersets of GM. The usual General MIDI programs are in the first bank, which is the default bank, and the extra programs are found in additional banks. Each bank available on the synth has a unique identifying number using a combination of two parameters, called LSB (Least Significant Byte) and MSB (Most Significant Byte). The standard GM bank on every GM-compliant synth has an LSB/MSB address of 0 0.

Controllers

MIDI allows for 128 controllers. These controllers typically work at a channel level, and are used to control things such as pan (how far to the left or right the sound will play), volume (the overall maximum volume for the channel), pitch bend (used to simulate guitar and harmonica bends, play quarter tones, as well as numerous other uses), reverb (makes notes on the channel sound like they're in a concert hall) and sustain (causes the note to keep playing unhampered until the sound finally dies away, like the sustain pedal on a piano). There is enormous variability in this area, and you will find some equipment that ignores them all, while other instruments will use nearly all 128 of them. You will need to know what kind of controllers your equipment (or software synth) supports if you are to configure Rosegarden to make use of them, though it does come out of the box aware of a limited subset of the most common controllers.

Appendix C: The Author and His Studio

I have been surprised at some of the questions I have been asked since I began writing this book in 2002. I've been doing the whole PC soundcard thing since the very earliest beginnings of the technology, and I've been playing with MIDI in one form or another since the '80s. I had assumed that the archetypical Rosegarden user would be someone like me. Perhaps someone who grew up using Cakewalk, or some similar MIDI sequencer package on another platform, and needed only to understand how to translate familiar concepts to a new environment. It seems in retrospect that many of you are new to all of this, and that you're not quite sure what is even possible when it comes to setting up your studio. I find it wonderful that so many people have been empowered to explore new territory thanks to Rosegarden, so I've decided to describe my own setup in some detail, to provide an example of one possible scenario.

Mine is not a pro studio by any stretch of the imagination. I'm not a pro musician. I just like to play around every once in a blue moon and have a bit of fun with music. I have an old Sound Canvas, an old clunky controller keyboard (a FATAR MIDI-72 with broken pitch and modulation wheels), and a new but hardly exciting Sound Blaster Live! that I bought pretty much so I could experience it and write about it for my purposes here in this book. It's not much of a studio, but it's really all I need for the kind of hack amateur work I do. This diagram attempts to explain how I have all the cabling routed.

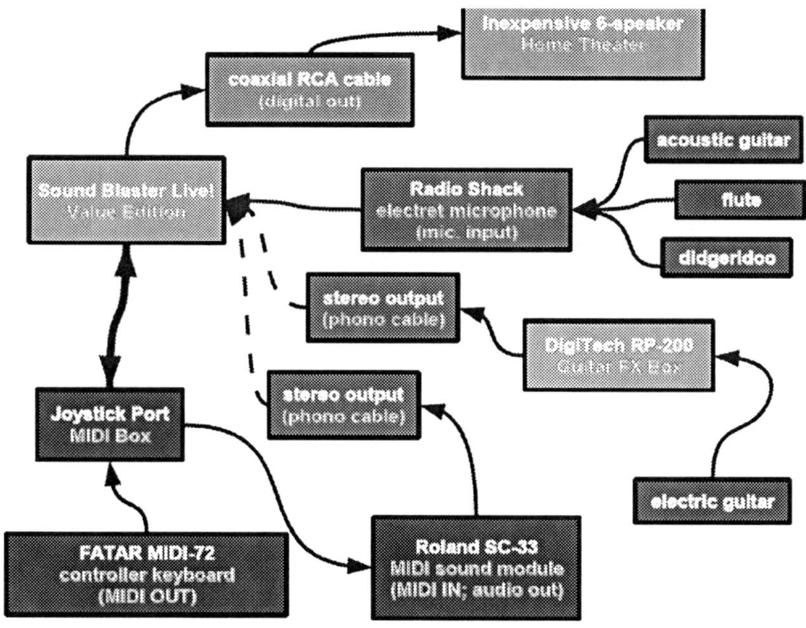

At the center of my studio is the SB Live!. I use the on-board mixer to control the levels on various channels for recording and playback, and I use the MIDI interface to connect my keyboard to Rosegarden, and to connect Rosegarden to my Sound Canvas. The audio mixer output is routed through the orange jack on the card, through a digtial coaxial cable to a cheap $50 home theater system from Wal-Mart.

On the internal MIDI side of things, the SB Live! offers four output ports of 16 channels each, and 64-voice polyphony using commonly-available soundfonts. It has no effects processor, and no reverb or chorus, so the voices sound rather flat and lifeless. However, the flexibility in choosing soundfonts means I can usually find a reasonably good approximation of whatever instrument I'm after. On the external MIDI side, my Sound Canvas can receive on 16 channels, and can play a maximum of 28 voices simultaneously. It has excellent on-board effects, but the instruments are hit or miss. Some sound quite good, while others are decidedly pitiful. It is also dreadfully short on polyphony. It still sounds better than anything else I have, and it's 10 years old.

On the audio side, I have a Radio Shack microphone plugged into the red jack on the SB Live!, and I share the blue jack between the audio output from my Sound Canvas and the audio output from my DigiTech RP-200 guitar effects processor (represented by the dashed lines on the diagram). This arrangement is inconvenient, since I can't play the Sound Canvas through my soundcard's mixer while recording the guitar, but I have to live with this unless I want to lay out the cash for a real mixer.

Appendix D: General MIDI Program Names

I have provided this zero-based list for your convenience when inserting program change events by hand using the event list editor.

Piano

0 Acoustic Grand Piano

1 Bright Acoustic Piano

2 Electric Grand Piano

3 Honky-tonk Piano

4 Electric Piano 1

5 Electric Piano 2

6 Harpsichord

7 Clavi

Bass

32 Acoustic Bass

33 Fingered Bass

34 Picked Bass

35 Fretless Bass

36 Slap Bass 1

37 Slap Bass 2

38 Synth Bass 1

39 Synth Bass 2

Reeds

64 Soprano Sax

65 Alto Sax

66 Tenor Sax

67 Baritone Sax

68 Oboe

69 English Horn

70 Bassoon

71 Clarinet

Synth FX

96 FX 1 (rain)

97 FX 2 (soundtrack)

98 FX 3 (crystal)

99 FX 4 (atmosphere)

100 FX 5 (brightness)

101 FX 6 (goblins)

102 FX 7 (echoes)

103 FX 8 (sci-fi)

Chromatic Percussion

8 Celesta

9 Glockenspiel

10 Music Box

11 Vibraphone

12 Marimba

13 Xylophone

14 Tubular Bells

15 Dulcimer

Orchestral

40 Violin

41 Viola

42 Cello

43 Contrabass

44 Tremolo Strings

45 Pizzicato Strings

46 Orchestral Harp

47 Timpani

Pipes

72 Piccolo

73 Flute

74 Recorder

75 Pan Flute

76 Blown Bottle

77 Shakuhachi

78 Whistle

79 Ocarina

Ethnic

104 Sitar

105 Banjo

106 Shamisen

107 Koto

108 Kalimba

109 Bag pipe

110 Fiddle

111 Shanai

Organs

16 Drawbar Organ

17 Percussive Organ

18 Rock Organ

Ensembles

48 String Ensemble 1

49 String Ensemble 2

50 SynthStrings 1

Synth Leads

80 Lead 1 (square)

81 Lead 2 (sawtooth)

82 Lead 3 (calliope)

Percussive

112 Tinkle Bell

113 Agogo

114 Steel Drums

115 Woodblock

19 Church Organ

20 Reed Organ

21 Accordion

22 Harmonica

23 Tango Accordion

Guitars

24 Acoustic Guitar (nylon)

25 Acoustic Guitar (steel)

26 Electric Guitar (jazz)

27 Electric Guitar (clean)

28 Electric Guitar (muted)

29 Overdriven Guitar

30 Distortion Guitar

31 Guitar harmonics

51 SynthStrings 2

52 Choir Aahs

53 Voice Oohs

54 Synth Voice

55 Orchestra Hit

Brass

56 Trumpet

57 Trombone

58 Tuba

59 Muted Trumpet

60 French Horn

61 Brass Section

62 SynthBrass 1

63 SynthBrass 2

83 Lead 4 (chiff)

84 Lead 5 (charang)

85 Lead 6 (voice)

86 Lead 7 (fifths)

87 Lead 8 (bass+lead)

Synth Pads

88 Pad 1 (new age)

89 Pad 2 (warm)

90 Pad 3 (polysynth)

91 Pad 4 (choir)

92 Pad 5 (bowed)

93 Pad 6 (metallic)

94 Pad 7 (halo)

95 Pad 8 (sweep)

116 Taiko Drum

117 Melodic Tom

118 Synth Drum

119 Reverse Cymbal

Sound Effects

120 Guitar Fret Noise

121 Breath Noise

122 Seashore

123 Bird Tweet

124 Telephone Ring

125 Helicopter

126 Applause

127 Gunshot

Index

Printed in the United States
118957LV00002B/17/A

9 782915 925180